Responsibility and Responsibilisation in Education

Concerns with the nature of and relationship between responsibility and responsibilisation pervade contemporary social, political and moral life. This book turns the analytical lens on the ways in which responsibility and responsibilisation operate in diverse educational settings and relationships, and social, policy and geographical contexts in the USA, Europe, the UK, New Zealand and Australia. Scholars have sought to explain the genealogy and the mélange of rationalities, technologies, bio-politics and modes of governmentality that bring responsibility and responsibilisation into being, how they act on and are taken up by individuals, groups and organisations, and the risks and possibilities they create and delimit for individuals, social collectives and their freedoms.

Contributors to this collection have diverse views and perspectives on responsibility and responsibilisation. This disagreement is a strength. It underlines the importance of unravelling both the differences and similarities across scholars and contexts. It also issues a salutary warning about assumptions that reduce the complex concepts of responsibility and responsibilisation to simplistic, fixed categories or to generalising and universalising single cases or experiences to all areas of education.

This volume was originally published as a special issue of *Discourse: Studies in the Cultural Politics of Education*.

Christine Halse is Chair Professor of Intercultural Education in the Department of Education, Policy and Leadership, The Education University of Hong Kong. Her research focuses on the manifestation of sociological themes in bodies and biographies, particularly in interracial and intercultural relations.

Catherine Hartung is Lecturer in Education Studies at the University of Otago College of Education, New Zealand. Her research draws on feminist poststructural theory to critically examine how various educational, cultural and political institutions govern children and young people, as well as the ways that children and young people negotiate and resist this institutional governance.

Jan Wright is Emeritus Professor in the Faculty of Social Sciences at the University of Wollongong, Australia. Her most recent research draws on feminist and poststructuralist theory to critically engage issues associated with the relationship between embodiment, culture and health.

Responsibility and Responsibilisation in Education

Edited by
Christine Halse, Catherine Hartung
and Jan Wright

LONDON AND NEW YORK

First published 2018
by Routledge
2 Park Square, Milton Park, Abingdon, Oxon, OX14 4RN, UK

and by Routledge
711 Third Avenue, New York, NY 10017, USA

Routledge is an imprint of the Taylor & Francis Group, an informa business

Introduction, Chapters 1-6 & 8-11 © 2018 Taylor & Francis
Chapter 7 © 2018 Harry Torrance. Originally published as Open Access

With the exception of Chapter 7, no part of this book may be reprinted or reproduced or utilised in any form or by any electronic, mechanical, or other means, now known or hereafter invented, including photocopying and recording, or in any information storage or retrieval system, without permission in writing from the publishers. For details on the rights for Chapter 7, please see Open Access footnote to Chapter 7.

Trademark notice: Product or corporate names may be trademarks or registered trademarks, and are used only for identification and explanation without intent to infringe.

British Library Cataloguing in Publication Data
A catalogue record for this book is available from the British Library

ISBN 13: 978-1-138-57105-1

Typeset in Myriad Pro
by RefineCatch Limited, Bungay, Suffolk

Publisher's Note
The publisher accepts responsibility for any inconsistencies that may have arisen during the conversion of this book from journal articles to book chapters, namely the possible inclusion of journal terminology.

Disclaimer
Every effort has been made to contact copyright holders for their permission to reprint material in this book. The publishers would be grateful to hear from any copyright holder who is not here acknowledged and will undertake to rectify any errors or omissions in future editions of this book.

Contents

Citation Information   vii
Notes on Contributors   ix

Introduction: Responsibility and responsibilisation in education   1
Christine Halse, Catherine Hartung and Jan Wright

1. Responsibility for racism in the everyday talk of secondary students   2
   Christine Halse

2. Global citizenship incorporated: competing responsibilities in the education of global citizens   16
   Catherine Hartung

3. Homophobia, transphobia, young people and the question of responsibility   30
   Mary Lou Rasmussen, Fida Sanjakdar, Louisa Allen, Kathleen Quinlivan and Annette Bromdal

4. Reframing responsibility in an era of responsibilisation: education, feminist ethics   43
   Julie McLeod

5. Growing up after the GFC: responsibilisation and mortgaged futures   57
   Peter Kelly

6. Ghostings, materialisations and flows in Britain's special educational needs and disability assemblage   70
   Julie Allan and Deborah Youdell

7. Blaming the victim: assessment, examinations, and the responsibilisation of students and teachers in neo-liberal governance   83
   Harry Torrance

8. Academic responsibility: toward a cultural politics of integrity   97
   William G. Tierney and Daniel J. Almeida

9. The implications of contractualism for the responsibilisation of higher education   109
   Shaun Rawolle, Julie Rowlands and Jill Blackmore

CONTENTS

10. Responsibilisation and leadership in the neoliberal university: a New Zealand perspective 123
    Mark Amsler and Cris Shore

11. From State responsibility for education and welfare to self-responsibilisation in the market 138
    Michael A. Peters

    Index 147

Citation Information

The chapters in this book were originally published in *Discourse: Studies in the Cultural Politics of Education*, volume 38, issue 1 (February 2017). When citing this material, please use the original page numbering for each article, as follows:

Introduction
Responsibility and responsibilisation in education
Christine Halse, Catherine Hartung and Jan Wright
Discourse: Studies in the Cultural Politics of Education, volume 38, issue 1
(February 2017), pp. 1

Chapter 1
Responsibility for racism in the everyday talk of secondary students
Christine Halse
Discourse: Studies in the Cultural Politics of Education, volume 38, issue 1
(February 2017), pp. 2–15

Chapter 2
Global citizenship incorporated: competing responsibilities in the education of global citizens
Catherine Hartung
Discourse: Studies in the Cultural Politics of Education, volume 38, issue 1
(February 2017), pp. 16–29

Chapter 3
Homophobia, transphobia, young people and the question of responsibility
Mary Lou Rasmussen, Fida Sanjakdar, Louisa Allen, Kathleen Quinlivan and Annette Bromdal
Discourse: Studies in the Cultural Politics of Education, volume 38, issue 1
(February 2017), pp. 30–42

Chapter 4
Reframing responsibility in an era of responsibilisation: education, feminist ethics
Julie McLeod
Discourse: Studies in the Cultural Politics of Education, volume 38, issue 1
(February 2017), pp. 43–56

Chapter 5
Growing up after the GFC: responsibilisation and mortgaged futures
Peter Kelly
Discourse: Studies in the Cultural Politics of Education, volume 38, issue 1 (February 2017), pp. 57–69

Chapter 6
Ghostings, materialisations and flows in Britain's special educational needs and disability assemblage
Julie Allan and Deborah Youdell
Discourse: Studies in the Cultural Politics of Education, volume 38, issue 1 (February 2017), pp. 70–82

Chapter 7
Blaming the victim: assessment, examinations, and the responsibilisation of students and teachers in neo-liberal governance
Harry Torrance
Discourse: Studies in the Cultural Politics of Education, volume 38, issue 1 (February 2017), pp. 83–96

Chapter 8
Academic responsibility: toward a cultural politics of integrity
William G. Tierney and Daniel J. Almeida
Discourse: Studies in the Cultural Politics of Education, volume 38, issue 1 (February 2017), pp. 97–108

Chapter 9
The implications of contractualism for the responsibilisation of higher education
Shaun Rawolle, Julie Rowlands and Jill Blackmore
Discourse: Studies in the Cultural Politics of Education, volume 38, issue 1 (February 2017), pp. 109–122

Chapter 10
Responsibilisation and leadership in the neoliberal university: a New Zealand perspective
Mark Amsler and Cris Shore
Discourse: Studies in the Cultural Politics of Education, volume 38, issue 1 (February 2017), pp. 123–137

Chapter 11
From State responsibility for education and welfare to self-responsibilisation in the market
Michael A. Peters
Discourse: Studies in the Cultural Politics of Education, volume 38, issue 1 (February 2017), pp. 138–145

For any permission-related enquiries please visit:
http://www.tandfonline.com/page/help/permissions

Notes on Contributors

Julie Allan is Professor of Equity and Inclusion and Head of the School of Education at the University of Birmingham, UK.

Louisa Allen is Professor in the Faculty of Education at the University of Auckland, New Zealand.

Daniel J. Almeida is Assistant Professor in the School of Education at Cal Poly San Luis Obispo, USA.

Mark Amsler is Associate Professor in the Faculty of Arts at the University of Auckland, New Zealand.

Jill Blackmore is Alfred Deakin Professor and Professor of Education at the School of Education, Deakin University, Australia.

Annette Bromdal is Lecturer in Sport, Health and Physical Education at the School of Linguistics, Adult and Specialist Education, University of Southern Queensland, Australia.

Christine Halse is Chair Professor of Intercultural Education in the Department of Education, Policy and Leadership, The Education University of Hong Kong.

Catherine Hartung is Lecturer in Education Studies at the University of Otago College of Education, New Zealand.

Peter Kelly is Professor of Teacher Education in the School of Education at RMIT University, Australia.

Julie McLeod is Professor in the area of Curriculum, Equity and Social Change and Pro Vice-Chancellor (Research Capability).

Michael A. Peters is Associate Director of the Centre for Global Studies in Education at the Wilf Malcolm Institute of Educational Research, New Zealand.

Kathleen Quinlivan is Associate Professor at the School of Educational Studies and Leadership, University of Canterbury, Christchurch, New Zealand.

Mary Lou Rasmussen is Professor at the ANU (Australian National University) College of Arts and Social Sciences, Canberra, Australia.

Shaun Rawolle is Senior Lecturer in Education (Pedagogy and Curriculum) at the School of Education, Deakin University, Australia.

NOTES ON CONTRIBUTORS

Julie Rowlands is Senior Lecturer in Education (Education Leadership) at the School of Education, Deakin University, Australia.

Fida Sanjakdar is Senior Lecturer in the Faculty of Education at Monash University, Australia.

Cris Shore is Professor of Social Anthropology in the Faculty of Arts at the University of Auckland, New Zealand.

William G. Tierney is Co-Director at the Pullias Center for Higher Education, Rossier School of Education, University of Southern California, as well as a University Professor and Wilbur-Kieffer Professor of Higher Education.

Harry Torrance is based at the Education and Social Research Institute at Manchester Metropolitan University, UK.

Jan Wright is Emeritus Professor in the Faculty of Social Sciences at the University of Wollongong, Australia.

Deborah Youdell is Professor of Sociology of Education in the School of Education at the University of Birmingham, UK.

INTRODUCTION

Responsibility and responsibilisation in education

Christine Halse, Catherine Hartung and Jan Wright

Debates about responsibility and responsibilisation pervade contemporary social, political and moral life. For this reason, how they are configured, operate, inter-relate and their effects have been the subject of theoretical work across multiple disciplines and sub-disciplines, including but not limited to sociology, economics, business and accounting, ethics, health and psychoanalysis. Here, scholars have sought to document and account for the *mélange* of rationalities, pressures, technologies and practices of responsibility and responsibilisation that act on and/or are taken up by individuals, groups and organisations, and how they work to both delimit and create possibilities for individual and collective freedoms.

This special issue adds to this body of knowledge by turning an analytical lens on the ways in which responsibility and responsibilisation operates in different sites, jurisdictions and relationships in education. This focus, as Michael Peters observes in his concluding article, makes this collection of articles 'the first of its kind in education'.

Contributors are all renowned experts in their respective fields. Individually, their articles consider questions of responsibility and responsibilisation in relation to different populations, from children and young people inside and outside of schools, to teachers and students and managers in higher education. The discussions are located in very different social, policy and geographical contexts, including the USA, Europe, the UK, New Zealand and Australia, and attend to both formal and informal educational contexts. Individually and collectively, they provide nuanced insights into the multiplicity of ways that responsibility and responsibilisation work differently in different educational contexts to construct particular social orders and ways of being in the world.

This does not mean our authors agree with each other. A strength of this collection, we propose, is that it presents very different views and perspectives on the operation and effects of responsibility and responsibilisation based on the analyses of different educational sites and actors. These differences send a salutatory caution against making universalised assumptions about responsibility and responsibilisation in education, and about generalising single case findings to the entire field of education. In doing so, the diverse perspectives presented in this collection reinforce the foundational principles of scholarly educational research. They demonstrate the importance of exploring the complex ways in which individuals, groups and contexts are differentiated from one another and of resisting the temptation to reduce key concepts, such as responsibility and responsibilisation, to simplistic categorical oppositions (for example, good/bad) that are fixed in time and space.

Responsibility for racism in the everyday talk of secondary students

Christine Halse

ABSTRACT
This article examines the attributions of responsibility for racism in the everyday talk of secondary school students. It draws on focus groups with a cross section of students from different ethnic backgrounds in three, very different, secondary schools. In these focus groups, students deploy six different, sometimes contradictory, racialised discourses. Each discourse attributes responsibility for racism in very different ways that testify to the immanence of the past in the present and students' positioning in specific social and political conditions. In all but one instance, these discourses work to dismiss, deny and/or deflect responsibility for racism by averting responsibility from the self to other individuals, groups or entities. The empirical data, it is argued, show that the individualisation of responsibility for racism has not seeped its way into students' race-thinking. This testifies to the persistence of race-thinking, the difficult challenge of finding non-racist ways of being in the world, and cautions against assuming that responsibilisation is a universal descriptor of all contemporary social relations.

Introduction

Responsibility, in its various guises and insinuations, lies at the heart of all social relations. For this reason, how students view ethnic groups in an increasingly diverse world is intimately entangled with race-thinking and the question of the responsibility for racism. Race-thinking, as Gilroy (2000) reminds us, is the precondition for racism. These are the beliefs, attitudes, values and behaviours that racialise and differentiate between social groups based on physical and cultural characteristics, such as language, religion and ethnic customs and traditions, and that work to privilege the social majority and to discriminate against and disadvantage ethnic minorities.

Contemporary conditions have increased the imperative to recognise how race-thinking shapes the ways in which individuals and societies understand and enact their responsibilities to others. Global travel, migration and transnational mobility have produced greater ethnic, cultural and linguistic diversity within nation states. In many countries, these changes have escalated anxieties about strangers, increased racialised tensions, discrimination and conflicts, and led governments to limit the movement of refugees and migrants across borders and their access to basic social services, such as employment, education, health and welfare.

Supranational agencies, such as the United Nations Education, Scientific and Cultural Organization (UNESCO), have responded to these social and political conditions by assigning schools the responsibility for ensuring young people have the intercultural knowledge and skills necessary to halt racism and build inclusive, cohesive multicultural societies (2006, 2013). The UNESCO report on *Education for Intercultural Understanding* is explicit on this point: 'Education systems, schools and teachers are therefore responsible for strengthening the child's cultural identity and values, while also promoting respect and understanding for the culture of others' (2010, p. 9).

In Europe, nations have sought to build positive relations between different racial and ethnic groups and their various social, cultural and religious traditions through 'intercultural education' – the pseudonym for fostering positive relations between racial and ethnic groups through schooling policies and curricula designed to promote cultural knowledge, cultural exchanges, and skilful interethnic interactions (Puzic, 2008). In a similar vein, the national Australian Curriculum requires 'Intercultural Understanding' to be integrated into all subject areas to develop students who possess the three personal dispositions that policy leaders believe are needed for a cohesive, multicultural society: expressing empathy, demonstrating respect and taking responsibility (Australian Curriculum, Assessment, Research Authority, 2014).

This specific configuration constructs intercultural relations as a consequence of specific personal attributes and psycho-social capacities, and *individualises responsibility* for relations with/between ethnically and culturally different social groups. In doing so, the curriculum echoes the *responsibilisation* of individuals that characterises contemporary society. It assigns personal responsibility to individuals for adhering to the normative values, attitudes and behaviours decreed by governments, institutions and wider society, and for exercising the 'self-care' (Lemke, 2001, p. 201) needed to cultivate appropriate intercultural dispositions and behaviour, and correct their wrong ways of thinking and behaving.

The concept of responsibilisation presumes the existence of the archetypal modernist subject: the unique, rational, independent individual who is equal to all other members of society and has the free choice and agency to think and act beyond their specific social, political, economic and racial circumstances (Boyd, 2004). The characteristics of the 'liberal individual' – ontological uniqueness, symmetrical positioning, intentional rational agency, capacity for transcendence – underpin the principles of autonomy, equality, human dignity, respect and justice that are the basis of the social, legal, political and economic institutions of Western democracies (Boyd, 2004). Yet locating responsibility for intercultural relations in the rational, moral, modernist subject papers over the ways that race-thinking and racist practices are legitimised and rendered invisible by being embedded in the daily interactions, communications and exchanges between individuals and in the operation of the social, economic and political structures of society (Young, 1990).

The everyday talk of students is a primary means by which the racial coding and judgement of race-thinking is kept 'close to the surface, ready to spring into action' (Amin, 2010, p. 1). It is everyday talk that voices race-thinking, perpetrates the racial micro-aggressions that constitute ethnic groups as different and Other to the social majority (van Dijk, 1992), and that communicate, share and embed the concept of responsibilisation and accounts of *who* is responsible for racist attitudes and actions in society (Sue, 2010; Young, 1990).

There is substantial research literature on the discourses – the attitudes, values and behaviours – immanent in schools and schooling that hail raced and racialised minorities into being and work to subjugate them while privileging the social majority (e.g. Gillborn, 1990, 2008; Giroux, 1993; Leonardo, 2009; Lewis, 2001). There is also a sizable literature on how the different ways that students *do* racism shapes their identities and relation to racialised Others (e.g. Bennett & Lee-Treweek, 2014; Dolby, 2000; McLeod & Yates, 2003). Absent from this literature is any empirical discussion of how the discourses immanent in and shared through students' talk work to convey, legitimate, deflect or deny *responsibility* for racism.

This article aims to begin to address this gap in knowledge though a discourse analysis of a series of focus groups with secondary students. Discourses embody the tacit, taken-for-granted theories about what constitutes the 'normal' and 'right' ways of behaving, interacting, valuing, thinking, believing, speaking and 'being in the world' (Gee, 1990/2008, pp. 3–4). They work to 'institute particular realities, establish regimes of truth, and organise particular ways of thinking about the world that shape subjects and subjectivities' (Halse, Honey, & Boughtwood, 2007, p. 222). In these ways, the discourses mobilised in students' talk work to simultaneously racialise *and* assign moral responsibility for racism, even if students are oblivious to these effects. Specifically, this article explores three questions: How is race-thinking articulated in secondary students' everyday talk? What discourses of responsibility for racism are communicated and shared through students' talk? What do these discourses reveal about the uptake of responsibilisation among this group of secondary students?

About the study

The focus groups discussed in this article were conducted in three schools that represent the spectrum of secondary schools in Melbourne, Australia, in terms of the number of students, their ethnic and language backgrounds and their families' socio-economic status.[1] The first school, Haskell Peak, is a large ($n = 1300$), co-educational, government school in which 65 nationalities are represented, mostly second- or third-generation migrants. A minority of students (22%) come from professional families but the majority (78%) come from families working in lowly paid, semi- and unskilled, and casual/part-time jobs with high levels of underemployment. The second school, Jardleigh College, is an average-sized ($n = 1000$), co-educational, government school where more than 50% of students speak a language other than English at home. The school's 54 nationalities include growing numbers of refugees from the Horn of Africa, Sri Lanka and Afghanistan, as well as international students from Vietnam, China, India and Korea. The school is located in a socio-economically disadvantaged district marked by high unemployment and generational poverty. The third school, Kirkswood, is a medium-sized ($n = 600$), single-sex, fee-paying, non-government school in an affluent, middle-class district with more than 30 nationalities represented across its students.

An average of six students from each of Years 7 and 8 and Years 9 and 10 participated in two focus groups across 2013 and 2014, except in Jardleigh College when only Year 9 participated, in 2013.[2] The focus groups comprised a balance of males and females in the co-educational schools and a cross section of different ethnic groups in each school.

The focus groups aimed to gain insights into students' perspectives of relations between different ethnic, cultural and religious groups and their experiences of racism inside and outside of school. The focus groups occurred at a time of hot debate in Australia about racialised issues and these issues were used as stimuli in the focus group discussions:

> There's a lot of discussion in the media and politics about asylum seekers arriving in Australia by boat, and what Australia should do. *If you were the Prime Minister, what would you do about the asylum seekers?* (2013)

> The government is changing the Racial Discrimination Act to lessen the punishment for saying something that is potentially offensive to somebody from a different ethnic/cultural background. *Do you think it is okay to say something that somebody from a different culture might find offensive?* (2014)

> The Human Rights Commission distinguishes between equitable and equal treatment of migrants: *Should your school treat migrants the same as other students or differently? If differently, in what way?* (2014)

Responsibility for racism in students' talk

In these focus groups, students deployed six dominant discourses of responsibility for racism. An illustrative example of each discourse is presented and briefly discussed. The examples were selected not just because they reveal the specific and different ways each discourse constructs and attributes responsibility for racism but, also, because they illustrate how the seemingly straightforward verbal exchanges that *responsibilise* can also involve contortions of logic and language and construct the micro-aggressions that racialise and perpetuate racism in society.

The moral discourse of multiculturalism

Across all focus groups, there was an almost unanimous support and reproduction of multiculturalism's liberal claim of social egalitarianism and equal treatment of all.

> Q: So what have you learnt in your classes about people who live in Australia?
> Student 1: It doesn't mean we're different; we're all alike in some way.
> Student 2: We're all alike, yet we're different. If that makes sense.
> Student 3: Yeah, we're all alike yet different, yeah.
> Student 2: It kind of –
> Student 4: It doesn't make sense –
> Student 2: It does make sense, but I think what it means is, like, we're all different; we might have different skin colour or a different religion –
> Student 3: Hair colour, eye colour –
> Student 1: Different ways, stuff like that, but really we're all friendly and we're all trying to get along with each other without conflict, so in that way we're all the same.
> Student 2: Yeah, we have, like, a multicultural society.
> Student 4: Yeah, like, we're – everyone's – different.
> Student 3: We're very multicultural [we've] been, like, taught to accept [that].
> Student 2: We all hang out together and we're all different, from different countries and different religions. Like, he's Arabic, and I'm Catholic, and etc.
> Student 1: And I'm a New Zealander. (Haskell Peak Year 9 Focus Group, 2013)

Kromidas (2010) describes multiculturalism as an *official moral discourse*. Something becomes an official moral discourse when it is entrenched in a nation's social, political, legal and educational policies and structures and, through these means, becomes the established social norm. Multiculturalism in Australia emphasises 'respect and support for cultural, religious and linguistic diversity' and that people of all ethnic groups are 'different but equal' (Australian Government, December, 2013, p. 5). Multiculturalism has been a touchstone of Australian social and political life and its schooling policies and curricula since the 1970s. Its place as an official moral discourse has been bolstered by anti-racism laws that prohibit and make punishable racist speech, vilification, behaviour and discrimination.

The students in this focus group demonstrate the embeddedness of multiculturalism in the national psyche and in the structure of schooling. They emphasise that they have been 'taught to accept' that Australia is 'a multicultural society' and repeatedly assert their understanding of multiculturalism as 'alike but different'. When one student questions this claim ('it doesn't make sense'), his classmates reject this moment of sedition by reaffirming and elaborating on the everyday mantra of multiculturalism as egalitarianism and the equality of all peoples.

The discourse of multiculturalism, however, presents a contradictory account of who is responsible for racism. On the one hand, the catch-cry of 'alike but different' implies that all members of society are *equally responsible* for racist thinking and behaviour. On the other hand, the rhetoric of *equal responsibility* also provides a rationale for evading individual or collective responsibility for racism. It offers a metaphorical loophole for ignoring the implications of ethnic diversity and difference in society, including how race-thinking and racialised inequities are immanent in everyday life, construct social, cultural and economic structures that divide society and disadvantage minority groups, and limit alternate ways of seeing and imagining being in the world. Further, the tolerance that multiculturalism promotes through its status as an official moral discourse makes it 'much more difficult for minority groups to challenge remaining inequalities, to take unified action and to gain credibility and support among the (white) dominant group' (van Dijk, 1992, p. 96).

Discourse of racism as a fact of nature

Yet the same group of students also acknowledges the pervasiveness of racism in society. It is not unusual for young people to voice seemingly contradictory positions on racial issues but these students invoke a stoic, fatalistic determinism. Racism, they argue, is a universal human characteristic and an inescapable fact of everyday life that cannot be controlled or prevented:

> Student 1: Because, like, wherever you go there's going to be racism. Like it's … it's a human thing.
> Student 2: You can't get away from it.
> Student 3: It's inevitable.
> Student 4: It's not a good thing but it's something that just happens. You can't control what people think or say.
> Student 5: It's also a form of – it's racism – but it's also a form of bullying as well. It's, like, it' something that just shouldn't happen, it's disgusting.
> Student 6: But then again you can't really stop people from saying …

Student 2: Bullying's going to happen, racism is going to happen.
Student 3: And that's the worst part I think, that you can't control it, you can't stop it.
Student 6: Yeah ... just like run away from it.
Student 1: You can't just be like 'Hey, I'm going to stop racism one day'. Look, it's not going to happen.
Student 6: Yeah. It's a hard topic. (Haskell Peak Year 9 Focus Group, 2013)

Students take an anti-racist stance ('just shouldn't happen, it's disgusting') but justify racism's presence by constituting it as a socio-biological truth – a universal characteristic of the human species ('it's a human thing') and a fact of Nature that cannot be controlled or stopped. In doing so, the students utilise the language of scientism 'to invoke an aura of truth, trustworthiness and transparency' (Halse, 2008, p. 47). The purpose of scientism, as Foucault (1972) points out, is to lure individuals into accepting a particular positivist account of an object (in this case racism) and to prevent them from seeing or questioning the social order it produces. In constituting racism as a fact of Nature, students summon, from the past, the elemental idea of the 'laws of Nature' as a causal explanation for events and relationships in the social world. The effect of this discourse, however, is to remove responsibility for race-thinking and behaviour from the realm of human history, society and politics, and to locate it in the world of Nature. Here, racism is immune to human intervention and control, and neither individuals nor society can be held responsible or be accountable for the attitudes, beliefs or behaviours that cause racism.

The discourse of racist bullying

Discourses never operate or exist in isolation. They are 'repeatedly colonized, extended by and conflated with other discourses within schools and in society more broadly' and 'at any time, an individual will be positioned in a discursive network of intersecting discourses' (Halse et al., 2007, p. 223). Students demonstrate their positioning in multiple discourses by interweaving the discourse of racism as a fact of Nature with the discourse of racist bullying.

The idea of racism as the result of the actions of a specific person – the racist bully – is widely promoted in anti-bullying school programmes, such as *Bully Stoppers* (DET, 2014), used in Victorian schools. These programmes define the racist bully as a socially deviant person who treats 'people differently because of their identity' (DET, 2014). Social deviance is a strongly held concept in medicine, psychology and branches of sociology. It constitutes and describes behaviours that diverge from those of the 'normal' population, and is used to authorise and legitimate expert intervention to correct and 'normalise' the deviant subject (Halse et al., 2007). The discourse of racist bullying responsibilises by locating racist attitudes and behaviours in a specific category of person: the socially deviant, racist bully. In doing so, it asserts the individualised responsibility of the autonomous, modernist subject by configuring racism as an individual psycho-social pathology: a mode of behaviour that is 'not normal' and for which the socially deviant individual must take responsibility for managing and correcting (DET, 2014).

Thus, the discourses of racism as an act of Nature *and* as racist bullying deflect responsibility for racism onto two disparate entities: the immutable force of Nature and the individual racist bully. These discourses shift responsibility for racism from humankind to the uncontrolled/uncontrollable force of Nature and attribute any exceptions to this rule to a specific, socially deviant person – the racist bully. Yet, the social effects of attributing responsibility for racism in these ways are similar. Both work to *de-responsibilise* by removing the responsibility of individuals to recognise and reform their *own* attitudes and behaviours or to consider how race-thinking and racism is perpetuated through the structures and organisation of society (see Bonilla-Silva, 1997).

Discourse of white victimhood

A responsible stance on racism implies a moral obligation to take up and enact anti-racist attitudes and behaviours. This possibility is obfuscated when the victims of racism are inverted and the responsibility for racism is deflected and reassigned.

> Student 1: I don't think it's okay to offend someone from a different culture, but then I don't think it's okay to offend anyone. Like, I think that it's made so much worse because it's not only controversial but … because they're from a different culture. So if I was to insult someone from a different culture to myself, people would say, not only was I being rude but I was also being racist … but then if I said the same thing to [someone from] my culture then they would just say that I was just being rude … there obviously are some racial things that are said, but I think sometimes racism is over-used. Like [racism is] not a good thing, I'm not saying that, but … sometimes even if you just address the fact that someone might be, I don't know, Asian or something, people say 'Oh no, don't say that. That's racist'. But it's like saying, 'Oh that person's white'. But nobody really from the white culture takes offence to that, but it's almost like … white people have to be very careful with what they say because it can be considered as racist very easily. But other people don't necessarily have to. (Kirkswood Years 7/8 Focus Group, 2014)

This student's talk alleges that charges of racism by 'other people' against the 'white culture' are unwarranted and untrue, and that these claims victimise the 'white culture' by forcing it to change its behaviours to escape accusations of racism. The denial of racism has been described as 'one of the defining aspects of contemporary racism in settler societies like Australia' (Dunn & Nelson, 2011, p. 589), but this student's talk contains subtle twists in logic and language that give it persuasive power. At the beginning and mid-way through the text, the student asserts an anti-racist identity: 'I don't think it's okay to offend someone from a different culture'; 'Like [racism is] not a good thing, I'm not saying that'. But he subtly manipulates language to disguise the racial prejudice intrinsic to his argument: deploying 'racism is over-used' as a proxy for 'racism is *mis-used*'; and papering over the damage racialised language does by equating it with less offensive verbal acts: 'offend', 'rude' and 'insult'. Those alleged to accuse/penalise the 'white culture' are not named but responsibility and blame is slated to this generalised group of 'other people' who are racialised by identifying them as not belonging to the 'white culture'.

The discourse of white victimhood invokes the race-thinking of contemporary, ultra-conservative, white supremacist groups such as the anti-Islam group *Reclaim Australia*, even though empirical evidence of the prevalence of such views is very contradictory (see Forrest & Dunn, 2010). It works to assign responsibility for racism in two ways. First, it denies any individual or collective responsibility by the 'white culture'. Second, it discredits the voices of discontent (Essed, 2002, p. 203) by reversing responsibility for racism and diverting the cause of racism onto the 'other people' who are not part of the 'white culture'. This is an example of where the targets of racism are 'in turn accused of inverted racism against whites, as oversensitive and exaggerating, as intolerant and generally as seeing racism where there is none' (van Dijk, 1992, p. 90). Such reversal is the 'strongest form' of denial and deflection of responsibility for racism because it is a 'strategy of (counter) attack' against the historical victims of racism (p. 94).

The next speaker shows how easily such discourses are reiterated, normalised and inscribe particular forms of race-thinking in others.

> Student 2: Yeah, it's a very thin line between like being racist and not. And it's almost like the minute you mention there being something different about you that includes race, it just becomes racist and you're not allowed to go there ... I'm not saying that people should be racist but I just think that sometimes it's overused. (Kirkswood Years 7/8 Focus Group, 2014)

Discourse of assimilation

The idea that minority groups ought to assimilate and conform to the cultural values and practices of the social majority has had a persistent presence in Australian social and political history. This past has resurfaced in recent decades as successive governments have placed an increasing emphasis on the importance of Australia's Euro-Christian history, the threat to shared values, social cohesion and national identity by immigration and multiculturalism, and the responsibilities of migrants to integrate and assimilate into Australian society. This trend manifests in political moves to prescribe Australian identity through a citizenship test for new migrants in 2006; an 'Australian Values Statement' in 2007; the revision of the national curriculum to emphasise 'Australia's Christian heritage' in 2015; and mandatory Civics and Citizenship education in schools to equip young people with the 'knowledge and understanding of Australia's democratic heritage and traditions, its political and legal institutions and the shared values of freedom, tolerance, respect, responsibility and inclusion' (Education Services Australia, 2015) (see also Fozdar & Low, 2015).

Australia's relationship with and moral responsibilities to asylum seekers, refugees and migrants pervaded national politics and media coverage in 2013–2014 when the focus groups were conducted. During this period, the Australian government tried (unsuccessfully) to ban the wearing of the burka in Parliament House (ostensibly for security reasons) and to remove penalties for racist speech from the Anti-Discrimination Laws (ostensibly to protect free speech). It was also a time when political parties vied to demonstrate their superior ability to manage/halt the growing numbers of asylum seekers arriving in Australia on boats. In the melee, asylum seekers were racialised as foreign, non-Christian, non-English speaking and Other to the national majority. Vitriolic stereotypes abounded: 'unlawful boats'; 'illegal immigrants'; and 'economic not humanitarian refugees'. Ignoring their personal histories and circumstances, these labels categorised *all* asylum seekers as: dishonest and self-serving; working against the national interest by seeking to exploit and benefit from Australia's economic wealth; and violating the sacred national value of a 'fair go for all'. Australia's care of asylum seekers also received repeated exposure during this period with revelations that both children and adults in Australia's detention centres on Manus and Christmas Islands lived in overcrowded living conditions, suffered high rates of mental health problems and sexual abuse, received inadequate medical treatment and care, and experienced long delays in progressing their applications for asylum.

The impact of this intense social and political context surfaced in the focus group discussions about the respective responsibilities of the state and of asylum seekers and migrants. Consistent across all focus groups was students' invoking of a discourse of assimilation that attributed all new arrivals with the responsibility to fit in with Australia's normative values, culture and behaviours.

> Student 1: If you're Australian, there are laws. It's like the burka issue. I just don't think that if you come to Australia you should try and make your own laws again to improve the system. Because – it's going to sound so petty – but we're Australians, like, we were here first. So if you're going to come to Australia and you get this opportunity – this amazing opportunity to start your life again – you're going to have to follow, kind of, our way.
>
> Student 2: Yeah, Australia is a very multicultural country, so I agree that people should have a right to speak their own language that their ancestors or previous family members have spoken and to carry on that kind of tradition, in a way. But I also don't agree when you see – I'm not picking on this because this is the least thing I want to be racist about, but, oh god – men with multiple wives! That's one big issue that I have a really big problem with in Australia, especially. In their own country I think that they should be allowed to uphold their tradition and custom, but once you come into another country, isn't that meant to be a symbol of a new beginning and new life? ... Like you wouldn't want, like, 60,000 wives following you around every day because that's not our way of doing it here. But I don't agree that we should ban languages and other multicultural beliefs and stuff. (Kirkswood, Years 7/8 Focus Group, 2014)

Students acknowledge that 'Australia is a very multicultural country' and voice acceptance of cultural practices they regard as inoffensive or unthreatening ('languages and other multicultural beliefs'). Nevertheless, they also insist that ethnic minorities adopt the Australian 'way' and abandon alien and confronting cultural practices, singling out particular Islamic traditions.

The discourse of assimilation uses words such as 'tradition' and 'culture' to assert 'the power of tribal affiliations' (Gilroy, 2000, p. 27) but it hinges on the assumption that the 'beliefs, values and practices of different ethnic groups are both distinctive and irreconcilable' (Amin, 2010, p. 2). This assumption is evident in students' talk but in ways that move beyond mere cultural racism (Leonardo, 2009). Rather, students merge two different but complementary positions: the civic responsibility to comply/not change Australian laws and the ethnic responsibility to adopt the culture, values and behaviour of the social majority (see Fozdar & Low, 2015). In short, they constitute the beliefs and social practices of ethnic minorities that are poorly understood or uncomfortable to the social majority as incompatible with Australia as a liberal democracy and a culturally cohesive nation.

Thus, the discourse of assimilation constructs the responsibility of ethnic minorities to integrate into Australian society as an issue of collective, national interest and well-being, *and* attributes these groups with responsibility for any negative, racialised tensions that might ensue if they fail to comply. In these ways, the discourse of assimilation deflects responsibility for racism from the social majority, reassigns this responsibility to ethnic minorities, and makes them responsible for any discrimination, exclusion or oppression they experience from neglecting their responsibilities: 'So if you're going to come to Australia … you're going to have to follow, kind of, our way'.

Discourse of mutual responsibility

How minority students viewed their responsibility for racism and the responsibilities of others emerged during a discussion about the role and impact of racialisation in jovial talk.

> Student 1: [It's OK] if something racist or something like culture is used in class as a joke and everyone is OK with it and everyone has a laugh and takes it the right way it's intended to – that's just how we live today, like, in our society. And that can be accepted and it's not really a bad thing. But if it's used in a different way, it's bad.
> I mean I muck around – people call me souvlaki because I'm Greek and I laugh – but it did hurt one of these Muslim kids in my class when one of the boys said 'You're going to blow us up' or something. And he really didn't like it and the kid did apologise to him and he's, like: 'Don't worry, I won't say those jokes again'. He's like, 'Oh, thank you'. That was good. Like, that boy didn't understand that it did really hurt him and it wasn't a funny joke [but] *it only hurts if you let it* [emphasis added]. I mean people call me souvlaki and I have an Indian friend [we call her] 'Curry'. She's like 'Yeah, I eat curry'. And I'm like 'Yeah, I eat souvlaki'. But you've got to make some good friends and not let it get to you. (Jardleigh Years 9/10 Focus Group, 2013)

This student identifies as both Greek *and* Australian. He endorses humourous, non-hurtful racialisation as an accepted, Australian cultural practice: 'that's just how we live today, like, in our society'. However, he attributes all parties involved in any racialised verbal exchange with equal responsibility for their actions: the speaker is responsible for ensuring that her/his jokes are 'funny' and do not cause 'hurt'; the targets of this speech are responsible for managing their responses: 'it only hurts if you let it … you've got to make some good friends and not let it get to you'.

The discourse of mutual responsibility, as Lewis (2001) shows, reflects social contexts where racialised humour is an accepted, everyday form of verbal interaction in which everyone participates and everyone is, therefore, responsible for the effects of their interactions. On the other hand, it is also a discourse that offers a pragmatic strategy for the social and emotional survival of minority groups in racialised contexts that turn a blind-eye to the race-thinking and prejudice immanent in racialised humour and the personal and moral damage that this can do. Regardless of the student's motives for summoning the discourse of mutual responsibility in this particular instance, the discourse of mutual responsibility *responsibilises* by attributing *all* subjects with equal responsibility for monitoring their attitudes, behaviours and responses to prevent racism.

Discussion

Students in these focus groups deploy different, and sometimes contradictory, racialised discourses, the effect of which is to convey, legitimate, deflect and deny *responsibility* for racism in distinct ways. These discourses work variously to deflect responsibility for racism by presenting it as a non-issue in an allegedly post-racial society (the moral discourse of multiculturalism) or by erasing all human responsibility and reassigning it to the elemental forces of Nature (racism as a fact of Nature). In other instances, students' talk deflects responsibility for racism to specific others, such as the socially deviant, racist bully (discourse of racist bullying), the racialised group of 'other people' who accuse the 'white culture' of racism (discourse of white victimhood), or to the minorities who fail to relinquish key aspects of their ethnic identity and adopt the cultural behaviours of the social majority (discourse of assimilation).

Some of these discourses are structural; they are embedded in the institutions, structures and psyche of the nation (discourse of multiculturalism). Others reflect long-established conceptions of the relationship between the natural and social world (racism as a fact of Nature). Others are deeply entangled in the history and politics of diversity, such as in the discourses of assimilation and white victimhood, while the discourses of racist bullying and mutual responsibility have their roots in contemporary social conditions and the practices of schooling.

The discourses deployed in these focus groups do not necessarily reflect the full repertoire of discourses circulating among students and in wider society. Nevertheless, each discourse embodies traces of the past. Amin (2010) asks how the remnants of the past evident in racialised talk can resurface so readily, even when they are inconsistent with each other and the lived experience of contemporary life. To explain this phenomenon, he draws on the ideas of the duration of time and the immanence of the past from French philsopher Henri Bergson. Amin proposes that time and the past are like vital energies that bleed into the present. Consequently, race-thinking from the past always 'lies close to surface things', ready to resurface and to delay, prolong and redirect the course of the present. Hence, the 'accumulated racial debris, variegated and dormant from different eras' always has the potential to be instantiated in daily life, providing the conditions and forces of its repetition are sufficiently strong (pp. 4–5). Thus, duration, immanence and the citational processes of reiteration enable racialised discourses from the past to be resurrected and reworked according to contemporary social conditions. In the focus groups, such traces of the past are evident, for example, in the discourses of racism as a 'fact of Nature', as 'white victimhood', and in the 'discourse of assimilation' and its eliding of legal and ethnic responsibility to meet the desires of the contemporary nation state.

With the exception of the discourse of mutual responsibility, each of the discourses taken up by students works to deny the responsibility of the social majority for racism and to deflect this responsibility to specific individuals (the racist bully), non-human entities (Nature) or those who are deemed Other to the social majority ('other people', migrants). Such denials have a social function; they work to manage the resistance and dissent of minority social groups, and to reproduce and sustain the hegemony of the social majority.

Herein lies the fundamental flaw in the logic of the autonomous, modernist subject and *individual* responsibility for racism. As race scholars such as Iris Young, David Boyd and Barbara Applebaum argue, different social groups come into being because they have their own social, cultural, linguistic and behavioural patterns that are the accepted, approved norms and ways of being in and belonging to the group. These norms are constituted, asserted and affirmed through the reiteration of specific attitudes, values and behaviours. They work to: constitute the *distinctive identity* of each group and the ways it is *different* to other groups; feed the race-thinking that filters how groups views social relations with others; and to constrain the possibilities for individuals to think, act and even imagine different ways of being in the world (Applebaum, 2005; Boyd, 2004). This reiteration operates through everyday talk and the daily interactions that are:

> ... embedded in the unquestioned norms, habits, and symbols, in the assumptions underlying institutional rules and the collective consequences of following those rules [and the] unconscious assumptions and reactions of well-meaning people in ordinary interactions, media and cultural stereotypes, and structural features of bureaucratic hierarchies and market mechanisms – in short the normal processes of daily life. (Young, 1990, p. 41)

As students' talk demonstrates, individuals are conscripted into and compelled to comply with the terms prescribed by discourse. This dynamic operates by silencing challenges to the discourse (multiculturalism), manipulating logic and language (white victimhood) and assigning blame to the historical victims of racism (assimilation). These micro-instances of daily life are powerful, situated moments of governmentality and subjection (Foucault, 1980) that reassert and inscribe the hegemony of the raced, social majority. It is through such strategies that race-thinking is articulated and embedded, the question of personal and/or collective responsibility for racism is denied and deflected, and ethical claims to respond well are obscured and silenced.

in concluding ...

With the exception of the discourse of mutual responsibility, the racialised discourses taken up in students' talk work to deny individual responsibility for racism and to deflect this responsibility onto various others. Contrary to the modernist subject who is individually responsible and capable of exercising sovereign choice to forestall racism, students in these focus groups do not appear to have been seduced or captured by the notion of responsibilisation immanent in curriculum policies or wider society. As such, the question of who and how responsibility for racism might/ought be (re)configured and enacted remains one of the 'moral dilemmas of the present' (Gilroy, 2000, p. 18). Tackling this difficult challenge is beyond the scope of the present article but students' talk reveals the diverse ways in which race-thinking and responsibility for racism are conveyed, legitimated, denied and deflected. It signals the importance of interrogating how everyday talk communicates, shares and embeds the racist values, attitudes and habits that divide and oppress. It calls us to vigilance about the persistence of race-thinking and racism, the imperative to put aside the talk and structures that deny our individual and collective responsibility for these attitudes and behaviours, and to find new ways of being in the world that subvert race-thinking and racism. It alerts us to be cautious about presuming that responsibilisation is a universal social phenomenon and an accurate descriptor of all social relations, and challenges us to extract ourselves from the limitations of its grasp.

Notes

1. The focus groups were part of larger, multi-method study: 'Doing diversity: Intercultural understanding in primary and secondary schools'. The study was funded by the Australia Research

Council [ARCLP 120200319] in partnership with the Victorian Department of Education and Training (DET), the Victorian Curriculum and Assessment Authority (VCAA), the Together for Humanity Foundation (THF) and Pukanui Technology.
2. Year 10 went on an excursion at short notice and the school could not find a suitable alternate time to reschedule the Year 9/10 focus group, so it was decided to progress the focus group with just Year 9 in this instance.

Acknowledgements

I would like to acknowledge the valuable feedback on earlier versions of this article by Caroline Mahoney and Ruth Arber, and two anonymous reviewers. I would also like to express my appreciation to my colleagues involved in the research study, and in organising and conducting the focus groups: Ruth Arber, Claire Charles, Ann Cloonan, Catherine Hartung, Julianne Moss, Joanne O'Mara, and Sarah Ohi.

Disclosure statement

No potential conflict of interest was reported by the author.

References

Amin, A. (2010). The remainders of race. *Theory, Culture & Society, 27*(1), 1–23.
Applebaum, B. (2005). On 'glass snakes'. In K. H. Rowe (Ed.), *Philosophy of education 2005* (pp. 149–157). Urbana: University of Illinois Press.
Australian Curriculum, Assessment, Research Authority. (2014). *Intercultural understanding*. Retrieved August 2014, from http://www.australiancurriculum.edu.au/GeneralCapabilities/intercultural-understanding/introduction/introduction
Australian Government. (2013). *Australia's multicultural policy – December 2013*. Canberra: Australian Government Printing Services.
Bennett, J., & Lee-Treweek, G. (2014). Doing race: How secondary school pupils in mainly white schools construct 'race'. *Power and Education, 6*(1), 32–45.
Bonilla-Silva, E. (1997). Rethinking racism: Toward a structural interpretation. *American Sociological Review, 62*(3), 465–480.
Boyd, D. (2004). The legacies of liberalism and oppressive relations: Facing a dilemma for the subject of moral education. *Journal of Moral Education, 33*(1), 3–22.
DET (Victorian Department of Education). (2014). *Bully stoppers*. Retrieved November 12, 2014, from http://www.education.vic.gov.au/about/programs/bullystoppers/Pages/default.aspx
van Dijk, T. A. (1992). Discourse and the denial of racism. *Discourse and Society, 3*(1), 87–118.
Dolby, N. (2000). The shifting ground of race: The role of taste in youth's production of identities. *Race, Ethnicity and Education, 3*(1), 7–23.
Dunn, K., & Nelson, J. K. (2011). Challenging the public denial of racism for a deeper multiculturalism. *Journal of Intercultural Studies, 32*(6), 587–602.
Education Services Australia. (2015). *Civics and citizenship education*. Retrieved September 2, 2015, from http://www.civicsandcitizenship.edu.au/cce/about_civics_and_citizenship_education,9625.html
Essed, P. (2002). Everyday racism. In D. T. Goldberg & J. Solomos (Eds.), *A companion to racial and ethnic studies* (pp. 202–216). Malden, MA: Blackwell.
Forrest, J., & Dunn, K. (2010). Attitudes to multicultural values in diverse spaces in Australia's immigrant cities, Sydney and Melbourne. *Space and Polity, 14*(1), 81–102.
Foucault, M. (1972). *Archeology of knowledge*. London: Routledge.
Foucault, M. (1980). *Power/knowledge: Selected interviews and other writings*. Brighton: Harvester Press.

Fozdar, F., & Low, M. (2015). 'They have to abide by our laws … and stuff': Ethnonationalism masquerading as civic nationalism. *Nations and Nationalism, 21*(3), 524–543.

Gee, J. (1990/2008). *Ideology in discourses*. Milton Park: Routledge.

Gillborn, D. (1990). *Race, ethnicity and education: Teaching and learning in multi-ethnic schools*. London: Unwin Hyman.

Gillborn, D. (2008). Coincidence or conspiracy: Whiteness, policy and the persistence of the black/white achievement gap. *Educational Review, 60*(3), 229–248.

Gilroy, P. (2000). *Against race: Imagining popular culture beyond the color line*. Cambridge, MA: Harvard University Press.

Giroux, H. A. (1993). Living dangerously: Identity politics and the new cultural racism: Towards a critical pedagogy of representation. *Cultural Studies, 7*(1), 1–27.

Halse, C. (2008). Bio-citizenship: Virtue discourses and the birth of the bio-citizen. In J. Wright & V. Harwood (Eds.), *Biopolitics and the 'obesity epidemic': Governing bodies* (pp. 45–59). London: Routledge.

Halse, C., Honey, A., & Boughtwood, D. (2007). The paradox of virtue: (Re)thinking deviance, anorexia and schooling. *Gender and Education, 19*(2), 219–235.

Kromidas, M. (2010). Cyberculture, multiculture and the emergent morality of critical cosmpolitanism: Kids (trans)forming difference online. In D. Chappell (Ed.), *Children under construction* (pp. 233–258). New York, NY: Peter Lang.

Lemke, T. (2001). 'The birth of bio-politics': Michel Foucault's lecture at the Collège de France on neo-liberal governmentality. *Economy and Society, 30*(2), 190–207.

Leonardo, Z. (2009). *Race, whiteness, and education*. New York, NY: Routledge.

Lewis, A. (2001). There is no 'race' in the schoolyard: Colour-blind ideology in an (almost) white school. *American Educational Research Journal, 38*(4), 781–811.

McLeod, J., & Yates, L. (2003). Who is 'us'? Students negotiating discourses of racism and national identification in Australia. *Race, Ethnicity and Education, 6*(1), 29–49.

Puzic, S. (2008). Intercultural education in the European context: Analysis of selected European curricula. *Metodika, 15*, 390–401.

Sue, D. W. (2010). *Microaggressions in everyday life: Race, gender, and sexual orientation*. Hoboken, NJ: John Wiley & Sons.

UNESCO. (2006). *Guidelines on Intercultural Education*. Paris: Author.

UNESCO. (2010). *Education for intercultural understanding*. Bangkok: Author.

UNESCO. (2013). *Intercultural competences: Conceptual and operational framework*. Paris: Author.

Young, I. (1990). *Justice and the politics of difference*. Princeton, NJ: Princeton University Press.

Global citizenship incorporated: competing responsibilities in the education of global citizens

Catherine Hartung

ABSTRACT
Interest in the education of young people to be 'responsible global citizens' has grown exponentially since the turn of the century, led by increasingly diverse networks of sectors, including government, community, business and philanthropy. These networks now have a significant influence on education policy and practice, indicative of wider changes in governance and processes of globalisation. Yet little of the academic literature on global citizenship education specifically examines the impact of these networks on the production of knowledge about young global citizens. This paper addresses this gap by analysing the discourses of global citizenship that underpin recent work by a youth organisation that works closely with a network of sectors in Australia. The paper finds that a particular kind of entrepreneurial global citizen is favoured, one that is simultaneously responsible for themselves, for the rights of others and for ensuring Australia's future economic prosperity.

Introduction

Notions of responsibility permeate public life in the twenty-first century. This is no more evident than in the field of global citizenship education (GCE) where the emphasis is on producing global citizens who are able to take responsibility for a plethora of global challenges in 'uncertain times'. While this global emphasis is not new, since the turn of the century, interest in GCE has intensified and expanded considerably beyond the traditional educational sites of the nation-state. This interest has arisen from a diverse network of national and transnational organisations and companies that are increasingly involved in the promotion of global citizenship and the education of young people as global citizens. This is indicative of wider changes in education policy reform and governance which is characterised by the increasing involvement of private or social enterprises due to a perceived failure of the nation-state (Ball, 2012). The intensification of interest in GCE is also evident in the academic literature; two-thirds of which has been published since year 2000 (Parmenter, 2011). This literature has examined GCE from a range of perspectives, some of which will be examined in this paper. However, very little of this literature has examined the impact of new networks that are playing increasingly influential roles in the production of GCE. This absence of examination is evident in the education policy literature more broadly. Indeed, despite the interest in globalisation and new forms of governance, 'most education policy analysis is still locked into a nation-state, policy-as-government paradigm' (Ball, 2012, p. xii) that fails to recognise the increasingly diverse spaces in which policy is now created.

This paper attends to Ball's call for analysis that takes into account the new educational sites of production beyond the nation-state. To do so, the paper examines some of the effects of these new networks on the responsibilities that are privileged or supported when it comes to GCE in the Australian context. There are a number of Australian institutions that could be considered for examination. However, the paper will focus on the work of the Foundation for Young Australians (FYA) because it is the only national independent non-profit organisation dedicated to young people in Australia and is therefore the epitome of an organisation that sits 'outside' traditional educational sites and has come to have significant influence on education in Australia. Further, the FYA is supported and funded by a diverse network of schools, government, corporations, philanthropists, research institutions and non-governmental organisations (NGOs). In order to make the examination of a manageable scale, the paper will focus on the FYA's website and 2013 publication 'Unlimited Potential'. These particular texts were chosen because at the time of analysis, the website and publication were the most up-to-date documents available to a wide audience. By examining the contents of both the website and publication, the aim is to examine the diverse ways in which young people are called upon to be responsible as global citizens and how these intersect and/or compete with the political agendas of the network of institutions that support the FYA's work.

While the FYA's work is not solely or specifically about 'GCE', young people are often referred to as 'global citizens' in their material and the FYA's mission is described on their website as:

> Together, with young people, we want to influence and shape education and career pathways, transform worldviews and lead communities in innovative ways. Together, we want to change the world.

The organisation has established its reputation in advocacy, education and research through collaborations with 10,000 educators and 1 million young people and has leveraged over $30 million in investment (FYA website, 2014). As a result, FYA has exercised substantial influence in relation to educational and youth policy in Australia. Given this significant track record and public presence, it is surprising that FYA has not been subject to more investigation from within the academy.

While the FYA has published a number of reports and publications, 'Unlimited Potential' is one of the organisation's most recent publications and was featured on the homepage of their website that is accessed by a diverse audience of potential and current funders, practitioners, young people and other interested members of the public. The website and 26-page publication provide information about the work of the organisation and some of their key initiatives, the majority of which centre around young people participating in work experience or volunteering. 'Unlimited Potential' also includes a number of recommendations and proposals for how key institutions, communities and governments can equip young people for life and work in the twenty-first century. The website and publication are stylishly designed with colourful graphic elements and professionally shot photographs of young people throughout. Text is presented in short paragraphs interspersed with quotations and statistics.

Defining global citizenship and GCE

Global citizenship encompasses a wide range of dimensions, from the political, moral and economic, through to the social, critical, environmental and spiritual. It has been a key interest of the education system, as well as industry and government, for centuries. Indeed, the term 'global citizen' can be traced back to the ancient Greek notion of the 'cosmopolitan', meaning 'citizen of the world' (Lettevall & Klockar Linder, 2008). In more recent times, the notion of global citizenship has gained popularity due its ability to incite and validate particular political action in times of uncertainty; it has been described as the 'great white hope' of international relations, as well as a 'counterbalance' to political and economic threats (Brysk, 2002, p. 243).

Strongly connected to this notion of global citizenship is a call for people to recognise themselves as democratic members of a global community not restricted by state borders. This call has been circulated and supported across the Western media, social entrepreneurs and 'transnational celebrity activists' like Bono and Jamie Oliver who campaign for a 'better world' through their own particular brand of citizenship (see e.g. Kelly & Harrison, 2009; Tsaliki, Frangonikolopoulos, & Huliaras, 2011). Moreover, many international corporations (e.g. Ernst & Young, Cisco, Coca-Cola and Cotton On) are 'tapping into' the popular discourse of global citizenship, funding campaigns and publishing materials focused on the promotion of responsible global citizenship.[1] Such a discourse tends to emphasise and promote individual responsibility as a means of finding solutions to global problems, epitomised in the oft-quoted line 'be the change you wish to see in the world'.[2]

GCE is also assigned a plethora of diverse meanings, though it is popularly concerned with the development of particular skills, knowledge and values in young people that are deemed particularly useful in their present and future interactions with diverse people and places. Much of the literature on GCE presents normative accounts of what a responsible global citizen 'should' look like. This is often supported by discourses of human rights and social justice, backed by respected international organisations, such as UNESCO and UNICEF. For example, the UNESCO website (2014) describes GCE as equipping:

> ... learners of all ages with those values, knowledge and skills that are based on and instil respect for human rights, social justice, diversity, gender equality and environmental sustainability and that empower learners to be responsible global citizens ... that promote a better world and future for all.

Rights-based discourses on GCE also often intersect with popular discourses of youth empowerment and voice, as a counterpoint to potentially damaging deficit models of young people that justify the exclusion of them based on their presumed vulnerability, immaturity, incompetence, rebelliousness or incompleteness. By contrast, positioning and educating young people as responsible global citizens offers a more optimistic and progressive view underpinned by honourable intentions to 'empower' them so that they have a 'voice' in political and social spaces from which they are traditionally excluded. This vision of young people, presented through GCE, has garnered support across a range of fields, including children's rights, children's participation and the sociology of childhood. It is a vision that not only positions young people as responsible for making decisions about their own lives, but as responsible for solving political, social and environmental issues at a national and global scale. Such a vision presents an alternative to a deficit model that views young people as 'silent, invisible, passive objects of parental and/or state control' (Stasiulis, 2002, p. 2) and is evident in much of the GCE literature, particularly that which seeks to identify select attributes and behaviours of an ideal global citizen, such as responsible, empathetic and interculturally aware (see e.g. Gerzon, 2010; Schattle, 2008; Veugelers, 2011). Here the notion of responsibility is accorded to young people through empowerment practices that highlight their capacities as global citizens and to distinguish between those young people who do the 'right thing' and those who are not yet equipped to do so, even though the 'right thing' is often vague, decontextualised and disconnected from the mechanisms deciding who or what is 'right'.

This position on GCE is also evident in the more critical literature on GCE. Much of this literature is concerned with distinguishing between 'good' and 'bad' practices and policies of GCE, often positioning these according to constructed binaries, such as 'above' vs 'below', 'north' vs 'south' and 'weak' vs 'strong' (see e.g. Andreotti, 2006; Shukla, 2009; Shultz, 2011). Structuring analysis of GCE around a binary is particularly evident in the work of Andreotti (2006), who argues that most approaches to GCE fall into one of two categories, 'soft' or 'critical'. 'Soft' GCE promotes a passive, uncomplicated engagement with the world that may reinforce inequality; 'critical' GCE combats these limitations by encouraging young people to critically and actively engage with notions of power, inequality and difference. Further, Andreotti (2006, p. 41) argues that if we fail to critically engage with GCE, 'we may end up promoting a new "civilising mission" as the slogan for a generation who take up the "burden" of saving/educating/civilising the world' and thereby 'project their beliefs and myths as universal and reproduce power relations and violence similar to those in colonial times'. While this critical work has been highly influential, drawing on binaries can disable more nuanced examinations that recognise the many 'grey areas' within and between the 'good' and 'bad' policies and practices of GCE.

There is also an increasing amount of critical literature that focuses on the underlying discourses and ideologies of GCE (see e.g. Arnot, 2009; Hartung, 2011; Oxley & Morris, 2013; Parmenter, 2011; Richardson, 2008; Schattle, 2008), often underpinned by Foucauldian and governmentality theory (such as Lemke, 2001; Miller, 1993; Rose, 1999) that highlights the neo-liberal processes by which individuals are governed so as to support economic and political needs. Critical GCE theorists argue that the popular discourse of global citizenship functions as a technology of subjection or 'an attempt at a remoralisation of young people' (Arnot, 2009, p. 227), one that produces an 'entrepreneurial self' (Peters, 2001). Rather than a 'byproduct of capitalism', Ruddick (2003, p. 334) argues childhood is located 'at its literal and figurative core'. Similarly, Prout (2000, p. 306) contends that with an increasingly complex, changing and uncertain world, 'children, precisely because they are seen as especially unfinished, appear as a good target for controlling the future'. Consequently, how children are constituted is strongly linked with wider societal demands. There is an increasing push to frame the education of citizens with solving global problems (Banks et al., 2005; Camicia & Saavedra, 2009; Parker, Ninomiya, &

Cogan, 2002). For example, when Parker et al. (2002, p. 162) surveyed the preferences of a multinational panel of 'experts' from business, scientific and educational fields, they found a significant consensus regarding the need for a 'multinational, deliberation-based school curriculum focused on complex worldwide ethical problems', with the primary objective to create 'multidimensional citizens'. Similarly, Banks et al. (2005) argue that children need to be knowledgeable about the world, as well as global problem-solvers and a force for positive change. Such a position is fuelled by an emphasis on particular human characteristics and responsibilities that are seen as necessary in a 'global world'. This take on young people's global role strongly intersects with what Ruddick (2003, p. 357) describes as the 'kind of future globalizations we wish to tolerate or create, and the social spaces and infrastructures we develop, who is included or excluded – and how'.

This critical literature suggests a notion of responsibility closely tied to neo-liberal processes by which young people are positioned to govern themselves and others, a process often referred to as 'responsibilisation'. Responsibilisation is a concept closely tied to other global regulatory processes that have become 'buzzwords' of the twenty-first century, such as 'individualisation', 'neo-liberalism', 'democratisation' and 'globalisation'. It is through such regulatory processes that the 'modern subject' is produced and reproduced; an increasing emphasis on self-determination and active citizenship is used to ensure realms outside the state (i.e. the social, private, market and civil society) 'function to the benefit of the nation as a whole' (Rose, 1996, p. 44). Lemke (2001, p. 201) argues that this neo-liberal rationality seeks to achieve congruence between a 'responsible and moral individual' and an 'economic-rational actor'. Through these neo-liberal processes of responsibilisation, Kelly and Harrison (2009, p. 8) argue that young people are compelled to carefully manage the risks of their own 'DIY project of the Self', a sort of institutionally determined autonomy.

GCE in the Australian context

Global citizenship has become increasingly embedded in Australian educational policy since the social movements and progressive pedagogies of the 1960s and 1970s, with particular intensification since the turn of the century as reflected in the Melbourne Declaration on Educational Goals for Young Australians (MCEETYA, 2008):

> Global integration and international mobility have increased rapidly in the past decade. As a consequence, new and exciting opportunities for Australians are emerging. This heightens the need to nurture an appreciation of, and respect for, social, cultural and religious diversity, and a sense of global citizenship. (p. 4)

The notion of global citizenship is evident in a range of state and national education curriculum frameworks and resources, including 'A better world for all' (Calder & Smith, 1993) and 'Global perspectives: a statement on global education for Australian schools' (Curriculum Corporation, 2002). The development of the Australian Curriculum and the various phases and amendments that have occurred since its initial inception in 2008 also point to the importance of GCE, which tends to overlap with other Australian educational priorities, such as intercultural understanding, civics and citizenship, Asia-literacy and engagement, sustainability and the environment, languages and values education, as well as the International Baccalaureate (Doherty & Mu, 2011). As an educational priority,

GCE asks young Australians to reflect on, and change, their cultural, political and social identities in accordance with particular democratic ideals.

Such curriculum activity indicates that there is significant interest in GCE in Australia. It is perhaps not surprising then that the academic literature tends to focus on curriculum documents and school-based initiatives as the bases for analysis (see e.g. Davies, Evans, & Reid, 2005; Doherty & Mu, 2011; Lingard & McGregor, 2014). However, an increasing number of GCE resources are based on partnerships between the state, the academy and various national and international NGOs (e.g., Primary English Teaching Association Australia, World Vision, Oxfam, Asia Education Foundation, Australian Agency for International Development). Consequently, the responsibility for promoting and delivering GCE in Australia has shifted to those organisations operating outside traditional educational spaces. This shift is reflected in the work of Black (2008) who argues that 'tinkering around the edges of schooling' will not rectify educational inequality and calls for:

> ... new models of schooling that recognise that the future of children and young people is the responsibility of the whole community, and which form the basis of a social alliance for all young people to take an active – if not leading – role in their community. (p. 2)

Framing the analysis

This paper draws on a poststructural discourse analysis and the genealogical work of Foucault (1981) in order to grapple with the contextual complexities described above. According to Foucault, discourse refers to both a body of knowledge and a set of practices that, when linked to a discipline, constitute and govern subjects in relation to that discipline. In this sense, knowledge is linked to power because it acts upon the actions of individuals, creating and restricting conditions of possibility. Consequently, this approach to discourse analysis focuses on the historical and social context of texts, rather than their linguistic features. While this approach does not imply a strict set of rules or prescribed steps for conducting an analysis, it does lend itself to a distinct type of questioning. Consequently, I pose three questions to frame this analysis:

(1) How did the FYA emerge and what institutions and discourses sustain its relevance in relation to young people's global citizenship?
(2) What language is used to describe young people and their responsibilities and are there instances where these descriptions contradict?
(3) What do the dominant discourses exclude and where have they been contested?

To answer these questions, I begin by tracing the emergence of FYA and the different ideas and institutional networks that are attributed responsibility for young people and upon which the FYA's continued work is contingent. I then analyse the discourses that are privileged within the texts and the underlying contradictions that exist in the language used to describe young people. Finally, I highlight some of the discourses and subjects that may be subjugated as a result.

It is important to note that my interest is not in forming judgements about whether the FYA's work is 'good' or 'bad', but in identifying the discourses that underpin the texts and their effects on how young people are constituted.

The Foundation for Young Australians

Formed in 2000 through a partnership between The Queen's Trust (1977–2000) and the Australian Youth Foundation (1987–2000), the FYA was originally a funding body focused on supporting young people from disadvantaged backgrounds. In 2010, with a new CEO, the organisation's focus shifted to being an 'initiative incubation space focused on education and social change' for *all* young Australians.

In the past few years the FYA's website has emerged as a key starting point for young people and potential funders who are interested in finding out more information about the organisation and their various initiatives. The website includes an extensive list of FYA's institutional partners across a multitude of sectors and industries. On the FYA's website they identify a range of 'major supporters', such as global engineering companies Kentz and Laing O'Rourke, Lotterywest, the National Australia Bank, Samsung, Shell, The Trust Company, UBS, Xero and The Myer Foundation, as well as the Victorian Government and the Northern Territory Government. The majority of these are large profit-making corporations. Consequently, they are primarily focused on the best financial return rather than on the interests of young people, per se.

Since the majority of the FYA's listed initiatives are supported by a combination of large companies and state governments, this has been reflected in the strong intermingling of discourses of business leadership with social change. For example, '$20 Boss', an initiative supported by the National Australia Bank and the Victorian Government, is aimed at inspiring young people to 'be more entrepreneurial whilst creating businesses that make the world a better place'. Similarly, the initiative 'Adappt', supported by Samsung, is described as 'a movement of young Australians using technology to solve humanity's biggest problems'. In addition, the high school-based program 'High Resolves' uses the motto 'Our world, our choice' and is aimed at helping 'students to realise that they have a personal role to play in how human society develops as a global community and that the choices they make in life will make a difference'. High Resolves is also seen as a stepping stone into other FYA initiatives, namely 'Young People Without Borders' and 'Young Social Pioneers' – both of which are highlighted as case studies in their publication 'Unlimited Potential' and will be discussed in more detail in the next section.

The website also lists FYA's team of almost 70 employees whose professional titles range from 'program managers' and 'coordinators' to 'engagement and partnerships officers'. Similarly, the website also includes a page dedicated to FYA's 'alumni' of young people, all of whom also have a range of professional titles, from 'entrepreneur', 'director', 'CEO', to 'founder', 'advisor' and 'chair'. This business-like language is particularly familiar and appealing to current and potential, and predominantly corporate, funders. Such language also reinforces a particular image of the ideal young citizen, whose empowered outlook is closely tied to their position within a corporate trajectory.

Although schools work in partnership on many of these initiatives, the FYA's work is contingent upon schools being inadequate in their support of young people or else how could one justify the existence of an external body like the FYA? For example, in the publication 'Unlimited Potential', where the picture of young people was 'relentlessly optimistic', the view of schools was much more critical. Schools are described in the publication as 'failing' young people and society, as 'out-dated' and 'irrelevant'. In doing so the publication presents a strong binary between schooling and industry, whereby engagement with the latter is seen as freeing young people from the limitations of the classroom. The negative view of schooling constituted in the publication sets up a space that needs 'filling' if young people are to meet the demands of industry. The FYA and other organisations are thus able to position themselves as key agents in supporting young people.

FYA's authority as an 'expert' on young people and youth policy in Australia is also contingent upon their being actively involved in the dissemination of, and engagement with, popular knowledge and up-to-date research on young people. Again, much of their engagement and dissemination activities reflect the FYA's strong network of government bodies, NGOs and business. For example, surveying the reference list in the 2013 publication, there are three general clusters of literature. The first and most dominant cluster of literature includes reports and papers published by Australian government departments, including the Australian Bureau of Statistics (ABS), the Australian Curriculum, Assessment and Reporting Authority (ACARA), Graduate Careers, Department of Immigration and Citizenship and the Department of Industry, Innovation, Science, Research and Tertiary Education. The second most popular source of knowledge came from reports from global corporations and organisations, including Cisco Systems, MTV, OECD and the World Bank. Third, there were also a small number of references to research coming out of research organisations, namely the Asia Education Foundation, based at the University of Melbourne. In addition to these references, the publication also drew on well-worn quotes by three famous dead thinkers to reinforce particular ideals about young people and education, namely Albert Einstein, John Maynard Keynes and George Bernard Shaw. Indeed, the references were primarily used to either provide a quick snapshot of quantifiable data to give a rationale for the FYA's work or to reinforce particular discourses about young people. A closer examination of the references suggest that they are primarily from sources that have certain interests in the production of particular kinds of young citizens; young citizens who might, for example, have the skills to facilitate business across state borders rather than to critically appraise the impacts of such business.

Contradictory responsibilities: global citizenship incorporated

> We need young Australians to be confident, connected, enterprising, innovative, optimistic, generous and happy. It begins with an equitable, world class and outward looking education system and the opportunity for young people to engage and become immersed in the real world. (Jan Owen, FYA CEO, 14 March 2013)

Building on the previous section's analysis, this section will analyse the contradictions that exist between competing discourses about young people and global citizenship that dominate FYA's publication and website. As indicated in the above quote from CEO Jan Owen, FYA presents a very bright image of young Australians. Throughout the publication, there is an absence of any negative language in relation to young people, perhaps a response to the need to move beyond a deficit model that so many other organisations have privileged in their work with young people from disadvantaged backgrounds. Instead, the FYA uses an array of positive attributes to describe young people, including: agile, enterprising, engaging, inspiring, empowered, persistent, resilient, willing, imaginative, optimistic, happy, confident, creative, passionate, effective, aware, active, generous, innovative, courageous and resourceful. They are spoken of as a 'source of energy', a 'driving force', as 'comfortable with change' and 'technology savvy', and with 'untapped talent'. Supporting these descriptions are photographs of young people standing confidently, face-on and often gesturing, as though making a speech. Other photographs show groups of young people in the midst of conversation or clustered around a computer screen. Positive descriptions of young people are also evident in the titles of the three key sections of the publication: 'future focused learners', 'enterprising changemakers' and 'confident global citizens'. Such labels place the emphasis on young people as 'beings' in the here and now rather than 'becomings' or future citizens. Within each of these sections an FYA initiative is highlighted alongside a case study of a young person who was involved. This focus on individual young people is consistent across much of the FYA's material. Indeed, aside from an occasional photograph of a small group of young people in the same room or studio, the website and publication privilege stories of individual young people rather than a collective.

By describing young people in relation to their potential contribution to both solving the world's problems and enhancing business relationships nationally and abroad, this language works to produce a particular kind of subject that is constituted in accordance with his or her institutional value. Further, in portraying young people in such a way, the publication separates young people from their context, placing them in one homogeneous group with similar needs, desires and capabilities. This suggests a process of responsibilisation, whereby underlying power relations are ignored and responsibility is placed on the young person to be exceptional.

Suggesting young people have responsibility over their own lives while also requiring that they be responsible for particular corporate or political needs points to a fundamental discontinuity within the work of the FYA. This discontinuity simultaneously supports young people to 'create the world they want to live in' while also 'meeting the demands of Australia's future economy' (FYA, 2013). For example, the introductory section of the publication states:

> Our collective role is to be relentlessly optimistic about the young people of this country and about their capacity and capability to envision and create the nation and world in which they want to live and work.

Here it would seem that the focus is clearly on the young people and what they want. Yet, further into the publication we find a shift in focus with the following:

> The predicted benefits [of youth engaging with Asia] are startling. For example, it is predicted that Australia could potentially lift its economic performance by up to $275 billion over the next 10 years through closer ties with Asia.

This passage shifts the focus from the young person's needs to the needs of the economy. Or rather, it relies on the assumption that the two will work harmoniously together. In marrying enterprise with a social person, the document presents a strongly neo-liberal view of a young person's national and global responsibilities built on market demands. This plays out in different ways across the three initiatives showcased in the publication. For example, in the two case studies featuring young men, the focus is on the attainment of business skills for the betterment of the individual and society, an atomised individual and an abstract society defined in economic terms. In the case study of Chris Raine, who started the website 'Hello Sunday Morning' that encourages young people to monitor their alcohol consumption, the emphasis is on 'enterprise with a social purpose'. Similarly, Kevin, a young Sudanese man, who took part in the FYA's work experience placement, 'World of Work project', describes meeting stockbrokers who advised him to 'trust self', 'watch less TV' and 'make goals'. Kevin reflects, 'I felt successful just by having spoken to you'. Both of these case studies place the emphasis on the young men's entrepreneurial aspirations coupled with their ability to govern themselves in more responsible ways by avoiding behaviours deemed unproductive such as watching television and drinking alcohol.

Notions of responsibility were also evident in the third initiative showcased in the publication which focused on a case study of the young woman, Chanoa, and her reflections and experiences of volunteering as an English teacher in China as part of the FYA's 'Young People Without Borders' (YPWB) initiative. According to the website, the YPWB initiative 'creates pathways and opportunities for young Australians to experience and become immersed in our Asian region'. Rather than an explicit focus on market goals and responsibilities, Chanoa's story focused on her fostering responsible global relationships. For example, Chanoa states:

> [I]t's amazing. They [the Chinese students] were all going on to uni and they really inspired me to go too. Before I went away I had a very stereotypical 'television' view of what Chinese people would be like, but now I have made so many friends for life. I've now got a home in China. They've now got a home in Australia.

The emphasis here is on learning about and connecting with other cultures, making friends and being motivated for tertiary study. While this focus is quite different from the previous case studies of the young men, there remains a focus on individual rather than collective gains. This gender disparity in how responsibility is understood and enacted – the male as responsible entrepreneur vs the female as responsible relationship manager – reflects the work of other researchers who have been concerned with issues of gender within GCE (see e.g. Arnot, 2009; Harris, 2004; Tormey & Gleeson, 2012).[3]

These three case studies demonstrate how young people and their global responsibilities are 'atomised' through an entrepreneurial or neo-liberal lens, whereby engagement with the world is limited to individual actions, jobs and relationships that potentially downplay the role of the collective and systemic.

Subjugated knowledges: beyond neo-liberal global citizenship

> [I]f one were to dislocate it [global citizenship] from the contextual historical embeddedness of neoliberal and imperial discourses of globalization, and begin afresh with it untainted, what questions might be asked of it? ... What does/might global citizenship actually mean? ... To whom might it mean this and why? What is demanded of an ethic of global citizenship in a world suffocating under poverty and environmental destruction and human degradation on a massive scale (Swanson, 2011, p. 122)

In this final section of the analysis the attention turns to highlighting knowledges that are subjugated in the process of producing particular ideas about young people and global citizenship. By 'subjugated knowledges' I refer to the ideas or people that become subordinated or marginalised when other ideas come to dominate. Consequently, in this last section the emphasis is on highlighting subjugated knowledges that become apparent when too much emphasis is given to an entrepreneurial or neo-liberal vision of the responsible global citizen.

One such 'subjugated knowledge' relates to those 'global responsibilities' that sit outside of, or even compete with, political or corporate agendas. As already indicated, the popular discourses reinforced through the FYA's website and publication rest on the assumption that what young people desire will also be what is 'best' for the nation and vice versa. In other words, there is an assumption that the world in which young people want to live and work will accord with an economic growth-oriented world. This subjugates different understandings of young people who may not be able, or desire, to fit into this entrepreneurial image. Furthermore, this subjugates research and perspectives which take a more critical stance on global citizenship, one which, for example, may opt for a 'degrowth' economy in order to respond to the environmental issues of our times.

Furthermore, through the FYA's network of businesses and government organisations, the knowledge that is privileged ignores a significant body of research literature that maintains a necessarily critical perspective on the neo-liberal discourses that position young people as entrepreneurial citizens. Such a literature, much of which was described in the opening sections of this paper, is a fairly undesirable entity among these new policy networks. As Gunter (2009, p. 94) contends in her paper on the fragile project of critical educational research, using the word 'critical' is becoming increasingly difficult even though 'being critical and doing critical work is not new or dangerous or necessarily oppositional, but it is vitally important in these neo-liberal hard new times'. Indeed, an uncritical focus on the individual responsibilities of young people also has the potential to 'apoliticise' the notion of global citizenship, which in turn may override or indeed reproduce systemic forms of inequality that exist within and between nation-states.

Conclusion

The young person as responsible global citizen has developed into a powerful idea in the twenty-first century, one supported and disseminated by an increasingly diverse network of sites beyond the nation-state. This paper has focused on one such networked site, the FYA, and the discourses that underpin the notions of young people's global citizenship evident on their website and a recent publication. In taking such a focus, the aim of the paper is not to cast judgement on whether the work of the FYA is 'good' or 'bad', but to consider the effects of the underlying discourses by which young people are constituted. As Foucault (1981) states:

> A critique does not consist in saying that things aren't good the way they are. It consists in seeing on just what type of assumptions, of familiar notions, of established and unexamined ways of thinking the accepted practices are based. (p. 456)

In examining the familiar, established and unexamined ways of thinking evident in the FYA's published material, the above analysis has identified how the networked nature of FYA is underpinned by intersecting neo-liberal discourses of enterprise and self-empowerment that in turn privilege a particular kind of entrepreneurial young person. The analysis has problematised the conflation of these discourses, highlighting the potential danger in assuming compatibility between the interests of business, the interests of the globe and the interests of young people. Yet, within the critical literature on neo-liberalism, such an argument is not particularly new. Indeed, criticism of the underlying neo-liberal agenda of global citizenship and youth empowerment has been highlighted in a number of papers within the last 20 years. So why then has this theoretical work failed to make a mark on publications such as FYA's 'Unlimited Potential', especially as FYA's diverse networks include research and practical initiatives with young people? Is it even reasonable to expect organisations to address the limitations of the discourses underlying their work in a context where they are competing for funding and critical reflection might work against them? There is a need to bridge the gap between the theoretical and critical work within the academy with the practices and policies in the field. This requires thinking differently about young people and responsibility and broadening critical work so that it takes into account the realities of networked sites, such as FYA. This is a point Rose (2014, p. 17) begins to address, highlighting the need to identify 'handholds' that enable 'a more optimistic intellectual and political engagement'. The sorts of handholds used by the FYA in the above analysis seem limited to hyperbolic descriptions of young people as infinitely powerful, if only in potential. It is our job now as researchers to offer new ways forward that challenge but also engage with these assumptions in ways that are productive and optimistic rather than dismissive or inaccessible.

Notes

1. For example, Cotton On and Coca-Cola's involvement in Bono's Global Citizen Festival and Cisco's reports on global, technology-driven education.
2. Quote has no clear origin although often misattributed to Mahatma Gandhi.
3. Such an observation does not suggest that all of FYA's material is consistent with these particular representations of young men and women.

Acknowledgements

The author would like to thank the two anonymous reviewers, as well as Christine Halse, Jan Wright, Trevor McCandless and Gary Levy, for their helpful feedback on earlier drafts of this paper.

Disclosure statement

No potential conflict of interest was reported by the author.

References

Andreotti, V. (2006). Soft versus critical global citizenship education. *Policy and Practice – A Development Education Review, 3*(Autumn), 40–51.
Arnot, M. (2009). *Educating the gendered citizen: Sociological engagements with national and global Agendas*. London: Routledge.
Ball, S. J. (2012). *Global Education Inc*. London & New York: Routledge.
Banks, J. A., Banks, C. A. M., Cortes, C. E., Hah, C. L., Merryfield, M. M., & Moodley, K. A. (2005). *Democracy and diversity: Principles and concepts for educating citizens in a global age*. Seattle, WA: Center for Multicultural Education, University of Washington.
Black, R. (2008). *Beyond the classroom: Building new school networks*. Camberwell, Victoria: ACER Press.
Brysk, A. (2002). Conclusion: From rights to realities. In A. Brysk (Ed.), *Globalisation and human rights* (pp. 242–256). Oakland, CA: University of California Press.

Calder, M., & Smith, R. (1993). *A better world for all: Development education for the classroom*. Books 1 and 2 (2nd ed.). Canberra: AIDAB.

Camicia, S. P., & Saavedra, C. M. (2009). A new childhood social studies curriculum for a new generation of citizenship. *The International Journal of Children's Rights, 17*(3), 501–517.

Curriculum Corporation. (2002). *Global perspectives: A statement on global education for Australian schools*. Carlton South: Curriculum Corporation.

Davies, I., Evans, M., & Reid, A. (2005). Global citizenship education? A critique of 'global education' and 'citizenship education'. *British Journal of Education Studies, 53*(1), 66–89.

Doherty, C., & Mu, L. (2011). Producing the intercultural citizen in the International Baccalaureate. In F. Dervin, A. Gajardo, & A. Lavanchy (Eds.), *Politics of interculturality* (pp. 173–197). Newcastle upon Tyne: Cambridge Scholars Publishing.

Foucault, M. (1981). So is it important to think? In J. D. Faubion (Ed.), *Power: Essential works of Foucault, 1954–1984* (R. Hurley, trans.) (pp. 454–458). New York: New Press.

Foundation for Young Australians. (2013). *Unlimited potential: A commitment to young Australians*. Melbourne: FYA.

Foundation for Young Australians. (2014). FYA website. Retrieved October 15, 2014, www.fya.org.au.

Gerzon, M. (2010). *American citizen, global citizen*. Boulder, Colorado: Spirit Scope Publishing.

Gunter, H. (2009). The 'C' word in educational research: An appreciative response. *Critical Studies in Education, 50*(1), 93–102.

Harris, A. (2004). Jamming girl culture: Young women and consumer citizenship. In A. Harris & M. Fine (Eds.), *All about the girl: Culture, power, and identity* (pp. 163–172). New York, NY: Routledge.

Hartung, C. (2011). *Governing the 'agentic' child citizen: A poststructural analysis of children's participation* (Unpublished PhD thesis). Faculty of Education, University of Wollongong. Retrieved from http://ro.uow.edu.au/theses/3504.

Kelly, P., & Harrison, L. (2009). *Working in Jamie's kitchen: Salvation, passion and young workers*. Hampshire: Palgrave Macmillan.

Lemke, J. L. (2001). Articulating communities: Sociocultural perspectives on science education. *Journal of Research in Science Teaching, 38*(3), 296–316.

Lettevall, R., & Klockar Linder, M. (Eds.). (2008). The idea of kosmopolis: History, philosophy and politics of world citizenship. *Södertörn Academic Studies, 37*, Södertörns högskola.

Lingard, B., & McGregor, G. (2014). Two contrasting Australian Curriculum responses to globalisation: What students should learn or become. *The Curriculum Journal, 25*(1), 90–110.

MCEETYA. (2008). *Melbourne declaration on educational goals for young Australians*. Retrieved January 20, 2015, from http://www.curriculum.edu.au/verve/_resources/National_Declaration_on_the_Educational_Goals_for_Young_Australians.pdf.

Miller, T. (1993). *The well-tempered self: Citizenship, culture, and the postmodern subject*. London: John Hopkins Press.

Oxley, L., & Morris, P. (2013). Global citizenship: A typology for distinguishing its multiple conceptions. *British Journal of Educational Studies, 61*(3), 301–325.

Parker, W. C., Ninomiya, A., & Cogan, J. J. (2002). Educating 'world citizens': Toward multinational curriculum development. In W. C. Parker (Ed.), *Education for democracy: Contexts, curricula, assessments* (pp. 151–184). Greenwich, CT: Information Age Publishing.

Parmenter, L. (2011). Power and place in the discourse of global citizenship education. *Globalisation, Societies and Education, 9*(3–4), 1–2.

Peters, M. (2001). Education, enterprise culture and the entrepreneurial self: A Foucauldian perspective. *Journal of Educational Enquiry, 2*(2), 58–71.

Prout, A. (2000). Children's participation: Control and self-realisation in British late modernity. *Children & Society, 14*(4), 304–315.

Richardson, G. (2008). Conflicting imaginaries: Global citizenship education in Canada as a site of contestation. In M. Peters, A. Britton, & H. Blee (Eds.), *Global citizenship education: Philosophy, theory and pedagogy* (pp. 115–131). Rotterdam: Sense.

Rose, N. (1996). The death of the social: Reconfiguring the territory of government. *Economy & Society, 25*(3), 327–356.

Rose, N. (1999). *Powers of freedom: Reframing political thought.* Cambridge & New York: Cambridge University Press.

Rose, N. (2014). *Making us resilient: Responsible citizens for uncertain times.* Invited keynote paper presented at the Competing Responsibilities Conference, Wellington, New Zealand, August 15–17.

Ruddick, S. (2003). The politics of aging: Globalization and the restructuring of youth and childhood. *Antipode, 35*(2), 334–362.

Schattle, H. (2008). Education for global citizenship: Illustrations of ideological pluralism and adaptation. *Journal of Political Ideologies, 13*(1), 73–94.

Shukla, N. (2009). Power, discourse, and learning global citizenship: A case study of international NGOs and a grassroots movement in the Narmada Valley, India. *Education, Citizenship and Social Justice, 4*(1), 133–147.

Shultz, L. (2011). Engaging the multiple discourses of global citizenship education within a Canadian university: Deliberation, contestation, and social justice possibilities. In L. Shultz, A. A. Abdi, & G. H. Richardson (Eds.), *Global citizenship education in post-secondary institutions: Theories, practices, policies* (pp. 13–24). New York: Peter Lang.

Stasiulis, D. (2002). The active child citizen: Lessons from Canadian policy and the children's movement. *Citizenship Studies, 6*(4), 507–538.

Swanson, D. (2011). Parallaxes and paradoxes of global citizenship: Critical reflections and possibilities of praxis in/through an international online course. In L. Shultz, A. A. Abdi, & G. H. Richardson (Eds.), *Global citizenship education in post-secondary institutions: Theories, practices, policies* (pp. 120–139). New York: Peter Lang.

Tormey, R., & Gleeson, J. (2012). The gendering of global citizenship: Findings from a large-scale quantitative study on global citizenship education experiences. *Gender and Education, 24*(6), 627–645.

Tsaliki, C., Frangonikolopoulos, C., & Huliaras, A. (2011). *Transnational celebrity activism in global politics: Changing the world?* Chicago: University of Chicago Press.

Veugelers, W. (2011). The moral and the political in global citizenship: Appreciating differences in education. *Globalisation, Societies and Education, 9*(3–4), 473–485.

Homophobia, transphobia, young people and the question of responsibility

Mary Lou Rasmussen, Fida Sanjakdar, Louisa Allen, Kathleen Quinlivan and Annette Bromdal

ABSTRACT
Young people may face conflicting and confusing messages about what it means to respond well in relation to homophobia and transphobia. Consequently, we ask – What might it mean to respond well to homophobia and transphobia? This strategy, inspired by Anika Thiem and Judith Butler, is recognition of the ambivalent conditions which structure attempts to respond well to bullying related to gender and sexuality. Such an approach is counter to educational responses that suggest a remedy in advance of the enactment of perceived bullying. Our paper draws on research conducted by the authors in four schools, two in Australia and two in Aotearoa/New Zealand. It is a deliberate turn away from focusing on who should be held to account for homophobia and transphobia.

Our specific focus in this article is on how to understand the question of responsibility in relation to what Pascoe (2013) has termed the 'sociology of bullying'. Inspired by Thiem's (2008) *Unbecoming Subjects: Judith Butler, Moral Philosophy, and Critical Responsibility*, we reconfigure responsibility in relation to the question – What might it mean to respond well to homophobia and transphobia? Thiem's work investigates the potential of thinking about responsibility as relational – rather than in terms of what we should do (2008, p. 5). This is a deliberate turn away from focusing on who should be held to account for homophobia and transphobia. It is also recognition of the ambivalent conditions which structure attempts to respond well (Thiem, 2008, p. 6). When responses to homophobia and transphobia are understood as relational, the impetus to craft a pedagogical or disciplinary response that suggests a remedy in advance of the enactment of perceived bullying is called into question.

The context of the investigation is public secondary schools in Australia and New Zealand (A/NZ) with culturally and religiously diverse student populations. We chose these sites because we recognize that attention to diversity is a fundamental characteristic of effective education related to gender and sexuality (UNESCO, 2009). Our paper draws on research conducted by the authors in four such schools, two in each country.[1] In embarking on this research we reasoned that many young people approach adulthood faced with conflicting and confusing messages about sexuality and gender and that they may experience conflicting advice and feelings about what it means to respond well in relation to homophobia and transphobia.

Responsibility, relationality and repetition

In thinking through the question of responsibility we begin by underscoring the need to see injury in relation to homophobia and transphobia. We also argue that we cannot just see injury. Homophobia and transphobia are the subject of numerous definitions and discourses, it is not possible of offer neat definitions of either – and part of the point of this paper is to resist defining these concepts. That said, we are in no doubt that young people and teachers experience violence related to gender and sexual identifications (real or perceived) and the associated injuries are important to acknowledge and address. We strongly believe that homophobia and transphobia can diminish all members of school communities because it impacts on those directly involved, those asked to intervene and as well as bystanders and allies. *This is not to say that responsibility and accountability no longer matter.* It is recognition that they are not straightforward or easily apprehended. To this end, we argue the need to separate accountability and responsibility, and to recognize that neither can be totally located in the individual, or a specific event, place or time.

We are not the first to make the observation that bullying needs a sociological response that recognizes the complex relations of power underpinning gender and sexuality (see Bansel, Davies, Laws, & Linnell, 2009; Pascoe, 2013; Ringrose & Renold, 2010; Walton, 2011). In a recent interview on the subject of responsibility, Judith Butler argues that:

> Sometimes the language of victimization strengthens the rationale of a paternalistic form of power ... at other times it can lead to practices of organized resistance. So we have to assess in what direction it works, and whose interest it serves. (Athanasiou & Butler, 2013, p. 115)

This argument suggests homophobia and transphobia in public schools might be understood as working in multiple directions, directions that we cannot necessarily anticipate in advance. If one concedes that transphobia and homophobia might work in many directions – what are the implications of this for how schools, students and researchers might analyze accounts of homophobia and transphobia, and then respond to these accounts?

We are also prompted to think about how the power dynamics of victimization related to homophobia and transphobia might potentially strengthen paternalistic forms of power that take various guises. Courtney Bailey (2011) explores an instantiation of this in his discussion of a US celebrity scandal related to homophobia and race. He draws attention to the way in which the high-profile black celebrity (Isaiah Washington) is characterized as 'the angry black man' perpetrating homophobia, simultaneously 'confirming white culture's fears about masculinity', and portraying Washington as a 'bad individual in need of reform' (2011, p. 2). Are there are other bad individuals and groups who are situated as in need of reform within the language of victimization related to homophobia and transphobia in school contexts? If so, how might these questions of responsibility relate to homophobia and transphobia?

In *Giving an Account of Oneself*, Judith Butler argues responsibility is not a question of responsibility that be conceptualized alone, in isolation from the other (2005, p. 85). In the scope of this conceptualization, individuals cannot take full responsibility for bullying – to do so would be a failure to recognize the fundamentally relational aspect of such an encounter. Applebaum (2010), in an article on ignorance and social justice education, notes that Butler's approach to theorizing responsibility has sometimes been misconstrued:

> … to assume that individuals are not responsible for their speech and, thus, should not be blamed for it … It is important, however, to underscore that most Butlerians, and Butler herself, do not reject individual responsibility, although the conception of responsibility they assume moves away from an exclusive focus on blame, control, and causality. (Applebaum, 2010, p. 326)

We share Applebaum's interpretation – this article is not about absolution from blame, rather our focus is on how young people and we as researchers apprehend and frame bullying and responsibility. In this article we are particularly interested in how blame, control and causality are conceptualized by students in response to homophobia and transphobia related bullying within school contexts.

Davies and McInnes (2012), also inspired by Butler, similarly recognize that the question of responsibility is not straightforward when it comes to gender and bullying. They argue:

> … perpetrators [of homophobic violence and we would add transphobic violence] are not the originators of their fear nor are they solely invested with or responsible for the power enacted through their injurious acts. Perpetrators of homophobic harassment and violence accumulate the power to injure through the repetition or citation of a prior set of practices – in this case, a set of practices that are understood to cause injury to the intended recipients. (p. 140)

While bullying is part of a practice of repetition and citation, the ways in which bullying is embedded in relations of power is not necessarily apparent to the bullies themselves, to the recipient of bullying, to teachers who are required to discipline and educate students about bullying, to parents whose children might be charged with bullying, or whose children may be the targets of harassment.

Bullying is ubiquitous within schools, but its racial, cultural, nationalist and religious politics, and the ways they are intertwined with heteronormativity, cisgenderism and shame are less apparent. Is it possible to avow certainty about bullying, when we may be in the dark about why we bully, and we may easily misconstrue the reasons that others bully. This is the basis of a mutual unrecognizability that lies at the heart of our social relations.

We recognize that cultural and religious differences are implicated in the repetition and citation of homophobia and transphobia. They are also implicated in attempts to speak back to and disrupt homophobia and transphobia. Yip's (2012) research on homophobia within ethnic minority communities in the UK is useful for thinking about how homophobia is linked to relations of power and resistance specifically linked to cultural and religious difference. Through his interviews, Yip grasps some of the complexities of labeling specific understandings as homophobic. For instance, he notes that for many of the heterosexual identified participants in his research the notion of homophobia evoked strong responses because they felt that it conflated ethical and moral concerns about homosexuality *with* irrational fears related to homosexuality – while the participants insisted upon the maintenance of this distinction.

Taking this style of thought to school contexts, it is possible that a student might feasibly question the morality of homosexuality at school – arguing that this objection is not irrational but reasoned. Yip is also careful to note that lesbian and gay respondents in his research refused this distinction. In thinking through these sets of relations, Yip argues that it:

> ... may prove to be more productive ultimately to frame unequal treatments of lesbians and gays as 'discrimination', 'hostility', 'prejudice', or 'negativity' (or a combination of these), which is more recognisable in the everyday lexicon, rather than 'homophobia', which is far more emotive; and to some, condemning. (Yip, 2012, p. 113)

Yip's approach does not deny the existence of unequal treatment. But he suggests a way forward that can recognize discrimination, hostility, bullying and so on, while calling into question the value of labeling particular acts as homophobic. For Yip, this is recognition that religious traditions and secular rights discourses frame unequal treatment of people based on their gender and sexual identity according to very different questions of accountability and responsibility.

Responsibility, bullying, and sexual and gender identity

Walton (2011) argues the importance of 'reconceptualizing bullying beyond behavior based approaches' in Canadian public schools where bullying is often addressed in a fashion which treats it as somehow divorced from difference. He believes that this is apparent in the production of generic safe schools policies that individualize school violence focusing on 'the actual moments of bullying. Doing so does not account for broader and social and political conditions that endorse bullying behaviours and the attitudes that are expressed as bullying' (p. 135). Walton goes on to argue that homophobic bullying is pervasive but frequently unaddressed in Canadian public schools and notes:

> ... parents' religious perspectives often clash with anti-homophobia initiatives. From an administrative standpoint, it therefore seems pragmatic as a strategy for evading controversy to draft policies that refer to bullying as generic behaviour. The problem, simply put, is this: Although masquerading as providing protection for all students, generic policies do not address the specific ways that particular children, and not others, are continual targets of peer violence. (p. 137)

In this passage Walton makes the point that parents' 'religious perspectives' might clash with anti-homophobia initiatives. It is worth mentioning that parents who are not religious may also have objections to anti-homophobia initiatives, and that students (like their parents) might also object to anti-homophobia initiatives. He goes on to argue, 'particular and prevalent forms of bullying (such as homophobia) have not drawn focused preventative action' (2011, p. 137). Here we wonder: What focused preventative action might look like? What is the goal of such action? Presumably the goal is to eliminate homophobia and transphobia. Does this also presume some agreement about what constitutes homophobia and transphobia? Can we agree in advance about how such things will be identified and addressed in school contexts? Does this depend on the community in which the school is located; the relations of power between students, teachers and parents; whether the school is public or private; secular or religious?

In concluding his discussion, Walton writes 'anti-bullying in schools must acknowledge, address, and educate about notions of difference so that children who are vilified for being different (or perceived as such) are accorded safer learning environments' (p. 142). There is a perception here that more education about difference will combat an apparent ignorance about difference, and therefore go some way towards combating bullying that is presumably linked to this ignorance about difference. We recognize the value of teaching about difference, but we wonder about Walton's conceptualization of bullying as 'fueled by antipathy toward difference' (p. 142). Within this framing, bullying is something that is associated with a knowledge deficit. Such a position invites an educative response whereby schools, teachers and students are invited to teach and learn about difference in the hope of constructing safer learning environments.

Applebaum's (2014) essay *Ignorance as a Resource for Social Justice Education?* is insightful in considering Walton's suggestion that bullying may be related to ignorance of, or antipathy toward difference. Opening her article with a brief discussion of ignorance, Applebaum notes that ignorance 'has often been simplistically perceived to be the primary culprit behind racism and many still believe that the remedy for racism is simply more knowledge' (p. 391). Similarly, homophobia and transphobia may be associated with the need for education about difference. In short, education about difference relating to sex, sexuality and gender may be seen as potentially ameliorative with regard to bullying. Drawing on the work of Judith Butler, Applebaum posits a different way of thinking about ignorance, and its uses in education, which is also instructive for our discussion of responsibility. We will return to this point in our conclusion, but now turn to data collected as part of our own research on cultural and religious difference in sexuality education in order to focus on how young people respond to our queries about homophobia and transphobia in public schools.

Taking responsibility for homophobia and transphobia?

Our ethnographic research explored how cultural and religious differences intersect with public school-based sexuality education. One element of this research tried to tease out how young people in these schools imagined what might constitute an appropriate response in relation to bullying related to homophobia and transphobia. Our research included observations of sexuality education lessons over two years in four religiously and culturally diverse high schools (two in Melbourne Australia and two in Aotearoa/New Zealand. Each of the researchers already had some type of relationships in the school, though this was still very difficult to negotiate in some instances (see Allen et al., 2014). Participants were in Year 8 or 9, aged 13 and 14 years, when the study commenced in 2012. This age group was selected partially because compulsory sexuality education in Australia is completed by the end of Year 10. In addition to our observations, at each school we conducted:

- Interviews with sexuality education teachers and their students (4–6 participants from each site).
- Focus groups (with all participants together – or with boys and girls split, depending on students' preferences).

As part of the interviews and focus groups, a range of scenarios were read out. In this paper our specific focus is on one scenario detailed below:

> A new boy has started in your class at school and he has been teased by other students because they think he is a sissy boy, his name is Joshua but he prefers to be called Jo. He mainly hangs out with a few girls and he likes to wear make up to school. His parents don't care what he wears or how he looks as long as he is happy. For as long as his family can remember he has enjoyed dressing up, wearing jewellery and putting on shows for his family.

- What advice would you give to Jo about being teased?
- Would you feel comfortable talking to your classmates about how they are treating him?
- Would you feel like you could invite him home or hang out with him outside school?
- What might teachers or students do to better support Jo?

In asking these questions we were partially interested in exploring in what ways, if at all, cultural and religious differences might mediate how participants would advise and support Jo. In retrospect, it is apparent to us that in our structuring of these questions we are implying that participants' must take responsibility for acting in relation to the teasing that Jo was experiencing. There is a demand to respond, in the framing of the question. This is problematic because the structure of the question effectively calls upon participants to recite how they will take responsibility for protecting Jo and educating their peers.

In reading excerpts from these data we want to contemplate how bullying, sexuality and gender might be read through a Butlerian-inspired understanding of the notion of responsibility. We begin with Abla, a student at Outer Suburbs High (a pseudonym), located on the urban fringe of Melbourne.[2] In the exchange below, Abla clearly interpreted our scenario as a call to be responsible for Jo. She is quick to suggest advice she might offer Jo – given the predicament in which we have placed Jo:

> Sanjakdar: What advice would you give Jo about being teased?
> Abla: Being teased, I'd tell him to actually try as hard as he could to ignore it. I know it's hard, because when you've been called something for a long period of time, a numerous amount of times, you're going to start to believe it. You're going to start – I know some people, they come to the point where they start self-harming themselves. I tell them to try to ignore it, to try and tell them, 'I was born this way. I like it. It's not my fault ... '

Accountability and responsibility are tangible for Abla in this exchange – she understands the teasing is problematic (primarily for Jo). Potentially Abla shares an understanding of how bullying and identity can be linked in Australian schools (Mansouri & Wood, 2008) based on her own or others' experiences of Islamophobia at school. Abla acknowledges that insistent bullying can lead to self-harm. For Abla, Jo is teased but he is not responsible for his predicament – she implies, because he has no choice – he was likely 'born this way'. Responsibility here might be read as being conferred upon and then removed from Jo. In the context of this discussion Abla also recalls an experience with a boy in her peer group at primary school who experienced gender-based bullying and who 'hung out with the girls'. Abla interprets this boy's desire to hang out with the girls as indicative of his need for protection – she does not consider that this affiliation might relate to his own desire/pleasure in spending time with the girls. In reflecting on this account, it is interesting to us that the possibility that a boy might prefer the company of women is obfuscated in Abla's story. What conditions of account have resulted in Abla structuring a narrative where such a choice is construed as unthinkable? Maybe part of responding well is recognition of young people's agency in choosing affiliations and questioning who can hang out with whom?

Bisar, another student at outer suburbs high, echoes some of Abla's sentiments in the exchange below:

Sanjakdar: What advice would you give Jo about being teased?
Bisar: If he doesn't care what people think, just don't think about them. If he wants to be like that, he can be like that, but if he actually gets offended at what people say, he should actually take it into consideration and try fixing it. So, he'll either ignore it, or he's got to fix it.
Sanjakdar: You think it's worth fixing it if he wants to?
Bisar: Yeah, if he wants to, he can fix it. If he wants to actually get a girlfriend and be like a man, he's got to fix it. But if he likes the way he is, who cares? ...

Both Bisar and Abla see the teasing of Jo as something to be dealt with by Jo. They also take some responsibility – through our injunction for them to respond. The notion of advising Jo to try and ignore the bullying comes up repeatedly in conversations with students across the schools. The participants in these exchanges (at least in part because of how the scenario is framed) continually turned their focus to how Jo might best negotiate this scenario – the responsibility is on Jo to fix it or ignore it. Both options seem unsatisfactory. These comments might be read as an expression of transphobia and heteronormativity. They could also be read as genuine by Bisar to offer a resolution to Jo's situation. What is most interesting to us about these exchanges is the ways in which they illustrate varied understandings of the difference between gender identity, sex and sexual identity. These understandings condition questions of responsibility in relation to the scenario we posed. We could not have predicted the responses made by these young women and find ourselves unsure about how to respond.

In his critique of school bullying policy in Canada, Walton writes 'particular and prevalent forms of bullying (such as homophobia) have not drawn focused preventative action' (2011, p. 137). What would 'focused preventative action' look like in response to Abla and Bisar's comments? Bansel et al. (2009), in their discussion of bullying and power in the context of schooling, suggest one way forward:

Teachers could work with students to become aware of the discourses and positionings and relations of power that are at play. Together they might turn their attention to the practices of schooling and their disciplining effects, and examine the tensions between conformity and conscience, between policing and questioning, and the tension between normalising practices and openness to difference. (p. 67)

We like this suggestion because it is propelled by a move away from the pathological character of the bully. The emphasis here is on education about relationality that circulates around incidents identified as bullying. But we wonder if teachers currently have the resources to identify and examine the tensions embedded in Abla and Bisar's responses to this particular scenario of bullying (see Martino, Lingard, & Mills, 2004). Bansel et al. (2009) go on to suggest:

> ... responsibility rests in the network of practices, discourses and relations of power through which subjects are constituted and for which schools have some considerable responsibility through the development of ethical reflexivity. (p. 67)

In thinking about homophobia within the context of the culturally and religiously diverse public schools – responsibility matters, but how we think about responsibility is crucial here.

Thiem's (2008) writing on responsibility in Butler's work is helpful in further teasing out this concept and how it might be useful in understanding participants' response to the scenario related to Jo. Thiem writes, 'we can never act fully responsibly' (p. 137). This is not to say that responsibility and moral action are an impossibility, but rather that 'it is the failure to become fully responsible that opens up the possibility for ethical life and for an inquiry into morality' (p. 137). Following this line of thought we can never become fully responsible because we are opaque to ourselves. This lack of understanding about the self, this opacity is apparent in the exchanges about Jo. How did Bisar come to a place where she thinks Jo might need fixing? How did Bisar come to a place where she thinks he does not need fixing, if he likes the way he is? How does she hold these two ideas together? These ideas have long histories that precede Bisar, but they are surely part of Bisar's reckoning of responsibility in relation with Jo.

The ways in which religious and cultural difference play a part in this framing is not straightforward. It appears that people continue to be undone by the prospect of realizing Bisar's proposition that 'if he likes the way he is, who cares?' People do care, these situations are not easily fixed. It is not clear to us who is responsible – though many popular commentaries in the press and online share Bisar's assessment that it is easy, he should have just 'come out'.

The ways in which the figure of Jo is constructed in these interactions also speaks of the challenges of incorporating people with diverse gender identities in such a way that onerous notions of responsibility and accountability are not invoked. Sanjakdar's response to Abla (which we think could have been uttered by any member of the team) is to reinforce Abla's approach 'That's very good advice, very supportive advice from a friend'. On reflection we do not find Abla's advice very helpful. Yet in the moment we would not have responded as such – articulating our own discomfort with this response feels inappropriate in the context of data collection. Yet, we are still unsure about what responding well here looks like.

In retrospect, the structure of the question we posed suggests that the participants are responsible for Jo. Or, if you are not responsible in your care for Jo, then you are somehow accountable for Jo's predicament – in this structure you are either with Jo or against Jo. Thiem (2008) writes:

> We become responsible not because actions can be attributed to us and we can be held accountable for them but because we are addressed by others in ways that demand we respond, and respond well. (p. 145)

Each of these interview exchanges shapes how we each imagine responsibility in relation to Jo. Relationality shapes our expectations and forms our different exchanges with participants upon asking these questions. In summary, these exchanges are instructive because of how suggestive they are of our own and participants' ingrained ways of thinking about, and desires for, responsibility and accountability. In part these ways of thinking command a response from our participants: Will you do this, or that? Will you intervene, will you stand up, will you be responsible for Jo? Rather than ask about how they understood the scenario (which may have been a more instructive line of questioning – or prompting them to devise their own scenario) we wanted to know what they would do for Jo.

Responsibility and queer youth suicidality

We now turn to Pacific High[3] (a pseudonym), one of the two schools in New Zealand in which we conducted our research. In response to our scenario Patrick's suggestions for how to engage with Jo, and his peers are not dissimilar to Abla and Bisar:

Patrick: It's all good. Being teased. I just tell him to ignore them. I know it's hard but just ignore what they say, and because some people do take what those bullies or those people who tease people, they take it to heart, 'Oh, why you wearing that much make up? Why you wearing jewellery?' They do take it to heart, and that's when sometimes they'll go overboard and then they will go and commit suicide. Just ignore what they say, but you should go to the teacher, otherwise the teasing will get worse.

Patrick's response to this scenario draws on his own experience at school. Like Abla, Patrick is highly aware that Jo might self-harm as a result of the teasing he receives. Later in the interview Patrick reports that in his sexuality education class he learnt about the correlation between identifying as lesbian, gay, bisexual and transgender (LGBT) and being suicidal. This correlation is clearly playing on Patrick's mind when responding to this prompt. But Patrick is also distant from Jo, but unwilling to risk a direct relation, instead suggesting that Jo should seek out the assistance of a teacher if the students 'go overboard'.

These young people's concerns about suicidality in relation to this scenario about Jo speaks to the ways in which responsibility and accountability have become inseparable from research and popular understandings that conflate suicidality and queer youth (Cover, 2012; Rasmussen, 2006; Waidzunas, 2012). LGBT identities in school are intertwined with notions of risk and our scenario ill-advisedly reinforces this perception. In his discussion of queer youth suicide, Cover (2012) argues that ethical responsibility is limited by the framework of identity politics (p. 144). He prefers a position that pays attention to the problems youth encounter that looks '*beyond* sexual categorization' (p. 144). Untying the knots that thread together queer youth, suicidality, accountability and responsibility is difficult work. In the context of this broader discussion of responsibility, we concur with Cover's observation of the need to challenge 'the notion that vulnerability is endemic to queer youth rather than a common, human, corporeal and shared attribute of humanity in relationality' (p. 145).

A way of thinking about Jo that might be taken as resonant with Cover's suggestion above is offered by students at Central High[4] (pseudonym). Of the four schools we observed, this school was the one that did the most to cultivate a climate that was accepting of diversity related to gender and sexuality. In responding to the scenario we developed in relation to Jo, Ted's impetus is to resist the temptation to call on a teacher to save Jo:

Rasmussen:	What advice would you give to Jo about being teased?
Ted:	I'd say basically just; giving advice to him for starters, I'd probably; if he looked like he wanted advice or he was upset, then I might start the subject. But if he seemed fine, I wouldn't; unless I felt that I'd be doing him justice if I didn't speak to him, I would go up and say, 'Listen. I know people are teasing you. You should do this'. The advice I'd give him would be, 'who cares? Stick around with your friends'. And just 'if you act like you just don't care, then people will probably feel like it's not worth it'.
Rasmussen:	What might teachers and student do to support Jo or people in that situation?
Ted:	Well teachers could just make sure that they keep an eye out on things and just if it looks like they're actually getting very seriously bullied, then they should step in. But in general, just if someone's being picked on a little bit, they should just keep an eye on the situation and make sure it doesn't escalate until it's out of control. And maybe if health teachers think it's necessary, they could also just make sure that everybody knows that this sort of thing is okay, it doesn't matter. And I think that would help.

This response does not assume that Jo will need an intervention related to the teasing. Like Patrick, Bisar and Abla, Ted keeps open the possibility that the teasing does not undo Jo. Responsibility, as configured in this scenario, involves asking the question as to whether it is best to engage with people who are teasing peers. Is ignoring hate speech sometimes an ethical response, one that can admit a shared vulnerability, but not assume this in advance on the basis of identity? Ted's impulse to stand back is echoed in Damian's comments below:

Rasmussen:	And just finally, what might teachers and students do better to support him?
Damian:	Well, sometimes I find if we have a problem the teachers point it out, and that's actually quite annoying I know they're trying to help but that's actually pretty annoying, so I guess the teachers could try to treat Jo with the same respect as everyone else so he doesn't stand out …

Damian sees the teacher's role in relation to Jo as potentially 'quite/pretty annoying' because to his mind teachers can compound problems by drawing attention to them. At first glance such an observation might seem counter-intuitive in terms of thinking about responsibility, teasing and gender identity. Damian does not suggest that the teacher should turn away from Jo – but his comments are a reminder that when teachers call attention to particular incidents of bullying they run the risk of underscoring difference. This observation is not necessarily contrary to Walton's worry that 'particular and prevalent forms of bullying (such as homophobia) have not drawn focused preventative action' (Cover, 2012, p. 137). But it is a reminder that focused preventative action needs to be mindful of the politics of identity and its relationship to ethical responsibility.

In a recent article *Teaching about sexual minorities and* 'princess boys', Martino and Cumming-Potvin (2014) discuss the strategic potential of bullying discourses in the production of what they call a 'depathologising pedagogy' (p. 8; italics in original) undertaken by Janice, an elementary school teacher working in Ontario, Canada. They illustrate how:

> Janice capitalized on a broader degree of consensus in the community about human rights and the unacceptability of bullying, which appeared to minimize or at least ameliorate their concerns or disapproval of the queer-trans focused content of her curriculum delivery. (p. 16)

They argue that the frame of bullying in this context:

> ... needs to be understood as a response to navigating a potentially threatening terrain as an openly queer teacher whose queerness is legible and visibilized through her embodied signification where she feels vulnerable to professional assault from religiously devout parents espousing conservative family values. (Martino & Cumming-Potvin, 2014, p. 15)

There is a strong sense here that vulnerability is expansive beyond the category of queer youth. Vulnerability is something which profoundly influences the pedagogical practices of teachers such as Janice (see also Gray, 2013). Vulnerability might also adhere to 'religiously devout parents' who negotiate school systems that they may view as increasingly divergent from their own beliefs about sex, gender and sexuality.

In closing

We return now to Applebaum (2010) and her discussion of ignorance and social justice education. Here she articulates the value of thinking responsibility as relational. She argues that such an approach understands responsibility as related to the 'critical interrogation of the limits of knowing' (p. 396). Following this, Applebaum suggests three points to consider about opacity responsibility, inspired by Butler's (2005) *Giving an Account of Oneself*. These are listed below:

(1) Ignorance about the self is the source of our ethical connection to others.
(2) We are all implicated in the maintenance of norms 'that determine the livability of subjects' (p. 396).
(3) 'If one can acknowledge the limits of knowing then one can be open to the possibility of what has been foreclosed and from here new horizons of being can arise' (p. 397).

Bringing these points in relation to teasing and bullying related to gender and sexuality we can observe that such events take place in school contexts, which are not of young people's own making. They are also inflected by desires, fantasies and beliefs, which shape understandings of responsibility. Such a perspective runs counter to the idea that young people (and adults) who are engaging in teasing or bullying related to gender and sexuality are solely responsible for their behavior. It also interrupts the notion that education can repair ignorance, fear and anxiety that may infuse such scenes – because this too insinuates individuals have an awareness of what underpins homophobia and transphobia. For Thiem (2008), 'responding and responsibility are determined by how emotions, desires, and fantasies condition our opacity to ourselves as well as our way of relating to others and ourselves' (p. 145). This means that the way in which we relate to ourselves and to others within specific school cultures is conditioned by things we know, and things we cannot know, that also condition our responses and relations, desires and fantasies about gender, sex, sexuality and teasing.

In this way of thinking about the 'subject in terms of its formation, rethinking responsibility consequently becomes a pressing question, since we no longer have the subject unquestionably as that of a self-conscious and self-knowing moral agent' (Thiem, 2008, p. 144). In the context of this discussion of accountability and responsibility in relation to young people and homophobia and transphobia, we argue the need to see injury, but we cannot just see injury. We are all implicated in homophobic and transphobic bullying and teasing. Accountability and responsibility cannot be located in a specific individual, nor a specific event, place or time. This is not to say that responsibility and accountability no longer matter. It is recognition that neither are they virtues, straightforward or easily apprehended. To our minds, the dialogues presented in this paper illustrate this opacity of accountability and responsibility. That is precisely their significance.

By tracing different attempts to respond to Jo in the scenario we manufactured – it is possible to see how responsibility is conditioned by different ways of thinking about gender identity, care, accountability, the role of the teacher, the vulnerability of Jo. None of these things are necessarily transparent to any of us. Accountability and responsibility in this paper are structured by temporalities, spatialities, desires and structures of knowledge that opaquely shape our responses to Jo. In short, maybe none of us can really know what responding well looks like – which does not stop us trying to respond well in the hope of generating new horizons of being.

Notes

1. This article draws on data gathered in 2011 and 2012 as part of a research project led by the first author entitled *Sex Education in Australia and New Zealand: Responding to religious and cultural difference*. DP110101173. The investigators on this project were Mary Lou Rasmussen and Fida Sanjakdar, Monash University; Kathleen Quinlivan, University of Canterbury, Christchurch, New Zealand; Louisa Allen, University of Auckland, New Zealand; Clive Aspin, Independent researcher.
2. This school is in a community that is populated by a lot of new immigrant families. The average income is classified by the Australian Bureau of Statistics as below the Victorian and national averages. In terms of religious diversity, Catholicism is still the largest religious group represented on the census (nearly 40%), followed by Islam (nearly 30%). The community also has significant populations that identify as Eastern Orthodox and Buddhist.
3. It is a co-educational, secondary school in an urban location with a mixed population in terms of socio-economic status with populations of students that identified as Maori, Pasifika and Christian, Anglo and Christian, Muslim and Hindu, as well as students from who identified as having no-religious identification. It is classified as a decile four school (NZ Schools in decile one have the highest proportion of students from low socio-economic backgrounds while schools in decile ten have the highest proportion of students from high socio-economic backgrounds).
4. An inner city Melbourne school that has the largest proportion of students who identified as having no religion. This school is located in a culturally diverse suburb with an average income significantly above state and national averages.

Acknowledgments

Thanks to the reviewers for their thoughtful responses and their valuable feedback.

Disclosure statement

No potential conflict of interest was reported by the authors.

Funding

Thanks to the Australian Research Council (ARC) for funding this research on sexuality and secondary schooling as part of its Discovery Program. This was the first time the ARC funded such research in Australia.

References

Allen, L. E., Rasmussen, M. L., Quinlivan, K. A., Aspin, C., Sanjakdar, F., & Bromdal, A. C. G. (2014). Who's afraid of sex at school? The politics of researching culture, religion and sexuality at school. *International Journal of Research and Method in Education, 37*(4), 31–43.

Applebaum, B. (2010). When projects of critique are complicit with the object of their critique. *Philosophy of Education*, 323–332.

Applebaum, B. (2014). Ignorance as a resource for social justice education? *Philosophy of Education Archive*, 391–399.

Athanasiou, A., & Butler, J. (2013). *Dispossession: The performative in the political*. Cambridge: Polity Press.

Bailey, C. W. (2011). Coming out as homophobic: Isaiah Washington and the Grey's Anatomy scandal. *Communication and Critical/Cultural Studies, 8*(1), 1–21.

Bansel, P., Davies, B., Laws, C., & Linnell, S. (2009). Bullies, bullying and power in the contexts of schooling. *British Journal of Sociology of Education, 30*(1), 59–69.

Butler, J. (2005). *Giving an account of oneself*. New York, NY: Fordham University Press.

Cover, R. (2012). *Queer youth suicide, culture and identity: Unliveable lives?* London: Ashgate.

Davies, C., & McInnes, D. (2012). Speaking violence: Homophobia and the production of injurious speech in schooling cultures. In S. Saltmarsh, K. Robinson & C. Davies (Eds.), *Rethinking school violence: Theory, gender, context* (pp. 131–148). New York, NY: Palgrave Macmillan.

Gray, E. M. (2013). Coming out as a lesbian, gay or bisexual teacher: Negotiating private and professional worlds. *Sex Education, 13*(6), 702–714.

Mansouri, F., & Wood, S. P. (2008). *Identity, education and belonging: Arab and Muslim youth in contemporary Australia*. Carlton: Melbourne University Press.

Martino, W., & Cumming-Potvin, W. (2014). Teaching about sexual minorities and 'princess boys': A queer and trans-infused approach to investigating LGBTQ-themed texts in the elementary school classroom. *Discourse: Studies in the Cultural Politics of Education*. Advance online publication. doi:10.1080/01596306.2014.940239

Martino, W., Lingard, B., & Mills, M. (2004). Issues in boys' education: A question of teachers' threshold knowledges? *Gender and Education, 16*(4), 435–454.

Pascoe, C. J. (2013). Notes on sociology of bullying: Young men's homophobia as gender socialization. *QED: A Journal in GLBTQ Worldmaking, 1*, 87–103.

Rasmussen, M. L. (2006). *Becoming subjects: Sexualities and secondary schooling*. New York, NY: Routledge.

Ringrose, J., & Renold, E. (2010). Normative cruelties and gender deviants: The performative effects of bully discourses for girls and boys in school. *British Educational Research Journal, 36*(4), 573–596.

Thiem, A. (2008). *Unbecoming subjects: Judith Butler, moral philosophy, and critical responsibility*. New York, NY: Fordham University Press.

UNESCO (2009). *International guidelines on sexuality education: An evidence informed approach to effective sex, relationships and HIV/STI education*. France: UNESCO.

Waidzunas, T. (2012). Young, gay, and suicidal: Dynamic nominalism and the process of defining a social problem with statistics. *Science, Technology and Human Values, 37*(2), 199–225.

Walton, G. (2011). Spinning our wheels: Reconceptualizing bullying beyond behaviour-focused approaches. *Discourse: Studies in the Cultural Politics of Education, 32*(1), 131–144.

Yip, A. K. T. (2012). Homophobia and ethnic minority communities in the United Kingdom. In L. Trappolin, A. Gasparini, & R. Wintemute (Eds.), *Confronting homophobia in Europe: Social and legal perspectives* (pp. 107–130). London: Hart Publishing.

Reframing responsibility in an era of responsibilisation: education, feminist ethics

Julie McLeod

ABSTRACT

Late modern social theories and critiques of neoliberalism have emphasised the regulatory and negative aspects of responsibility, readily associating it with self-responsibility or analytically converting it to the notion of responsibilisation. This article argues for stepping back from these critiques in order to reframe responsibility as a relational disposition and practice in education that warrants a fresh look. Feminist scholarship on the ethics of care, affective equality and relational responsibility are revisited in light of a consideration of teachers' work and educational purposes. It is argued, first, that there is an urgency for repositioning responsibility as a productive orientation and practice, given definitions of teaching are increasingly instrumental. Second, feminist theories of care and relational responsibility remain relevant to normative discussions of education and its knowledge and person-making purposes. Third, critical engagements with the affective and social circumstances of precarity bring new challenges for how educational institutions might respond to a pervasive sense of vulnerability, and accompanying opportunities and demands for care, interdependence and relational responsibility – towards others, not only the self.

Introduction

> I mean things were changing [late 1950s] and you knew you could do anything, that was the sort of feeling you had, especially as you had Miss Jones, that was really ... she was an inspiration ...
> Well Miss Jones if we needed any help would've been the one. You know, she was very supportive ...
> I just would've liked to have said to Miss Jones and Miss Stitchnoff, thank you, thank you, so inspirational. (Marilyn H., oral history interview 10 June 2010, reflections on being a secondary school student in the 1950s, small country town, Australia)

It is a familiar experience for teacher educators to hear from aspiring teachers that they are motivated by a desire to make a difference, relishing the opportunity to work with young people, helping to mould their individual and collective futures. I suspect my own experience of school teaching was framed by similar ambitions, even if it is a matter of looking back now with a mix of nostalgia and scepticism about the redemptive discourses of teaching. Nevertheless, similar desires have fuelled the work of generations of teachers. This came home to me forcefully while I recently listened to life-history narratives of former teachers who were working in Australia during the mid-decades of the twentieth century.[1] The vivid memories of turning points in their lives commonly pivoted not on the formal curriculum, but on acts of thoughtfulness and care, on special efforts teachers made towards them when they were students themselves, or the personal and sometimes transformative encounters they had with their own students across their teaching careers. None of this is likely to be surprising, but the fond intensity of these recollections was striking, warranting more critical attention than a simple acknowledgement of the memory of strong feelings. Equally striking was the sense of social responsibility many of them carried into teaching – responsibility for education in the abstract, as a public good, as part of a social mission or a radical politics, and as an individual right or entitlement, alongside a sense of responsibility for the lives of individuals and classes of students.

These observations gave rise to a number of questions about how the idea of responsibility is articulated in contemporary educational discourses. What does a 'sense of responsibility' mean in discussions about education today? What are the dominant terms in which responsibility is understood, and how might it connect to an ethics of responsibility towards other? What kind of pedagogical and subjectivity work does responsibility enable or oblige? How are the gendered dimensions of responsibility playing out or reconfiguring? And what theoretical resources might be helpful for opening up renewed thinking about responsibility in and for education today?

Such questions arise at a particular historical moment of widespread feelings that we are living in especially precarious times, when issues of care and interdependence become more pressing. Concomitantly, across social policy, high theory and popular advice, notions of individual and social vulnerability have a renewed visibility (Eccelstone, 2015), with vulnerability represented variously as a sign of personal pathology, a fragility that registers our humanity and a characteristic of the contemporary socio-politico-affective era (McLeod, 2012). In her 'affective histories of the present', Berlant (2012, p. 166) writes of vulnerability and precarity as 'magnetizing concepts' (see too Butler, 2004), citing a sense of precariousness in response to war and military aggression, unstable economies and uncertain futures: her notion of 'cruel optimism' captures feelings of precarity in the face of the attrition of the 'good life' fantasy (Berlant, 2011). Berlant's interest in precariousness lies in 'the relation between its materiality in class and political terms, its appearances as an affect, and as an emotionally invested slogan that circulates in and beyond specific circumstances' (Berlant, 2012, p. 166). In her view, the reach and intensity of precariousness has become 'a rallying cry for a thriving new world of interdependency and care that's not just private, but it is also an idiom for describing a loss of faith in a fantasy world to which generations have become accustomed' (Berlant, 2012, p. 166). Of particular relevance to the arguments explored here is Berlant's (2012) observation that 'precarious politics' signifies a shift 'from an idiom of power to an idiom of care as grounds for what needs to change to better suture the social'. Trying to figure out what a shift to an 'idiom of care' might involve in the field of education in the specific circumstances of now (and not in a universalist or ahistorical sense) is one background provocation, including what such a shift enables and what it recedes from view, as suggested by the description of a move away from an idiom of power. Looking afresh at responsibility, and revisiting earlier and recent feminist debates about care and ethics offers one route into this.

A sense of responsibility is not the same as techniques of responsibilisation

The idea of teaching as a vocation has a long lineage, tied to the religious origins of educational provision as well as to the civic ambitions of state schooling. Notions of duty, obligation, service, responsibility as well as care have historically framed the practice of teaching. These have been powerfully constituted as gendered qualities (Warin & Gannerud, 2014), with the care work of teaching both romanticised and devalued – materially and symbolically: women care, men lead. This has produced mixed messages about heroic and charismatic teachers (the 'Dead Poets' Society' syndrome) alongside the ambivalent ideal of self-sacrificing and mythically kind teachers. There is an urgency to revisit questions of teaching and responsibility now, at a time when teachers' work is increasingly being recast in instrumental terms (metrics of performance, merit pay). Amidst checklists of 'professional standards' and measures of teaching effectiveness, where does the work of care and relational responsibility fit? Listening to former teachers reflecting on their educational experiences underscored the extent to which these vital aspects have become sidelined in recent discussions about teaching.

A further context is the reach of late modern social theories and critiques of neoliberalism that have emphasised the regulatory and negative aspects of responsibility. Responsibility is commonly rendered as self-responsibility or analytically converted to the notion of responsibilisation, referring to the diverse processes by which individuals not only assume greater and greater responsibility for their own destinies but in so doing re-configure relationships between individuals and social and political life. Following a line of work influenced by the arguments, among others, of Beck (1992), Giddens (1991) and Rose (1996), responsibilisation is typically associated with intensified pressures on individuals to be self-governing, emphasising a pessimistic account of rampant individualisation. A raft of critical educational scholarship informed by such work has documented the damaging personal and social effects of responsibilisation, particularly for young people (e.g. Furlong & Cartmel, 2006; Kelly, 2001). Such discussions draw attention to various compulsions to govern and discipline citizens, teachers and students, inducing them to be relentlessly responsible for their own destinies. In blunt terms, social mobility and educational success are represented in individualistic terms, of sticking to personal goals and ambitions (e.g. Reay, 2013), children are seen as increasingly responsible for their own futures and the normative pupil and future citizen of curriculum is a self-starter, the opinion-forming individual able to make judgements and determine their own (unique) path through a mass of competing messages (e.g. McLeod & Yates, 2006). An accompanying sociological critique is that such injunctions and norms of responsibilisation work more or less effectively for groups depending on their cultural and social positioning: they exacerbate relations of privilege and poverty; favour cultures that prize autonomy as a virtue; have gendered and classed consequences; and contribute overall to insinuating the divisiveness of neoliberalism into the pores and minutiae of everyday existence.

I present a case for stepping back from these critiques to allow space for other ways of thinking about responsibility in education. The immediate context is educational debates within Australia, but given transnational policy logics, as well as the travelling discourses of feminism, the arguments are likely to have a wider resonance. While remaining cognisant of the effects of a pervasive responsibilisation and the historical circumstances which produced both the phenomenon and its various critiques, I want to re-position responsibility as a productive and affirming orientation to self and other in educational work, particularly in teaching. I argue that responsibility should be reclaimed as a relational disposition that warrants a fresh look outside late modern and neoliberal critiques that have harnessed it to quite specific analytic and political purposes. To do so, I revisit a body of feminist scholarship on care and ethics which offers helpful directions for shifting the critical gaze form a predominant focus on self-responsibility to recognition of relational responsibility towards others. This encompasses feminist work that has theorised care and responsibility (Beasley & Bacchi, 2005; Warin & Gannerud, 2014; Young, 2011) as well as work that seeks to revalue the affective, ethical and relational dimensions of education (Baker, Lynch, Cantillon, & Walsh, 2009; Zembylas, Bozalek, & Shefer, 2014).

Before proceeding, a brief caveat is noted. In some respects, the case made here might be working from a 'false antithesis', in that there is not necessarily an exclusive opposition between self-responsibilisation and responsibility towards and for others. Conventionally for women, this has not been perceived as a straightforward either/or identification. Indeed, being oriented to obligation and care for others is a conventional hallmark of femininity – deeply implicated in its normalisation and repetition – often positioned in tension with the pursuit of freedom to make one's own life (a dilemma elaborated by Gilligan 1982 among others, as the tension between autonomy and connection). It could be also argued that developing a habit of orienting to others is, in Foucauldian terms, a technology of the self (Foucault, 1988), a mode of gendered self-making that is simultaneously ethical in expressing care for others and a mode of subjectification that inscribes gender difference and asymmetrical relations of power and autonomy. While these observations warrant a larger discussion, they nevertheless suggest that responsibility is not usefully characterised as either principally about regulation or relationality, and that gendered resonances of responsibility belong in the forefront, especially when looking to the field of education.

Affirming responsibility and its scope in education

The responsibilisation thesis, while influential today, is of course not the only way in which notions of responsibility have shaped the educational field. Before turning to its uses in education, it is helpful to signal briefly some of the diverse ways in which responsibility surfaces in social discourse. As Hage and Eckersley (2012) observe, the 'language of responsibility permeates social life': its 'everyday usage is more often than not closely associated with questions of causality and the formal/legal, or informal, attribution of liability' and encompasses questions of 'duty, accountability and morality' (p. 1). Responsibility is, they argue, a concept that touches on many aspects of people's lives, noting that: 'All spheres of belonging that encompass our social being are delimited by explicit or implicit attempts at defining, assigning, assuming, questioning or resisting such conceptions of responsibilities and their scope' (p. 2). They explore the legal and political dimensions of responsibility and accountability – for example, the responsibilities of states in international relations or the responsibility and accountabilities of elected governments.

Legal and political responsibilities are often construed in terms of liability and blame, as Young (2011) elaborates in her proposal for an alternative account of responsibility to address structural injustice. In contrast to the 'liability model' dominant in moral and legal discourse, Young proposes a 'social connection model' of responsibility, which posits that 'all those who contribute by their actions to structural processes with some unjust outcomes share responsibility for the injustice. This responsibility is not primarily backward-looking, as the attribution of guilt or fault is, but rather primarily forward-looking' (Young, 2011, p. 95). Being responsible means 'that one has an obligation to join with others who share that responsibility in order to transform the structural processes to make their outcomes less unjust' (p. 95). Linking responsibility to collective and personal action and structural change resonates with debates about individual, institutional and state responsibilities to distant and intimate others, to strangers and to those closer to home (one's family or friends, networks of affiliation, citizens of the same nation state). Many of the big moral and political dilemmas of our time such as the nature of hospitality, belonging, movements of people, citizenship claims and rights (Benhabib, 2004; Somers, 2008) as well as ecological crises, call up notions of responsibility – towards others and the other-than-human, towards principles and universal values, towards places. According to the political philosopher Seyla Benhabib, working out how to respond and act in the face of such multi-layered issues requires an ongoing mediation of 'moral universalism with ethical particularism' (2004, p.16). This formulation also speaks to the universal and particular dimensions of responsibility and the type of principles (absolute, contextual) and motivations called upon to guide our sense of acting and being responsible. These matters are especially pressing in the field of educational work, where, for example, classrooms bring together intimates and strangers (in fact complicate such distinctions) and teachers' daily actions and decisions navigate normative and contextual factors as well as affective relations.

The attribution or claiming of rights is often paired with responsibility to honour, recognise or enact those rights, and this alliance extends into more informal injunctions in everyday life. This is manifest in admonitions for children and young people to exercise responsibility as they acquire more freedoms and rights. Similar notions of responsibility are woven into developmental accounts of subjectivity, with acquiring a sense of responsibility aligned to gaining autonomy and adult status. Remaining in the realm of intra- and inter-subjectivity, responsibility can also be invoked by its absence, as suggested by Ahmed (2014) in her dazzling analysis of the gendered 'wilful subject' in literary and cultural texts. The figure of the wilful subject has her own mind and a kind of excess of will that makes her stubborn, disobedient, contrary and *not* responsible in the sense of not adhering to social norms or a conforming femininity, nor subjecting herself to the containment of will. Even this small snapshot of how the idea of responsibility is variously invoked suggests its centrality in political, social and interpersonal life.

Responsibility has long been a pivotal notion in education, from formal philosophical deliberations on norms and purposes to more vernacular accounts of how schools 'ought to fix' whatever the prevailing problem is said to be. Looking to classic formulations in the philosophy of education, Peters (1973/1959), for example, articulated the value of personal responsibility for individual actions, in contrast to what he observed as a modern malaise, with too many attributing their failures or problems to external causes of a psychological or social nature. This illustrates Hage and Eckersley's (2012) observation that responsibility is often allied to questions of cause and liability, and it also links the exercise of responsibility in education to a kind of a robust and self-reliant individualism.

In the contemporary era, educational work is shaped and defined by shifting regimes of governance and policy rhetorics that mark out the pragmatic as well as aspirational responsibilities of schools and teachers, as much policy sociology has shown (Ball, 2005); it is embedded in local/global political and social conditions (Rizvi & Lingard, 2010) and it carries with it promises of transformation and responsibilities to students and larger social collectivities. Moreover, teachers' work is defined by an almost overwhelming repertoire of responsibilities. Key attributes of the good teacher encompass responsibility for the learning of children, their well-being and future success, effective classroom management and good results on tests. The multiple responsibilities of schools in educating the next generation are articulated in the *Melbourne Declaration on Educational Goals for Young Australians* (Ministerial Council on Education, Employment, Training and Youth Affairs [MCEETYA], 2008): these principles underpinned the development of an Australian national curriculum. Responsibility is represented as a social duty, with schools seen as vital in 'promoting the intellectual, physical, social, emotional, moral, spiritual and aesthetic development and wellbeing of young Australians, and in ensuring the nation's ongoing economic prosperity and social cohesion'. This role is conceived as a 'collective responsibility', shared with 'students, parents, carers, families, the community, business and other education and training providers' (MCEETYA, 2008, p. 4). The attribution of weighty responsibilities to schools is not new, and while this statement of admirable principles affirms a rhetorical commitment to the full development and well-being of individuals, elsewhere, including in associated assessment regimes, a more instrumental sense of the reach and responsibilities of schools is evident.

An influential strand of transnational educational policy discourse is reframing teaching as an activity principally concerned with testing and improving student learning and outcomes (Lingard, 2011). From this viewpoint, pedagogical responsibility is properly discharged through ensuring that measurable forms of learning take place and improvement can be documented. This represents, as others also argue, a narrowing of the vision and purposes of education (Yates, 2012). Education becomes synonymous with learning and normative questions regarding the person-forming and knowledge-building aims of education or the nature of the ethical relation between student and teacher virtually disappear (Biesta, 2012). A sense of responsibility becomes re-articulated as being professionally responsible for student learning. As Lynch, Lyons, and Cantillon (2007) argue, the 'teacher's role as an affectively engaged caring person is not attributed much significance, not least because the teacher is largely seen as midwife for delivering student performance' (p. 14).

Increasing concerns with testing and measurement of effective schools and quality teaching are part of the context in which consideration of care and relational ethics appear to have dropped off the educational agenda. There are other likely factors as well – perhaps as a critical response to shun naïve conceptions of teaching as 'merely' caring work and a refusal to trivialise the feminisation of the profession. Or, given widespread concerns about childhood abuse, a response to the perceived and actual dangers of teachers being 'too close' to pupils, which gives rise to a different set of issues about responsibility, protection and duty of care. Others (such as Lynch et al., 2007) argue that matters to do with caring for others have never been part of the mission of schools, because of an 'implicit if not explicit assumption that the development of autonomous, rational, public citizens remains the core educational project' (p. 4). Critics themselves have contributed, even inadvertently, to this sidelining of care: as Lynch et al. argue, 'research in the sociology of education has also been quite indifferent to the importance of other-centred work, the work arising from our interdependencies and dependencies as affective, relational beings' (p. 2).

In contrast, other scholars have lamented a perceived influx of 'feelings' into schools, noting a therapeutic turn that has displaced attention from what children should know or are learning, with an over-focus on how they feel about themselves. Critics of the rise of self-esteem agendas in schools have argued that concerns with 'feeling good about myself' have displaced the moral and knowledge functions of schooling, emptying out the curriculum in favour of a self-focussed agenda (Stout, 2000). In reference to the UK and the USA, Furedi (2009) has observed that 'the therapeutic objective to make children feel good about themselves is [increasingly] seen as the primary objective of schooling' (p. 190). Such orientations have been criticised for their individualised solutions to complex social and structural problems (Kenway & Willis, 1990) and for overstating the efficacy of an introspective gaze for navigating social life (McLeod, 2015). Critics of therapeutic culture in schools have exposed the excesses of individualised self-esteem, however, it would be mistaken to conflate their targets of critique with the more relational and socially oriented account of responsibility and care proposed here. In these latter accounts, tendencies to self-absorption and personalisation of care and self-responsibility are equally criticised as problematic and dangerous (Tronto, 2013). Nevertheless, debates about therapeutic culture point not only to the mixed views on emotions in education but also to the repeated polarisation of learning and emotion.

The partitioning of affective realms in the work of education echoes longstanding distinctions between the public and private sphere, which have been at the core of much political theory, aligning emotions and relationality to the private sphere and valorising the public domain as the space of rationality and freedom from affective ties. These old dualisms have been comprehensively challenged by a range of feminist work (Arnot & Dillabough, 2006; Pateman, 1988; Tronto, 2013), including recent accounts of 'public feelings' and the affective charge of social life (Berlant, 2011), all of which collapse neat oppositions between private and public, and bring into sharp relief the significance of inter-subjectivity and relationality cutting across both domains. To develop these arguments, I revisit feminist debates about care and relational responsibility as they offer useful directions for re-articulating responsibility and for drawing out its ethical, transformative and affective dimensions in educational work.

Ethics of care and relational responsibility in teachers' work

A resurgence of feminist interest in the ethics of care (Baker et al., 2009; Beasley & Bacchi, 2005) exists alongside growing attention to the politics of vulnerability and precarity (Berlant, 2012; Butler, 2004; Eccelstone, 2015). It follows earlier work from second-wave feminism associated with figures such as Noddings (1984), Tronto (1993) and Gilligan (1982). While this influential early work emerged from different philosophical positions – which deserve more attention than is possible here – in combination it brought centre-stage questions about gender and morality, care relations in the public and private spheres and notions of women's way of knowing (caring, learning, writing …). As Beasley and Bacchi (2005) argue, 'care was refreshingly recast as a resource for both private and public life', challenging ideas of the public sphere having 'a monopoly on the political imaginary' (2005, p. 50). While the salience of this work did not recede, it met an increasingly critical reception, in part because of charges of essentialism and the emergence of new feminist theoretical hotspots.

A wave of new work is opening up a fresh appraisal of the importance of these debates and an associated reconsideration of responsibility. Across different styles of theorising, responsibility as a practice and mode of inter-action is emphasised. Walker (2007) argues it is 'fruitful to locate morality in *practices of responsibility* that implement commonly shared understandings about who gets to do what to whom and who is supposed to do what for whom' (p. 16, original emphasis). While much rests upon and is even repressed in claims of 'commonly shared understandings', Walker proposes that in 'the ways we assign, accept, or deflect responsibilities, we express our understandings of our own and others' identities, relationships, and values' (p. 16). In her philosophy of 'agential realism', Barad (2007) foregrounds responsibility as an inter-action with the world around us, arguing that '[W]e are responsible for the world of which we are a part … because reality is sedimented out of particular practices that we have a role in shaping and through which we are shaped' (p. 390). Barad's distinctive take on this general proposition is the challenge of 'learning how to inter-act responsibly as part of the world' while 'understanding that "we" are not the only active beings' (p. 391). The social connection model of responsibility advanced by Young (2011) also emphasises practices and collectivities, focusing on responsibility for actions to address injustice. Framing responsibility as a practice and inter-action directly speaks to the specific characteristics of educational work and the relational encounters of teaching.

Working from this rich body of theorising, I highlight three related clusters of argument that directly engage with education, and which together suggest approaches for forging a multi-dimensional conception of responsibility, one that seeks to address the ethical and affective in conjunction with the social, distributive and knowledge aspects of schooling. The first concerns the idea of relational ethics, between self and other in pedagogy, as explicated in the work of Sharon Todd (Todd, 2003); the second is relations of care, love and solidarity in education, building on a critical social justice and equality framework (Baker et al., 2009; Lynch et al., 2007) and the third is the concept of relational responsibility, drawing from Tronto's (2013) work and its application in educational settings (see also Zembylas et al., 2014).

In her analysis of 'learning from the other', Todd (2003) proposes that one aim of social justice education has been for teachers and pedagogies 'to arouse responsibility through "developing" concern for and connection to the lives of "Others"'(p. 66). This is often incited by 'exposure to another's suffering' (p. 66) and a *committed* regard' for the suffering of another has the 'potential to lead to responsibility and hopefully responsible action' (p. 66). She stages an encounter between Levinasian philosophy and psychoanalysis to help understand how ethical responses such as guilt, shame, love, responsibility – all dimensions of encounters between self and other – take place in classrooms and pedagogies. Todd argues that, despite their seeming incommensurability, these two views 'may be held in tension' in productive ways. 'Both discourses offer education a way of thinking through the relationship between self and Other that refuses to ignore affect as significant not only to learning but to engagements with difference' (p. 13). Together they show how negotiating 'complex ethical formation[s] involves the subject inescapably in both a psychical history and a metaphysical dimension' (p. 92). An ethical responsibility of teaching, then, is to cultivate in students a sense of social responsibility: this might include teachers seeking to evoke in students feelings of shame or love in relation to Others, in order to forge a 'more complex understanding of responsibility' (p. 91). In this account, responsibility both encircles the pedagogical encounter and is 'responsibly' produced in it. The role of the teacher is critical in evoking a sense of responsibility beyond the self and towards others. Conceiving responsibility in education in this way brings affective relations and inter-subjectivity into the foreground, along with the notion of teaching as an ethical practice, with the teacher more than a facilitator of assessment regimes.

Lynch et al. (2007; Baker et al., 2009) advocate for 'affective equality', a conception of equality that takes as integral the emotions of love, care and solidarity. They define equality as encompassing five core dimensions: respect and recognition; resources; love, care and solidarity; power; and working and learning (Baker et al., 2009, p. 24). There are resonances with the social justice frameworks debated in feminist political theory, notably in the work of Fraser (1997) and Young (1990, 2011). Lynch et al.'s (2007) contribution is distinctive, however, in its insistence on the centrality of love, care and solidarity and linking these emotions to reconceiving the core practices and purposes of schooling. They argue that recognition of these fundamental relations has traditionally been excluded from the realm and practices of education, which has typically 'been indifferent to other-centred work arising from our interdependencies and dependencies as affective, relational beings' (p. 2) and, as noted above, more focused on educating for an ideal of the rational, autonomous citizen-subject.

Relations of love, care and solidarity build on and evoke a sense of responsibility toward others, not only toward one's (performative) self, and are deeply embedded in the purposes and work of education. They are not to be trivialised as mere 'feelings' or personal affairs to be relegated for teaching through 'values education' or 'personal development' (the non-core, soft options) curriculum. Rather, these relations are essential to the citizenship-forming and knowledge-building purposes of schooling, with educational institutions understood as 'arbiters of what is culturally valuable, not only in terms of what is formally taught, but also in terms of the manner in which it is taught, to whom, when and where' (Baker et al., 2009, p. 142). Moreover, love, care and solidarity are inter-connected with the sociological and distributive dimensions of education and crucial to understanding forms of inequality in education. Baker et al. (2009) argue that 'equality in education has generally been a matter of dividing education, and education-related, resources more equally or fairly. Inequalities of status and power have been defined as secondary, while issues of love, care and solidarity have been largely ignored' (p. 143). The role of emotions in education more generally has been neglected, they argue, despite the central importance of emotional work in teaching and learning. This is in terms of, for example, providing the care students need 'as well as helping them to learn to care for and to develop bonds of solidarity with others' (p. 164). Education is thus crucial for people in learning how 'to recognise and appreciate the feelings of others, to know how to care for others and to develop supportive relations' (p. 167). There are echoes here with the broad argument proposed by Todd in teaching to foster a sense of responsibility towards others.

So far, I have been using caring for and responsibility towards others in relatively interchangeable ways. Similarly, in discussing the idea of affective equality, I have configured responsibility into the mix, not as a substitute but to suggest how responsibility is linked to care work and solidarity; and I have situated responsibility as part of relational affects that are firmly within the remit of educational work and theories of social justice. Tronto (2013) offers a differentiated account of these ethical orientations, distinguishing between four phases in her analysis of a feminist ethics of care in which she emphasises care as both a 'disposition and a practice' (Zembylas et al., 2014, p. 200). First, there is 'Attentiveness – caring about'; the second is 'Responsibility – caring for', the third is 'Competence – care giving' and the fourth is 'Responsiveness – care receiving' (Tronto, 2013, pp. 34–35). To these four, she adds a fifth suggested by Sevenhuijsen, and which also captures elements of the affective equality emphasis on care and solidarity: 'Plurality, communication, trust and respect: solidarity – caring with' (p. 35). These latter qualities, Tronto proposes, 'make it possible for people to take collective responsibility, to think of citizens as both receivers and givers of care, and to think seriously about the caring needs in society' (p. 35). This is not a call for greater 'personal responsibility', a notion that Tronto sees as 'an embodiment of neoliberal ideology' (p. 47) and at odds with building a democratic politics in which care is at the heart of how societies are organised. Moreover, Tronto (pp. 46–64) argues that as a moral position, elevating personal responsibility is insufficient and even dangerous as it allows some people to 'pass' on being responsible for others and for the care work of responsibility to be differentially distributed – along gender, class and ethnic lines, for example. This, in turn, allows certain groups to live in a state of 'privileged irresponsibility', in which they both depend on but fail or refuse to acknowledge the systems of care that support and make possible their life – domestic labour, cleaning and maintenance, care of young children, the elderly, the ill and infirm; while those who do the care work of society are necessarily highly aware of the labour of their responsibilities.

Although Tronto's arguments are not specifically directed to the field of education, there are important implications for teaching and educational work, particularly in its emphasis on responsibility as a disposition *and* a practice: some of these implications are explored by Zembylas et al. (2014) in a discussion of critical pedagogies of emotion in higher education. Focusing on the notion of 'privileged irresponsibility', Zembylas et al. argue that:

> Tronto's political ethics of care framework enriches the transformative potential of critical pedagogies ..., because it helps educators expose how power and emotion operate through responsibility – that is, how responsibility is connected with the meaning and practices of power and the place of emotion in caring practices. (p. 201)

In pedagogical practice, this could include encouraging 'students and educators to be attentive to their own emotional positions with regard to caring responsibilities and privileged irresponsibilities' (Zembylas et al., 2014, p. 210). Critical attention to such emotional investments is not intended to replace recognition of structurally differentiated relations to responsibility, but rather to show how these dimensions intersect and have a hold on people's caring practices and expectations: and in doing so to 'locate individuals and decision-making in emotional investments, relationships, and structural contexts' (p. 211).

The role of the teacher in this account, as with Todd's arguments, is attributed with significant responsibilities, emphasising how pedagogical encounters can be personally and ethically transformative, especially in the context of understanding education's role in achieving social justice and democratic aims. Yet, as I have noted, educational institutions also have responsibilities for curriculum and knowledge building (Yates, 2012), and this is a vital element of teachers' work. I have been arguing for a reframing of responsibility as a relational and productive practice, seeing it not only in terms of self-responsibilisation and techniques of governance. As I have emphasised, this is not a proposal for relational and ethical responsibilities to override or stand in for schooling's other normative and epistemological purposes. Rather, my argument is that relational responsibility and care are central (neither add-ons nor replacements) to the work of schools, implicated in the inequalities they produce, reinscribe or challenge, and fundamental to philosophical and policy debates about curriculum content and educational purposes.

Concluding comments

I began with questions prompted by a teacher remembering her own school teachers, and the strong impact their support had upon her at the time and subsequently. Such vivid memories of teaching-as-care were not an isolated example in the suite of oral histories, offering an embodied 'feel' of the power of relational and affective dynamics in teaching, and the significance of expressing care and responsibility for and towards others. From the preceding discussion of feminist ethics, three main propositions are highlighted that together speak to how responsibility might be re-imagined in teaching and educational work. First, an ethical pedagogical role for teachers is to foster a sense of social responsibility in students and to cultivate a sense of openness to others. Second, relations of love, care, solidarity *and* responsibility belong within frameworks of equality as well as in debates and policies about the purposes and curriculum of educational institutions. Third, responsibility is relational, a practice and a disposition; it is linked to democratic imaginaries, and has a collective remit, rather than a singular focus on personal responsibility (or responsibilisation). Attention to the effects of responsibilisation and technologies of individualisation in education has offered valuable insights into modes of subjectivity and governance in the contemporary era, and it is important to bear these analyses in mind in any re-assessment of responsibility and its potentially double-edged qualities as both regulatory and relational. However, I have also argued that the responsibilisation thesis can be reductive if it eclipses from view other equally significant dimensions of the movement, practice and sense of responsibility in education.

Overall, I have argued, first, that there is an urgency for repositioning responsibility as a productive orientation and practice, linked to framing education as a transformative and relational endeavour, particularly given the current educational climate where definitions of teachers' work are becoming more and more instrumental. Critical analyses abound of this and the performative measures that govern teachers' work. While such critiques have been necessary, they – and their targets of critique – can also serve to mute the pleasures and sense of purpose that both propels and keeps people teaching. This was touched on in my necessarily brief opening remarks regarding the oral history memories of teachers. Second, I have proposed that feminist theories of care and relational responsibility remain relevant to normative discussions of education and its knowledge and person-making purposes. There are risks in emphasising the affective realm of schooling – downplaying (inadvertently) the knowledge functions of schooling, fostering a self-involved individualism, romanticising feelings at the expense of understanding schools' role in credentialing and the differential distribution of educational success and pathways. The discussions canvassed here, however, advocate placing relations of responsibility and care as integral to, not instead of these epistemological and distributive aspects of schooling, and as relational – other-directed, not self-focused. Third, critical engagements with the affective and social circumstances of precarity bring new challenges into view for how schools and other educational institutions might respond to a pervasive sense of vulnerability. Berlant (2012) points in the direction of interdependence, a concept aligned to the idea of relational responsibility that has been elaborated here. Finally, Berlant's remarks about an 'idiom of care' as now the mode of managing the social forcefully brings our attention to the specific circumstances of the historical present in which these various discussions about ethics and relational responsibility take place. In doing so, it brings us back to ground, to the insecurities and divisiveness of contemporary life, and to the motivations for trying to rethink responsibility towards others, not only towards the self.

Notes

1. The oral history interviews were undertaken by Julie McLeod and Katie Wright as part of the project *Educating the Australian Adolescent: An Historical study of Curriculum, Counselling and Citizenship, 1930s – 1970s*. Australian Research Council Discovery Grant 2009–11 (DP0987299). The oral history archive comprises more than 80 interviews with former teachers and students from the 1930s, 1950s and 1970s. Project website: http://education.unimelb.edu.au/news_and_activities/projects/eaa.

Acknowledgements

I acknowledge with thanks discussions with Katie Wright and Fazal Rizvi and helpful feedback from two anonymous reviewers.

Disclosure statement

No potential conflict of interest was reported by the author.

Funding

This article draws from research undertaken as part of two ARC Projects: 'Educating the Australian Adolescent: An Historical study of Curriculum, Counselling and Citizenship, 1930s – 1970s', (DP0987299, Discovery Grant); and 'Youth Identity and Educational Change since 1950: digital archiving, re-using qualitative data and histories of the present' (FT110100646, Future Fellowship.)

References

Ahmed, S. (2014). *Willful subjects*. Durham, NC: Duke University Press.
Arnot, M., & Dillabough, J. (2006). Feminist politics and democratic values in education. In H. Lauder, P. Brown, J. Dillabough, & A. H. Halsey (Eds.), *Education, globalization, and social change* (pp. 161–178). Oxford: Oxford University Press.

Baker, J., Lynch, K., Cantillon, S., & Walsh, J. (2009). *Equality: From theory to action* (2nd ed.). Basingstoke: Palgrave Macmillan.

Ball, S. (2005). *Education policy and social class: The selected works of Stephen Ball*. London: Routledge/Falmer.

Barad, K. (2007). *Meeting the universe halfway: Quantum physics and the entanglement of matter and meaning*. Durham, NC: Duke University Press.

Beasley, C., & Bacchi, C. (2005). The political limits of 'care' in re-imagining interconnection/ community and an ethical future. *Australian Feminist Studies, 20*(4), 49–64.

Beck, U. (1992). *Risk society: Towards a new modernity*. London: Sage.

Benhabib, S. (2004). *Rights of others: Aliens, residents and citizens*. Cambridge MA: Cambridge University Press.

Berlant, L. (2011). *Cruel optimism*. Durham, NC: Duke University Press.

Berlant, L. (2012). Virtual roundtable discussion. In J. Puar (Ed.), Precarity talk: A virtual roundtable with Lauren Berlant, Judith Butler, Bojana Cvejic, Isabell Lorey, Jasbir Puar, and Ana Vujanovic. TDR: *The Drama Review, 56*(4), 163–177.

Biesta, G. (2012). Philosophy of education for the public good: Five challenges and agenda. *Educational Philosophy and Theory, 44*(6), 581–593.

Butler, J. (2004). *Precarious life: The powers of mourning and violence*. London: Verso.

Eccelstone, K. (2015). Vulnerability and wellbeing in educational settings: The implications of a therapeutic approach to social justice. In K. Wright & J. McLeod (Eds.), *Rethinking youth wellbeing: Critical perspectives* (pp. 35–54). Singapore: Springer.

Foucault, M. (1988). Technologies of the self. In L. H. Martin, H. Gutman, & P. H. Hutton (Eds.), *Technologies of the self: A seminar with Michel Foucault* (pp. 16–49). London: Tavistock Publications.

Fraser, N. (1997). *Justice interruptus*. New York: Routledge.

Furedi, F. (2009). *Wasted: Why education isn't educating*. London: Continuum International Publishing Group.

Furlong, A., & Cartmel, F. (2006). *Young people and social change* (2nd ed.). London: McGraw-Hill.

Giddens, A. (1991). *Modernity and self-identity: Self and society in the late modern age*. Cambridge: Polity Press.

Gilligan, C. (1982). *In a different voice: Psychological theory and women's development*. Cambridge, MA: Harvard University Press.

Hage, G., & Eckersley, R. (Eds.). (2012). *Responsibility*. Melbourne: Melbourne University Press.

Kelly, P. (2001). Youth at risk: Processes of individualisation and responsibilisation in the risk society. *Discourse: Studies in the Cultural Politics of Education, 22*(1), 23–33.

Kenway, J., & Willis, S. (Eds.). (1990). *Hearts and minds: Self-esteem and the schooling of girls*. London: The Falmer Press.

Lingard, B. (2011). Policy as numbers: Ac/counting for educational research. *The Australian Educational Researcher, 38*(4), 355–382.

Lynch, K., Lyons, M., & Cantillon, S. (2007). Breaking the silence: Educating citizens for love, care and solidarity. *International Studies in Sociology of Education, 17*(1/2), 1–19.

Ministerial Council on Education, Employment, Training and Youth Affairs (2008, December). *Melbourne declaration on educational goals for young Australians*. Melbourne: Author.

McLeod, J. (2012). Vulnerability and the neo-liberal youth citizen: A view from Australia. *Comparative Education, 48*(1), 11–26.

McLeod, J. (2015). Happiness, wellbeing and self-esteem: Public feelings and educational projects. In K. Wright & J. McLeod (Eds.), *Rethinking youth wellbeing: Critical perspectives* (pp. 179–196). Singapore: Springer.

McLeod, J., & Yates, L. (2006). *Making modern lives: Subjectivity, schooling and social change*. Albany, NY: SUNY Press.

Noddings, N. (1984). *Caring: A feminine approach to ethics and moral education*. Berkeley: University of California Press.

Pateman, C. (1988). *The sexual contract*. Cambridge: The Polity Press.

Peters, R. S. (1973/1959). *Authority, responsibility and education* (3rd ed.). London: Allen and Unwin.

Reay, D. (2013). Social mobility: A panacea for austere times. *British Journal of Sociology of Education, 34*(5–6), 660–677.

Rizvi, F., & Lingard, B. (2010). *Globalizing educational policy*. London: Routledge.

Rose, N. (1996). *Inventing ourselves: Psychology, power and personhood*. Cambridge: Cambridge University Press.

Somers, M. (2008). *Genealogies of citizenship: Markets, statelessness, and right to have rights*. New York, NY: Cambridge University Press.

Stout, M. (2000). *The feel-good curriculum: The dumbing down of America's kids in the name of self-esteem*. New York, NY: Perseus Publishing.

Todd, S. (2003). *Learning from the other: Levinas, psychoanalysis, and ethical possibilities in education*. Albany: State University of New York Press.

Tronto, J. C. (1993). *Moral boundaries: A political argument for an ethic of care*. New York, NY: Routledge.

Tronto, J. C. (2013). *Caring democracy: Markets, equality, and justice*. New York: New York University Press.

Walker, M. U. (2007). *Moral understandings* (2nd ed.). New York, NY: Oxford University Press.

Warin, J., & Gannerud, E. (2014). Gender, teaching and care: A comparative global conversation. *Gender and Education, 26*(3), 193–199.

Yates, L. (2012). My school, my university, my country, my world, my Google, myself … what is education for now? *The Australian Educational Researcher, 39*(3), 259–274.

Young, I. M. (1990). *Justice and the politics of difference*. Princeton, NJ: Princeton University Press.

Young, I. M. (2011). *Responsibility for justice*. Oxford: Oxford University Press.

Zembylas, M., Bozalek, V., & Shefer, T. (2014). Tronto's notion of privileged irresponsibility and the reconceptualisation of care: Implications for critical pedagogies of emotion in higher education. *Gender and Education, 26*(3), 200–214.

Growing up after the GFC: responsibilisation and mortgaged futures

Peter Kelly

ABSTRACT

In this paper I argue that in the aftermath of the Global Financial Crisis of 2008–2009 young people, certain populations of young people in particular, are being made to bear a heavy burden, carry significant responsibilities for re-imagining their lives as a enterprise – an enterprise in which an *investment* in education and training and work increasingly looks like a *mortgaging* of an uncertain future. In mortgaging their future, many young people are confounded by the possibility of repaying this debt, or of leveraging it into a life that was promised them if only they stayed in education and training, if only they got a job, if only they studied and worked hard, and had an eye to the future. The paper will explore some of the characteristics of the self as enterprise, the challenges and opportunities that shape the fields of possibilities from which this self emerges, and which require us to practise our freedom in particular, always limited, ways and to carry responsibilities for more and more aspects of our lives, in circumstances that mostly escape our differing, individual abilities and capacities to shape these circumstances.

Introduction

In a number of spaces, over a number of years, I have argued that the self as enterprise is a *figure*, a 'material-semiotic node or knot' (Haraway, 2008), that points to the sort of person that we should become if we want to be, and remain, employable in the globalised, precarious labour markets of the twenty-first century, flexible capitalism. The self as enterprise, and the 'ethically slanted maxims for the conduct of a life' (Weber, 2002/1930), the 'technologies of the self' (Foucault, 2000), that promise to give shape to this form of personhood, assume that we are, or should become, rational, autonomous, choice making, risk aware, prudential, responsible and enterprising in the conduct of ourselves, our lives (see e.g. Kelly, 2013, 2007).

However, the self as enterprise is not imagined as the raw material, the essence of what it is to be a person. Rather, the self as enterprise has to be 'made up' (Rose & Miller, 1992) – in families, in schools, in relationships, in labour markets, in training programmes – and continuously worked on (*for the term of our natural life*). Technologies of the self as enterprise imagine that we, as individuals, are responsible for the always in-process, always provisional, always precarious state of our Do It Yourself (DIY) project of the self (Beck, 1992). These processes of individualisation and responsibilisation have a particular character in the lives of young people as they are made the subjects of a diverse array of governmental programs – in families, schools, workplaces – that promise to equip them to secure some sort of parlous redemption in the globalised, increasingly precarious labour markets of twenty-first-century capitalism (Kelly & Harrison, 2009).

In the aftermath of the Global Financial Crisis (GFC) of 2008–2009 young people, certain populations of young people in particular, are being made to bear a heavy burden, carry significant responsibilities for re-imagining their lives as an enterprise. This is an enterprise in which an *investment* in education and training and work increasingly looks like a *mortgaging* of an uncertain future. In mortgaging their future many young people are confounded by the possibility of repaying this debt, or of leveraging it into a life that was promised them if only they stayed in education and training, if only they got a job, if only they studied and worked hard and had an eye to the future. Drawing on the work of Bauman, Foucault, Law and Haraway (among others) this paper will explore some of the characteristics of the self as enterprise. The challenges and opportunities that shape the fields of possibilities from which this self emerges, and which require us to practise our freedom in particular, always limited, ways, and, in the end, to carry responsibilities for more and more aspects of our lives, in circumstances that mostly escape our differing, individual abilities and capacities to shape these circumstances.

The GFC and generations

In many of the Organisation for Economic Co-operation and Development (OECD) economies, young people appear to be carrying a particularly heavy burden for many of the downstream effects of the 2008–2009 GFC. These downstream effects have compounded the educational and labour market effects and consequences of 30 or 40 years of heightened globalisation, the emergence of a more flexible capitalism, and the ways in which 1980s Thatcherism and Reaganism have morphed into the globalised triumphalism of neo-Liberalism (Hall, Massey, & Rustin, 2013).

The unfolding effects of what some are calling the Great Recession in Europe and the USA, and the emergence of sovereign debt crises and significant austerity programs in many European Union (EU)/OECD economies represent a largely successful framing of responses to the downstream effects of the GFC as being principally about State debt levels. In this discourse those that depend most on State provided services, payments and programmes will be the ones to carry the greatest burden of government austerity measures. In an appearance before the UK's House of Commons Treasury Committee in early 2011, the then Governor of the Bank of England Mervyn King claimed that those made unemployed or who had their benefits cut as a consequence of the GFC, recession and austerity 'had every reason to be resentful and voice their protest'. In his submission to the Committee he suggested:

> that the billions spent bailing out the banks and the need for public spending cuts were the fault of the financial services sector: 'The price of this financial crisis is being borne by people who absolutely did not cause it'. (cited in Inman, 2011)

One example from the North East of England illustrates some of my concerns here. In an article in *The Guardian* on 4 February 2013, John Harris discussed some of the debates and possible consequences related to Newcastle City Council's (UK) published budget plans. According to reports on these plans the Council was to cut a third of its budget, or £100m spread over three years to 2016, and shed 1300 jobs as it struggled to deal with budget cuts imposed by the Tory/Liberal Democrat coalition government in the name of a sovereign debt crisis, fiscal responsibility, austerity and the need to show the UK's *strivers* that the coalition was serious about dealing with a 'culture of entitlement' among the nation's *skivers*. In the week prior to the publication of Harris' article, the UK's National Audit Office (NAO) had issued a report titled *Financial sustainability of local authorities*. This report, referenced by Harris (2013), suggested that not all Councils in the UK were in the same position as a consequence of Tory/Liberal Democrat austerity measures. According to the NAO: 'councils in the most deprived areas have seen substantially greater reductions in government funding as a share of revenue expenditure than councils in less deprived areas'. In other words, claimed Harris (2013), the likes of 'Hackney ... Liverpool, Manchester and Newcastle take a big hit, but Elmsbridge, Winchester and Richmond-upon-Thames have got off very lightly indeed.' He goes on to suggest that this 'kind of imbalance' is also reflected in the ways in which these sorts of cuts are reported:

> In the London-based media, Newcastle is currently a byword for the 100% drop in the council's arts budget ... Unfortunately, there [seems to be no one] who will speak up for the youth services set to be killed by a 100% cut in their budget, the Sure Start provision soon to be restricted to 'those who need it most', the respite services for parents of disabled children that will shut, the city's remaining educational psychologists or the imperilled swimming pools. (Harris, 2013)

Harris (2013) suggested that in this sort of environment 'you get a keen sense of bright, shining hypocrisies that extend into the distance'. Tory and Liberal Democrat ministers 'still parrot the political class's habitual platitudes about "aspiration" and "opportunity", while in places such as this they are self-evidently meaningless'. The idea of *intergenerational theft* becomes, in this sense, less about passing on public debt to future generations, and more about changing the 'life chances of millions of young people'. What is at play here, Harris argued, is some sort of fantasy in which the 'barren expanses' being created 'will sprout new centres of entrepreneurial zeal'. In such fantasies those young people that are 'refused extra educational help or denied a local library', well, they become 'tomorrow's genius digital tycoons, or something ... '.

It is in this sense that I want to suggest that today's young people and young adults, and the generations who will follow and grow up in the unfolding aftermath of the GFC, will carry a particularly heavy burden in terms of changed education and employment circumstances and opportunities; consequences for physical and mental health and well-being; consumption, housing, relationship and parenting aspirations; and a sense of self in relation to the possibilities for participation in the liberal democracies.

In the EU, for example, youth unemployment and long-term unemployment rates in many Member countries have reached record levels; and the numbers of young people not in employment, education or training have also risen. At the start of 2013 the youth unemployment rate (for 15–24-year-olds) ranged from 7.7% (Germany) to 59.1% (Greece). In the EU these percentages translate to more than 5.7 million unemployed young people (European Commission, 2013). As many have suggested, these sorts of aggregate figures do not reveal the ways in which different groups and communities and different localities are differently impacted, how different labour markets offer more or less opportunities for particular populations of young people, or what combinations of social class, gender, ethnicity and geography shape the exclusion and marginalisation of young people from education, from work, from housing, from consumption, from the possibilities of family relationships. For example, a recent Australian study suggested that data from the Australian Bureau of Statistics indicated that in early 2014 the youth unemployment rate (for 15–24-year-olds) was 12.2%. Importantly, this rate was much higher in certain towns/cities/regions: 21% in West and North West Tasmania, including Burnie and Devonport; 20.5% in Cairns (Queensland); 19.7% in northern Adelaide, including Elizabeth and Gawler (SA); 17.5% in Hume (Victoria), including Goulburn Valley, Wodonga and Wangaratta; 17.3% in Mandurah (WA) and 16.8% in Parramatta (NSW) (Brotherhood of St Laurence, 2014). These *gross* and regionally segmented unemployment figures also do not tell us much about the types of work, the sorts of jobs that are available to many people, young and old.

In addition, in many OECD and EU economies governments have, for the last few decades, been shifting the burden for the cost of higher education to students. In the UK, in 2010, the newly elected Tory/Liberal Democrat government partially deregulated the structure of University undergraduate tuition fees to increase competition between providers (in the process breaking a key pledge in the Liberal Democrat election manifesto not to increase tuition fees). As a result there was a race to the top of the government imposed £9000/year cap on tuition fees as nearly all providers priced their degrees the same (even though there must be a self-evident difference in what students are 'buying' for that price). Students, who take out loans to pay these fees, and to provide a small annual allowance, are likely to graduate with debts of £40,000. Millions of young people in the OECD economies can now look to start their 'working lives' (if they can find a job) with large debts that are to be repaid through an array of student loan schemes (McQuillan, 2014).

Young people: a future mortgaged?

At this time I want to briefly examine some of the ways in which young people in different parts of the globe have taken up some of the challenges of growing up after the GFC. During the last five years or so, we witnessed how many young people around the world had both begun to experience what some of these consequences might be and to give voice to much of their anxiety, uncertainty and anger about their experience of these consequences. Space does not permit me to spend any time analysing young people's involvement in groups and movements such as the Spanish *Indignados* or the global Occupy movement, or in the various and different revolutions in the Arab Spring, or in the riots in many cities in the UK during August 2011. But I do want to suggest that high levels of youth unemployment and precarious employment, student debt accompanying increased costs for higher education, housing costs that lock many out of home ownership, and the challenges for young people's physical and mental health and well-being are re-shaping young people's sense of self and of their chances for meaningful participation in relationships and settings that traditionally identified someone as an adult, as a citizen.

These concerns are well captured by the many hundreds, even thousands of contributions from young people to a Tumblr page called *We Are the 99%*.[1] Those who posted to this page were asked to upload an image, and to contribute some text about the image and why they imagined themselves as being part of the 99%. I want to present just a small number of these posts. In the first one a forlorn looking young woman, wearing headphones and looking into her computer's camera, holds up a notebook where she has written:

I CAN'T FIND MY FUTURE.
I looked in college.
I found debt.
I looked to my parents.
I found debt and heartbreak.
I looked at my friends.
I found grief and sorrow.
I looked at the land.
I found MY COMMONS DESTROYED, MY LAKES AND RIVERS AND SOIL AND TREES AND BEES AND WORMS DESTROYED.
I looked at my fellow humans.
I found disease, debt, sorrow, dissonance, hate, greed, misery, AND NO ONE CARES ANYMORE.
well. I CARE. an awful lot.
I'M TAKING MY FUTURE BACK.
(IT'S MINE)
I AM THE 99%

Another post shows an image of white board with words that appear to have been written with much passion, emotion, anger, anxiety:

I am 20
I earned a culinary degree
I had to move back w/my parents
I have $$$$ in student loans
I make and have never made more than $9.50/hr
I vow never to have children, for I fear for their future like I fear for my own
I feel this life is almost not worth living …
I live 4 change
I AM THE 99%
#OCCUPYWS

In the final post, the following text accompanies an image of a digital clock showing 0:01 (orange figures against a black background):

I'm on an internship for school. I'm not getting paid for it. I'm in a strange city. I don't know anyone here. I have applied at almost every fast-food restaurant, retail store, gas station, and whatever else I can think of, but have heard nothing back. My bank account is almost completely empty. I'm writing this on the laptop I can't sell because I need it for school, and while I write, I eat the last of my groceries. My car is almost out of gas. I don't even have enough money to pay rent on the first of the month. I don't have a lot of personal possessions that I can sell, and the ones that I can, probably won't get much for. I don't have health insurance, and I dread getting sick or having an accident that leaves me in the hospital. If I give up now and go home, I won't graduate. I'm already several thousand dollars in student loan debt, I hope to at least have something to show for it. But how long can I last at my

internship when I have to choose between putting gas in my car and doing laundry? My life is a ticking time-bomb, and the last few seconds are counting down before my eyes.
I am the 99 percent. And I am out of ideas.

We can see in these and the thousands of similar posts, and in a variety of other spaces, a powerful questioning of many of the markers of adulthood that have framed young people's identity, their sense of self, both in *being*, and in *becoming*: *becoming* an adult, *becoming* a citizen, *becoming* independent, *becoming* autonomous, *becoming* mature, *becoming* responsible. These markers frame accounts of what it is to be an aspirational, enterprising young person who has a prudential eye to the future: to *their* future as adults with some sort of investment in an education, a career, relationships, consumption, housing, possibly parenting (Kelly, 2007, 2012). For many young people it now appears that what is needed to realise these aspirations is less an investment in *becoming*, and more a mortgaging of these possibilities with few, if any, means to meet the obligations that these debts demand. And in seeing these aspirations and hopes mortgaged many young people see little chance for their concerns to be heard and met through the traditional institutions of the liberal democracies.

We are the 99% represents, in this sense, an attempt to re-imagine what it means to be a person who is connected to others in various spheres of life. Of course not everyone who might qualify will imagine themselves as being a member of the 99%. But it can be argued that the material concerns of those who imagine themselves as being part of the 99% are able to be reframed via the networking that is promised by social media. That is, I can imagine myself as being part of this thing called the 99% because social media enables me to imagine that such a thing exists, or exists as imagined by those who come to identify themselves in this way. These 'experiments' in new 'cultures of democracy' (Taylor, 2007) are uncertain and open-ended. In many instances they have been transformed, or have 'failed', or been suppressed and dispersed by the powerful forces at the disposal of governments and globalised corporations. The nature and consequences of these experiments are of interest, but are not my primary concern in this paper. Instead, I want to situate the burdens and responsibilities that will be carried by the generations who will grow up after the GFC in processes that have made individuals in the neo-liberal democracies increasingly responsible for managing their lives as an enterprise. And for the experience of the ambivalence that inevitably accompanies the obligation to make choices, to exercise an always limited freedom, and to carry the responsibilities for the ways in which we exercise our freedom.

Precarious work and twenty-first-century capitalism

A number of influential sociologies of work have claimed that at the start of the twenty-first century the nature and meaning of work has changed. In many respects workers in the OECD economies remain as participants in a classic capitalist exchange relation in which they sell their labour (physical, mental, creative) in variously regulated labour markets. Those individuals and organisations that purchase labour then have some claims – often negotiated, contested, arbitrated – over what individuals are expected to do in terms of work processes and practices; when and where they are expected to do work; and the manner in which they should think, act and feel in relation to these paid work tasks and duties. Not much has changed then since the likes of Marx and Engels, and later Weber, were formulating frameworks for understanding capitalism and work. Yet, in many other ways work, work opportunities, work identities, the meaning of work, the place of work in our lives, the times and spaces and places in which work occurs have been, and continue to be, transformed (Bauman, 2005; Beck, 2000).

Long-term trend data (1982–2005) shows that at a fundamental level paid work in many of the OECD economies is no longer primarily a male pursuit (although, of course, to suggest that at one time it was is to think of paid work from a middle-class perspective: large numbers of women from the working classes had to participate in the paid labour market to secure household livelihoods). In many of these economies women now make up at least 40% of the labour force, and in many economies at least 60% of women of working age (15–64 years) are active participants in the labour force (OECD, 2006). At another level paid work requires fewer and fewer of the workforce to manufacture a physical object; fewer and fewer to plant, sow, harvest or otherwise engage in the production of foodstuffs or agricultural products; fewer and fewer to dig or mine minerals, ores and fuels above or below ground. The percentage of the labour force engaged in mining and primary production in most OECD economies declined significantly from 1982 to 2005, as did the numbers involved in the manufacturing industries; while greater numbers of those who participate in labour markets are engaged in the provision of a vast variety of services (OECD, 2006).

In this context there has been discussion about the emergence of core and peripheral labour markets in which the core workforce trades excessively long hours of work for a measure of security and access to a range of non-salary benefits. The so-called peripheral workforce has been characterised as low/minimum wage, casualised and part-time, denied access to employment conditions such as sick leave, pension and health care entitlements, and a general lack of security in an employment context. In many of the OECD economies, the labour force has become characterised by increased levels of casualised and part-time work, and the over-representation of particular populations – females and young people – in part-time and casual employment (also Hochschild, 2001, 2003; OECD, 2006; Thrift, 2005). Standing (2011a) has recently canvassed many of these concerns in his book *The precariat*. Elsewhere he summarises a number of his key ideas in arguing that the precariat:

> … consists of a multitude of insecure people, living bits-and-pieces lives, in and out of short-term jobs, without a narrative of occupational development, including millions of frustrated educated youth who do not like what they see before them, millions of women abused in oppressive labour, growing numbers of criminalised tagged for life, millions being categorised as 'disabled' and migrants in their hundreds of millions around the world. They are denizens; they have a more restricted range of social, cultural, political and economic rights than citizens around them. (Standing, 2011b)

Sennett (2006) identifies three key, unfolding, processes shaping the emergence of what he calls *flexible capitalism* – a form of capitalism that energises and is energised by precariousness. The changes Sennett describes are complex; they unfold unevenly and with a variety of consequences (intended and unintended); they may look different and impact differently in different configurations of time/space/place – such as in different organisations (large/small, startup/established), or in different towns, cities, regions, nations, free trade communities. Sennett's framework enables a discussion of changes in twenty-first-century work regimes that foregrounds the powerful demands for flexibility, both at the level of the organisation, and at the level of the self.

The first of the processes, Sennett (2006, pp. 37–47) identifies is the 'shift from managerial to shareholder power' in many, mostly larger, organisations. Sennett locates the energising moment for this shift in the 1970 breakdown of the Bretton Woods agreement, and the subsequent freeing of vast amounts of capital to find optimal returns anywhere around the globe. Takeovers, mergers, acquisitions and buyouts became the playthings of increasingly mobile capital. All enabled by the frenzied activity of wealth holders seeking wealth creation; and facilitated by the demands for the interests of mobile, digitised capital to be accorded more currency/value that those of more *territorially fixed players* such as nation states and *flesh and blood* workers (Beck, 2000).

This globalised circulation/flow of often predatory capital ushered in the second process that Sennett identifies as energising the flexibilisation of capitalism. Sennett (2006, pp. 39–40) argues that 'empowered investors' in greatly enhanced, globalised circuits of capital demanded short term rather than long-term results: 'whereas in 1965 American pension funds held stocks on an average for 46 months, by 2000 much in the portfolio's of these institutional investors turned over on an average of 3.8 months'. As Sennett (2006, pp. 40–41) indicates, there is little new in money chasing money. However, organisations have had to transform their institutional processes, practices and structures to satisfy the fetishisation of the short term by impatient, globalised, digitised capital: 'Enormous pressure was put on companies to look beautiful in the eyes of the passing voyeur.' In Sennett's understanding of flexible capitalism this is a profound change, and a continuing driver of change: the re-engineering, re-working, re-invention of the organisation – and I would add, of the self – that accompanies the myriad, complex demands for flexibility, nimbleness and innovation signals a highly consequential break from the *steel hard shell/iron cage* of the Weberian bureaucracy.

The third driver of this post-bureaucratic, flexible capitalism is, for Sennett, the information, communication and transportation revolutions of the last four decades that have transformed the nature of all productive activities. Under the sometimes uneven influence of the global development and deployment of these technologies twenty-first-century work looks different, is imagined and regulated in different ways. It can be undertaken by micro-processor governed machines and hardware that displace humans on a massive scale. It can be organised within organisational architecture that, ideally, looks less like a *pyramid*, is *flatter* with less layers, and which constantly strives for *real time* rather than *lag time* in processes of command and control, but also of innovation and development. These forces are not just felt at the organisational level, at the level of being an attractive object of mobile, digital, impatient capital. They are highly consequential for the individual, the self, that constantly encounters these *norms* of economic activity, and must make choices, fashion a self, practice his/her freedom in the spaces structured by these demands and expectations (Kelly, 2013).

These, and other claims, have figured prominently in a broad literature concerned with the sociology of so-called *new work orders* that has emerged in the last few decades. This literature highlights the emergence of widespread anxieties and uncertainties as individuals work away at constructing a coherent and continuing narrative of self, of identity, in an adult world of work that is increasingly precarious, uncertain, flexible (Bauman, 2001,

2005; Beck, 2000). These understandings should not be seen as determining the forms of selfhood that we are encouraged and/or compelled to practise in the labour markets of twenty-first century, flexible capitalism. But if twenty-first century, flexible capitalism structures the fields of possibility in which we practise our freedom, then these fields, following Foucault, should be understood as not being entirely open, and as not being wholly constrained. There is always the possibility of acting otherwise, but in acting otherwise there are always consequences for a self.

The self as enterprise and the ambivalence of freedom

In this final section I want to situate this discussion in a brief account of why it is productive to think about the self as an enterprise, and the ways in which neo-Liberalism, as an art of government (Foucault, 1991), seeks to make the individual responsible for the choices, outcomes and consequences of managing this enterprise. In *The Protestant ethic and the 'spirit' of capitalism,* Weber (2002/1930) explored the particular virtues that should be seen as attaching to work, and the particular influence that certain Protestant sects had on articulating these virtues. Weber's concern was with investigating the relationship between a Puritan/Calvinist view that hard work, done well, was its own reward, and a so-called *spirit of capitalism*. Weber (2002/1930) provides a 'provisional illustration of what is meant here by the "spirit" of capitalism' via a 'document of that "spirit" which encapsulates the essence of the matter in almost classical purity'. What follows in *The Protestant ethic* are extended passages from the 18th century pamphleteer Benjamin Franklin, including:

> Remember, *that time is money* ... The most trifling actions that affect a man's credit are to be regarded. The sound of your hammer at five in the morning, or eight at night, heard by a creditor, makes him easy six months longer ... It shows, besides, that you are mindful of what you owe; it makes you appear a careful as well as an *honest* man, and that still increases your *credit.* (pp. 9–11, original emphases)

Weber (2002/1930, p. 11, original emphasis) makes no claims for the representativeness, even truthfulness of Franklin's incitements and advice. Yet, for Weber there is little doubt that what he calls 'this little sermon' is the 'characteristic voice of the "spirit of capitalism", although clearly it does not contain everything that may be understood by the term'. Moreover, the 'essence of this "philosophy of avarice" is the idea of the *duty* of the individual to work toward the increase of his wealth, which is assumed to be an end in itself'. This *spirit* has, for Franklin, 'the character of an *ethically* slanted maxim for the conduct of life [*Lebensführung*]. *This is the specific sense in which we propose to use the concept of the "spirit of capitalism"*'.

Weber saw in the Protestant Ethic only one of the motive forces for the emergence of rationalised capitalism. A Protestant ethic promised heavenly salvation, and an earthbound redemption as the outcome of the pursuit of the individual's calling. Twenty-first century, flexible capitalism is energised by a spirit that sees in the cultivation of the self – as an ongoing, never ending enterprise – an *ethically slanted maxim for the conduct of a life*. This spirit is made explicit in the ways in which American management consultant Peters (2005), for example, imagines the type of person one must be, the forms of personhood that one must cultivate, in order to succeed in the *monstrous cosmos* of twenty-first-century flexible capitalism. In his *100 ways to help you succeed/make money*, Peters (2005, pp. 41–42) claims that:

> 100 WAYS TO SUCCEED #23:
> DESIGN MEANS YOU!
> Sure, 'design' means DHL spending Gazillion$$$$ on … YELLOW. IT'S THE NEW BROWN.
> But that's not all.
> *Design means* … me … at age 61 and somewhat successful … going through more than 25 drafts of a mere update of my Official Bio … that will be circulated to Clients for the next several months.
> *Design means* … that every action I take is Consciously Mediated by my implicit-explicit 'design filter': That is … HOW DOES THIS COME ACROSS? COULD IT BE CLEARER? CRISPER? MORE EXCITING?
> I 'am' design!
> It works for me.
> I invite you aboard!
> It's a daunting journey … and an exciting one.
> It's near the Heart of the Matter in a BrandYou World.
> (Hint: We live in a BrandYou World … like it or not.)
> You = Desire to Survive = BrandYou = Branding Fanatic = LoveMark Fanatic (thanks, Kevin Roberts) = Design Fanatic.
> Q.E.D.

Michel Foucault's later work on the care of the self; the central part played by an analysis of the relationships between knowledge/power/subjects in this work; the focus on the ways in which forms of management and regulation, and practices of the self interact to shape the ways in which we practise our freedom in neo-Liberal spaces; and a refusal to ground this analytic in a theory of the Subject provides a powerful framework for thinking about the self as enterprise and the processes of individualisation and responsibilisation at play in the conduct of this enterprise (Foucault, 1985, 1986, 1991). Foucault's work throws into relief questions about the ways in which we practise our freedom, and are managed and regulated as Subjects who are free to choose, and who must carry the consequences of the choices we make (Rose, 1999). An extensive literature that draws on Foucault's work argues that neo-Liberal governmentalities produce understandings of the self as an autonomous, self governing enterprise that should, ideally, be capable of identifying, navigating and managing the opportunities and risks of twenty-first century, flexible capitalism (Barry, Osborne, & Rose, 1996; Burchell, Gordon, & Miller, 1991; Gordon, 1991). The idea of the self as enterprise opens up for analysis our *willing* participation in globalised, precarious labour markets (Bunting, 2004). To practise one's freedom is to develop certain dispositions, behaviours, capacities and commitments – in settings and systems of interaction in which others seek to manage or encourage particular (appropriate) behaviours and dispositions. It is in the compulsion to choose, to make appropriate choices from a range of culturally and historically specific options that we, not only, *practise* our freedom, but also carry the responsibilities and obligations, or reap the rewards that flow from practising our freedom in these ways (Kelly, 2013).

Where the meanings of life are transformed into meanings which are structured by the market form, then the subjects of neo-Liberal rationalities of government emerge, argues Burchell (1996, pp. 22–23), as 'free', 'entrepreneurial', competitive and economically rational individuals. However, within these governmentalities this form of selfhood is not so much a 'given of human nature as a consciously contrived style of conduct'. That is, this subject has to be *made up* – encouraged, incited, directed, educated, trained – via the mobilisation of diverse techniques, as the active, autonomous, responsible entrepreneur of her or his own DIY project of the self. Rose (1996) argues that the self, in this sense, is conceived as an active, self-creating individual seeking to *enterprise* themselves. Individual biographical projects are the result, within this rationality, of the *maximisation* of the chances for a *good life* through *acts of choice* – through the practice of freedom. Life is accorded 'meaning and value to the extent that it can be rationalized as the outcome of choices made or choices to be made' (p. 57).

In this sense an ethic of enterprise is a fluid, shifting, generalised, and at the same time contingent and contextual body of thoughts, ideas, recipes, forms of advice, injunctions and suggestions for how it is that we should know and act on ourselves. This ethic emerges from and gives shape to an array of always limited fields of possibility in which we are encouraged to imagine ourselves, our choices, our aspirations in particular ways if we want to participate in precarious labour markets. Participation that will provide, it is hoped, the forms of salvation – even purpose and meaning – that paid work promises (Kelly, 2013). In the work of Tom Peters, for example, we see the moral imperatives to conduct one's self as an enterprise writ large. Indeed, the work one must do on oneself, the labour required to know oneself in terms of being the producer and promoter of one's own biography, and the diverse aspects of this biography that position the self in a favourable light in the precarious labour markets of twenty-first-century capitalism, are presented as imperatives. Success, on the terms demanded by this *monstrous cosmos* (Weber, 2002/1930), is dependent on being able to manage the self as a successful enterprise:

> Task one: Work on ourselves. Relentlessly!
> HE/SHE WHO HAS THE BEST STORY WINS! SO ... WORK ON YOUR STORY!
> You = Desire to Survive = BrandYou = Branding Fanatic = LoveMark Fanatic = Design Fanatic.
> (Peters, 2005)

Conclusion

Whether we have the capacity, the desire, the skills necessary to know or to recognise ourselves as an enterprise cannot be determined in advance. Despite the ambitions of neo-Liberal governmentalities the self as enterprise cannot be willed into existence. The regulation of the conduct of oneself and others is, always, an incomplete project. The responsibilities for managing the consequences of this enterprise, and the capacities to identify and manage the risks and opportunities that confront this enterprise are, in neo-Liberal mentalities of rule, imagined as residing in and with the individual. As individuals we are imagined as being responsible for the choices we make, for the outcomes of choices made (and not), for managing the material ambiguities (Bauman, 2001) and emotional costs of globalised, precarious labour markets (Elliott & Lemert, 2006). In the North East of England, in regional Australia, in Greek and Spanish cities, on Tumblr, the material ambiguities and emotional costs of globalised precarity are experienced in diverse ways by diverse groups of young people. And the possibility of thinking or acting otherwise in twenty-first-century capitalism is indeed limited. As Weber (2002/1930) argued in *The Protestant ethic*:

> *Today's* capitalist economic order is a monstrous cosmos, into which the individual is born and which in practice is for him, at least as an individual, simply a given, an immutable shell … , in which he is obliged to live. It forces on the individual, to the extent that he is caught up in the relationships of the 'market', the norms of its economic activity. The manufacturer who consistently defies these norms will just as surely be forced out of business as the worker who cannot or will not conform will be thrown out of work. (p. 13, original emphasis)

In the aftermath of the GFC, as a consequence of largely successful neo-Liberal attempts to re-configure this aftermath as being principally about sovereign debt crises, the need for austerity, and an end to the 'age of entitlement', we may be condemning generations of young people to a life-long burden of precariousness and debt. In this sense, a self as enterprise that grows up after the GFC is being made responsible for resolving the contradictions, the paradoxes, the limits and possibilities of fashioning a life in twenty-first-century capitalism. That is a burden of responsibility beyond the capacities of many us, and a burden that is that much harder to bear when you have mortgaged your future on the promise that education and training will secure an always parlous salvation in the globalised and precarious labour markets of twenty-first-century capitalism.

Note

1. Tumblr is a social networking/micro-blogging site. The *We Are the 99%* page can be found at www.wearethe99percent.tumblr.com. A methodological examination of research in these spaces is beyond the limits and intentions of this paper. See Campbell and Kelly (2013) for a more detailed discussion.

Disclosure statement

No potential conflict of interest was reported by the author.

References

Barry, A., Osborne, T., & Rose, N. (Eds.) (1996). *Foucault and political reason: Liberalism, neo-liberalism and rationalities of government*. London: UCL Press.
Bauman, Z. (2001). *The individualized society*. Cambridge: Polity.
Bauman, Z. (2005). *Work, consumerism and the new poor*. Berkshire: Open University Press.
Beck, U. (1992). *The risk society*. Cambridge: Polity.
Beck, U. (2000). *The brave new world of work*. Cambridge: Polity.
Brotherhood of St Laurence. (2014). *Youth employment – My chance, our future*. Retrieved March 23, 2014, from http://www.bsl.org.au/Advocacy/Youth-employment.aspx
Bunting, M. (2004). *Willing slaves: How the overwork culture is ruling our lives*. London: Harper Collins.
Burchell, G. (1996). Liberal government and techniques of the self. In A. Barry, T. Osborne, & N. Rose (Eds.), *Foucault and political reason: Liberalism, neo-liberalism and rationalities of government* (pp. 19–36). London: UCL Press.
Burchell, G., Gordon, C., & Miller, P. (Eds.). (1991). *The Foucault effect: Studies in governmental rationality*. Hemel Hempstead: Harvester Wheatsheaf.
Campbell, P., & Kelly, P. (2013). In/between feminism and Foucault: Iraqi women's warblogs and intellectual practices of the self. *Critical Sociology, 39*(2), 183–199.
Elliott, A., & Lemert, C. (2006). *The new individualism: The emotional costs of globalization*. Abingdon: Routledge.
European Commission. (2013). *Europe 2020: Youth unemployment*. Retrieved April 25, 2014, from http://ec.europa.eu/europe2020/pdf/themes/21_youth_unemployment.pdf

Foucault, M. (1985). *The use of pleasure*. New York, NY: Pantheon.
Foucault, M. (1986). *The care of the self*. New York, NY: Pantheon.
Foucault, M. (1991). Governmentality. In G. Burchell, C. Gordon, & P. Miller (Eds.), *The Foucault effect: Studies in governmental rationality* (pp. 87–104). Hemel Hempstead: Harvester Wheatsheaf.
Foucault, M. (2000). The ethics of the concern of the self as a practice of freedom. In P. Rabinow (Ed.), *Michel Foucault ethics, subjectivity and truth* (pp. 281–302). London: Penguin.
Gordon, C. (1991). Governmental rationality: An introduction. In G. Burchell, C. Gordon, & P. Miller (Eds.), *The Foucault effect: Studies in governmental rationality* (pp. 1–52). Hemel Hempstead: Harvester Wheatsheaf.
Hall, S., Massey, D., & Rustin, M. (2013). After neoliberalism: Analysing the present. In S. Hall, D. Massey, & M. Rustin (Eds.), *After neo-liberalism? The Kilburn manifesto*. Retrieved April 4, 2013, from http://www.lwbooks.co.uk/journals/soundings/pdfs/manifestoframingstatement.pdf
Haraway, D. (2008). *When species meet*. Minneapolis: University of Minnesota Press.
Harris, J. (2013, February 4). There is cold fear and resentment, but little sense of hope. *The Guardian*. Retrieved March 23, 2013, from http://www.guardian.co.uk/commentisfree/2013/feb/04/newcastle-cold-fear-little-sense-of-hope
Hochschild, A. R. (2001). *The time bind: When work becomes home and home becomes work*. New York, NY: Henry Holt.
Hochschild, A. R. (2003). *The commercialization of intimate life: Notes from home and work*. Berkeley: University of California Press.
Inman, P. (2011, March 1). Bank of England governor blames spending cuts on bank bailouts. *The Guardian*. Retrieved March 1, 2011, from http://www.guardian.co.uk/business/2011/mar/01/mervyn-king-blames-banks-cuts
Kelly, P. (2007). Governing individualized risk biographies: New class intellectuals and the problem of youth at-risk. *British Journal of Sociology of Education, 28*(1), 39–53.
Kelly, P. (2012, August 1–4). *Growing up after the GFC: Identity, democracy and enterprise*. Buenos Aires: The Second ISA Forum of Sociology, Social justice and democratization.
Kelly, P. (2013). *The self as enterprise: Foucault and the 'spirit' of 21st century capitalism*. Gower: Ashgate.
Kelly, P., & Harrison, L. (2009). *Working in Jamie's Kitchen: Salvation, passion and young workers*. London: Palgrave.
McQuillan, M. (2014). *The five options for student tuition fees that politicians have to choose from*. Retrieved October 19, 2014, from http://theconversation.com/the-five-options-for-student-tuition-fees-that-politicians-have-to-choose-from-32847
Organisation for Economic Co-operation and Development. (2006). *Labour force statistics, 1985–2005*. Paris: Author.
Peters, T. (2005). *100 ways to help you succeed/make money*. Retrieved February 22, 2007, from http://changethis.com/14.100Ways
Rose, N. (1996). Governing 'advanced' liberal democracies. In A. Barry, T. Osborne, & N. Rose (Eds.), *Foucault and political reason: Liberalism, neo-liberalism and rationalities of government* (pp. 37–64). London: UCL Press.
Rose, N. (1999). *Powers of freedom*. Cambridge: Cambridge University Press.
Rose, N., & Miller, P. (1992). Political power beyond the state: Problematics of government. *British Journal of Sociology, 43*(2), 173–205.
Sennett, R. (2006). *The culture of the new capitalism*. New Haven, CT: Yale University Press.
Standing, G. (2011a). The precariat – The new dangerous class. *Policy-Network*. Retrieved March 23, 2013, from http://www.policy-network.net/pno_detail.aspx?ID=4004&title=+The+Precariat+%E2%80%93+The+new+dangerous+class
Standing, G. (2011b). *The precariat: The new dangerous class*. London: Bloomsbury.
Taylor, C. (2007). Cultures of democracy and citizen efficacy. *Public Culture, 19*(1), 117–150.
Thrift, N. (2005). *Knowing capitalism*. London: Sage.
Weber, M. (2002/1930). *The Protestant ethic and the 'spirit' of capitalism: And other writings*. London: Penguin.

Ghostings, materialisations and flows in Britain's special educational needs and disability assemblage

Julie Allan and Deborah Youdell

ABSTRACT
In this paper we argue that the UK government's new special educational needs and disability (SEND) Code of Practice marks a further movement in the expansion of what Tomlinson has identified as the SEN industry. Yet at the same time, we suggest that the Code inaugurates a series of less familiar movements of policy, of governance and responsibility, of understanding SEND, and of the constitution of subjects identified in these terms. We make use of Deleuze's notion of assemblages and societies of control to think about the 'ghostings', 'materialisations' and 'flows' found within the Code and the ways in which these instantiate an 'empty architecture' which education, health and care professionals as well as children, young people and parents/carers must simultaneously furnish and navigate. We examine this new terrain for conceptualising, administering and responding to SEND and suggest that a new orientation to analysis and critique is needed.

Introduction

The UK Government's *Code of Practice for Special Educational Needs and Disability: 0 to 25 years*, (Department for Education/Department of Health [DfE/DoH], 2014) which came into force in September 2014, was offered as a means of enhancing assessment and provision for children and young people with special educational needs. This was offered as a necessary response to the 'serious flaws in the SEN system' (House of Commons Education and Skills Committee, 2006, p. 40) and to a recognition that 'the SEN system is failing' (p. 9), views also endorsed by the Audit Commission (2002) and Office for Standards in Education (2004). The Education and Skills Committee highlighted what it saw as confusion on the part of the Government and a rapid move away from its previous commitment to inclusion (Allan, 2008). Tomlinson (2012), however, suggests that the increases in the numbers of children with special educational needs included in mainstream schools have been maintained but notes the simultaneous expansion in special educational services and personnel, and concludes that there is now an 'expanded and expensive *SEN industry*' (p. 267, original emphasis). Tomlinson suggests that such an expansion has been 'irresistible' (p. 267) to governments and identifies a number of factors as having contributed to this expansion. These include the continued need for resourcing on the basis of a diagnosis; an increasing number and range of parents seeking such a diagnosis for their child; teachers, under pressure to raise standards, seeking to remove troublesome pupils from their classrooms; and an expanding number of professionals and practitioners needing to increase their client base.

In this paper we argue that the Code of Practice marks a further movement in the expansion of this SEN industry. Yet at the same time we suggest that the Code inaugurates a series of less familiar movements of policy, of governance and responsibility, of understanding special educational needs and disability (SEND), and of the constitution of subjects identified in these terms. We examine this new terrain for conceptualising, administering and responding to SEND and suggest that a new orientation to analysis and critique is needed in order to make sense of and respond to what we suggest, after Deleuze (1990), are emergent modulations of the societies of control.

Conceptual tools

The paper takes up conceptual tools offered by Deleuze and Guattari, in particular, their notions of assemblage (1987), code (1984), and corporation (Deleuze, 1990). As we do this we attempt to work with, rather than merely apprehend, the problematisations (Foucault, 1970) that arise from this 'education assemblage' (Webb & Gulson, 2012; Youdell, 2011) and which imbricate us as readers, requiring that we supply our own coding and decoding.

Deleuze and Guattari (1987) use the idea of 'assemblage' to think about how diverse elements come together in productive relations to form apparently whole but mobile social entities – 'public service assemblage', 'education assemblage' or 'SEND assemblage' might be understood in this way. Economy, money, legislation, policy, institutions, organisations, social and cultural forms, discourse, representation, subjectivities and affectivities are all potential components of assemblages. The Code of Practice, and the many pieces of legislation to which it refers, can be understood as productive elements in mobile relations in these assemblages.

In what can be seen as an attempt to demonstrate the continuities between his own thinking about assemblages and Foucault's thinking about the *dispositif*, Deleuze's (1992) 'What is a dispositif?' posits *dispositif* as a social apparatus (assemblage) 'composed of lines' that, rather than demarcate separate systems, 'follow directions' of all sorts (p. 159). The task is to untangle and map these lines as they emerge, move and mutate. That is, our concern is with 'the new', defined as 'the variable creativity which arises out of [*dispositifs*]' (p. 163). As we engage with the Code of Practice, we raise questions about the coincidence of a SEND *dispositif* or assemblage and the regimes of visibility and enunciation that appear with and are productive of it. This focuses on the 'new' or the 'emergent' – 'the current is not what we are but rather what we are in the process of becoming' (Deleuze, 1992, p. 164). As we consider the lines of the Code of Practice, Deleuze's work offers a methodology to pursue:

> In each apparatus we have to untangle the lines of the recent past and those of the near future; that which belongs to the archive and that which belongs to the present, that which belongs to history and that which belongs to the process of becoming; *that which belongs to the analytic and that which belongs to the diagnostic.* (p. 164, original emphasis)

Thinking in this way as we engage with the Code of Practice invites us to look for lines of the recent past – diagnostic apparatus, diagnosed subjects, customer-parents, struggles over inclusive education – and lines of the near future – a distant central legislature that mandates only a regulatory framework for others to populate, a responsibilised local bureaucracy and citizen-subject, a spectral SEND child/young person. By proceeding in this way, we begin to interrogate the Code's lines of visibility, enunciation and subjectification and suggest what the SEND assemblage is becoming. As we do this we offer a masochistic and intensive reading (Deleuze, 1997; Musser, 2012) of the Code, using twin processes of humour and inversion. This approach helps us engage with our own puzzlement over a document which is full of 'shifting, slipping, dislocations and hidden emissions' (Deleuze, 1995, p. 6) and which calls upon the reader to re-inscribe features – notably 'SEN' and 'disabled' students and associated services; and curriculum and pedagogies – that were central in the previous Code (2001) but have been omitted from the one we must now work with.

Deleuze's thinking in *Postscript on the Societies of Control* (Deleuze, 1990) is also deployed to examine the ghostings, materialisations and flows that are evident in the Code. We map what is ghosted by the Code. We show the spectres of directives and specifications for pedagogic and curriculum practices; of the specificities of special educational needs and disabilities, and the Diagnostic and Statistical Manual of Mental Disorders (DSM); of the field and principle of 'inclusive education'; of the quazi-market of education provision; and of the welfare state. We map what is materialised. We show a regulatory framework that mandates a series of required systems, actions, practices and timelines but simultaneously ghosts its own content, materialising what we call an 'empty architecture'. We argue that this empty architecture is less the prison panopticon that Foucault offers as the figure of the disciplinary institution and society, and more the labyrinthine interior of a Deleuzo-Guttarian rhizome, demanding that we follow its lines. We show professionals and citizens responsibilised not as neo-liberal producers and consumers but as corporate and citizen investors. We show a re-configured (disassembled?) local state responsibilised by this empty architecture as it is made ultimately responsible for materialising the returns on the investments it oversees but does not control. And we show our desire, as readers, to populate the empty architecture of the Code. Finally, we map the Code's flows. We show the flows of the child and young person through processes of definition and into categories; of provision and professionals; and of money.

We can see elements of a society of control being created around individuals within the Code, both in terms of the tactics of policy and the mode of governance. A control society captures individuals, but instead of being fixed and contained as subjects, they are created as malleable and moveable subjects that are subject to continuous change – 'deformable and transformable' (Deleuze, 1990, p. 6). Within the societies of control, the family, the school and the factory have been replaced by the 'corporation' (p. 7), an entity that Deleuze (1990, p. 4) describes as 'a spirit, a gas', with subjects that are 'undulatory, in orbit, in a continuous network' (p. 6). The key feature of the corporation is its capacity for dividing individuals, presenting 'the brashest rivalry as a healthy form of emulation, an excellent motivational force that opposes individuals against one another and runs through each, dividing each within' (p. 4). The corporation produced by the Code consists of parents, children and young people, professionals and local authorities, statutory health services, voluntary sector agencies and educational institutions and provisions that cross cut public, voluntary and private sectors. As it does so, these are grouped and split, placing them in mobile oppositions to one another and the Code acknowledges this potential, indicating that 'parents, teachers and others may have different expectations'.

The SEND Code of Practice

The UK Government's Code of Practice for SEND and the underpinning Children and Families Bill and associated regulations were passed during 2014, with the Code coming into force on 1 September 2014 and revised in May 2015. A number of shifts from the previous Code of Practice (Department for Education and Science [DfES], 2001) can be discerned. These include a stronger emphasis on the views of children and young people and their role in decision-making; a requirement for joint local assessment and service provision across education, health and social care; the introduction of a single co-ordinated plan for children with complex needs; and an emphasis on arrangements for transition from school to adulthood. The 2014 Code is, we argue, one movement toward a transformed approach to SEND, its regulation and provisions, and to governance more widely. Deleuze and Guattari's notion of code offers a helpful and plausible reading of the Code of Practice – as code – and we explore this below.

Reading the Code as code

> Over a society, over its social body, something flows [*coule*] and we do not know what it is, something flows that is not coded, and something which, in relation to this society, even appears as the uncodable … We encounter something that crumbles and we do not know what it is, it responds to no code, it flees underneath the codes. (Deleuze, 2007)

The Code of Practice, representing 'statutory guidance' for all who come into contact with children and young people with special educational needs and disabilities, is both coded and uncodable. It appears to function literally as a code, in the form of a 'password' (Deleuze, 1990, p. 5), which denotes entitlement to, access to, and control of information and knowledge. Yet, it also eludes our grasp as readers who are implicated directly, as professionals, or by proxy as concerned citizens.

Deleuze and Guattari's notion of a code does not denote a set of signifiers that are known in advance and can be used to communicate, such as Morse code, or to check whether an infringement has occurred, such as a civil code (Smith, 2012). Such a code, derived from genetics, is constantly being produced and transmitted in a domain of 'real inorganization' (Deleuze & Guattari, 1984), where:

> everything is possible, without exclusiveness or negation, syntheses operating without a plan, where the connections are transverse, the disjunctions included, the conjunctions polyvocal, indifferent to their underlying support, since the matter that serves them precisely as a support receives no specificity from any structural or personal unity. (p. 309)

The key feature of a code, according to Deleuze and Guattari (1984), is its absence of any complete essence in itself and its capability of being only apprehended, and even then never completely, in the moment of decoding. Every code requires a decoding of what has come before it – 'The genetic code points to a genic decoding' (p. 328) – and as a consequence, forms part of a chain that has no function other than of 'deterritorializing the flows', thereby decoding and undoing the codes. The decoding takes place through a chain that becomes 'a chain of escape and no longer a code' (Deleuze & Guattari, 1984) and it controls expertly by catching individuals in a constant cycle of obligation, incomprehension and apprehension. Codes, then, are vital for the distribution of desire or other elements and are thus essential for the maintenance of society (Bogard, 2000). We can see the Code of Practice operating as a code through its evasion of intrinsic meanings and the interpellation (Althusser, 1971) of professionals, parents and young people into the decoding processes as well as in its ghostings, materialisations and flows.

Ghostings

The Code effects a series of ghostings that have significant productive potential in terms of SEND subjects; educational institutions, philosophies and practices; the local and the relationship between the citizen and the state; and forms of governance. The act of ghosting is one that we understand as actively erasing a person or thing, while creating an impression of its continued presence. This is achieved, however, as Derrida (1994) underlines through a simultaneous:

> Specular circle: one chases after in order to chase away, one pursues, sets off in pursuit of someone to make him flee, but one makes him flee, distances him, expulses him so as to go after him again and remain in pursuit. One chases someone away, kicks him out the door, excludes him, or drives him away. But it is in order to chase after him, seduce him, reach him, and thus keep him close at hand. One sends him far away so as to spend one's life, and for as long a time as possible, coming close to him again. (p. 140)

While Derrida is all too aware of the frightening nature of our own ghostings, he also reminds us of their educative potential and urges that we 'learn to live' (Derrida, 1994, p. 176) by learning how to talk with the ghosts we create. There is little suggestion, however, of such an openness within the Code, written as it is, 'under the cloak' (Cixous, 2012, p. 20).

Our diagnosis of ghostings does not suggest straightforward erasures, but rather movements that render spectral certain elements that were previously (temporally or/and conceptually/discursively or/and practically) explicit, significant and perhaps central components of a SEND assemblage (see for instance the previous Code of Practice, DfES, 2001). In this sense an analysis of ghostings suggests those lines of movement from a recent past that continues to haunt a near future that is still emergent. Our suggestion that certain elements are ghosted in the Code does not suggest that these are no longer components of this assemblage, or that they are of diminished significance. Rather, it is to point to the ways in which these move through the Code, or are moved by the Code, and to underline the potentialities of these movements.

The first and perhaps most notable ghosting in the Code is the SEND subject, the child or young person. This may seem a counter-factual claim, given that the Code is all about children and young people with SEN and disabilities. Yet the Code seems to self-consciously and extraordinarily carefully ghost these subjects through the persistent practice of *not* naming them. The ephemeral grouping 'children/young people with SEND' is a refrain repeated in various forms throughout the Code, sometimes with 'SEN' and 'D' run together, and sometimes with 'special educational need' and 'disabilities' spelled and separated out. The absence of any specificity about the nature of these special educational needs or disabilities, and any diagnoses that might underpin them, is notable. Not only are these rarely specified, their specification seems to be actively eschewed. The DSM V receives not a single mention in the entire text and its annexes. It seems unlikely that this reflects a recognition of the negative consequences of diagnostic labels demonstrated by recent critiques (Allan, 2010; Youdell, 2011). Yet it does appear as a marked departure from the proliferations of diagnoses and 'psychopathologization' (Harwood & Allan, 2014) found in recent and indeed current approaches to the diagnosis of SEN and disability. From time to time specifications become unavoidable, the smooth surface of the text collapsing in on the striations of persistent diagnoses as the text names and constitutes the 'learning disabled', the 'autistic' and the 'chronically ill'. It is not that the Code calls on the reader (professional or citizen) to jettison diagnoses. Rather, in its refusal to name, the Code demands that the reader calls up these diagnoses him/herself and thereby makes him/herself responsible for the constitutive force of these interpellations. The spectres of children and young people already diagnosed and who will continue to be diagnosed in the medicalising and psychopathologising terms of the DSM worry at the backs and edges of the text, insisting that we notice them and reminding us that they are still very much there and that we are responsible for them.

Also ghosted by the Code are any directives or specifications for pedagogic and curriculum practices. Repeatedly throughout the text we encounter moments when we might anticipate being told what approaches 'should' or even 'must' be taken in relation to both curriculum and pedagogy. Yet these moments persistently disappoint – the directive is refused; the centrally sanctioned course of educational action is deferred; we are informed only (but powerfully) to devise our own practice based on 'evidence' and instructed that there is a wealthy 'evidence base' available. Hyperlinks are listed on the closing pages. While on one reading this offers up professional and institutional freedoms in relation to curriculum and pedagogy, it simultaneously refuses a specified entitlement for the child/young person identified as having SEND. Furthermore, the spectre of very particular sorts of expert knowledge (McGimpsey, in press) and a reified 'evidence-based practice' press on and constrict the apparent possibilities offered by the Code's absence of specification. Relatedly, as the specificities of curriculum and pedagogy are ghosted by the Code, so is the field and principle of 'inclusive education'. The term 'inclusive education' does not appear in the 261 pages of the Code, and where the notion of 'inclusion' appears it a vague and mobile notion that seems to also contain the possibilities of separation.

The final ghostings that we want to suggest here concern the welfare state and the quazi-market of education provision which the state has instantiated and through which it has sought to operate over the past 30 years. Again, this is not to suggest that these are absent, but that they take on a spectral quality as a mutated local state and competitive field of provision take shape. We turn to this below.

Materialisations

Over 261 turgid pages that have been almost (but only almost) expunged of any value position other than the primacy of data and evidence, the Code materialises a new but 'empty architecture' for/of 'SEND'. This is a regulatory framework that mandates an ever-turning sequence of required activities but simultaneously ghosts their content.

What is specified and so materialised by this empty architecture is a recurrent list of things that must be done – we must provide information and advice, we must inform, assess, consult, document, publish, plan and review, and all to specified timeframes, in this many weeks, and that many weeks. These are the becomings of the societies of control, where 'controls are modulations, like a self-deforming cast that will continuously change from one moment to the other' (Deleuze, 1990, p. 4). The content of this empty architecture is absent – it is repeatedly gestured towards, it is over there, but the reader must go and get it; the Central state has no need to detail it in its Code, all it details are modulations, and in detailing only modulations it moves responsibility to those individuals charged with furnishing this moving architecture. And so if we get it wrong, it is our problem. This refrain is repeated over and over again in sub-section after sub-section as our heads cloud, our grasp slips and our will to continue dissipates.

In the mobility of its modulations, in its 'ultrarapid forms of free-floating control' (Deleuze, 1990, p. 4), this empty architecture does not appear as the prison panopticon in which the central tower promises to see all and so incites us to see ourselves. Rather, it appears as a rhizomic, ever moving, labyrinth; we encounter passageways, thresholds and chambers in which we become stultified and lost, desperate and desiring of something to touch, to hold on to, to orientate ourselves by. And so we populate the empty architecture, following its lines, and making of it an unfamiliar home, reassembling the SEND that it disassembled (Youdell & McGimpsey, 2015). Our own desire to populate the Code with meanings, practices and subjects, including ourselves, that we recognise and that might be able to hold together the modulations of the Code with the values that it ghosts, such as inclusive education, is also materialised by the very ghostings it effects.

A key element materialised by the Code is the 'Local Offer'. While, again, the Code refuses to detail the students with whom it is concerned, the curriculum and pedagogy these students should encounter, or the context of inclusion in which they should be situated, it does specify the re-located site of responsibility for this specification and assurance of subsequent delivery: the 'Local Offer', led and overseen by the local state. The local state is called upon to lead complex alliances within 'Health and Well-being Boards' where education and children's social services as well as adult services, public health, primary and specialist health services must collectively develop a 'Joint Strategic Needs Assessment' and subsequently undertake and evaluate the 'Education, Health and Care Plans' of those deemed to need these. The local state must also coordinate the development, delivery and review of the wider 'Local Offer' for children and young people with SEND, including the myriad procurement and contractual arrangements across public service domains, sectors and professionals; relationships with civil society actors, parent-citizens, and young people with SEND; and flows of money through these. The local state, then, is responsibilised by this empty architecture. The local state is made ultimately responsible for materialising the array of services and related activities that will make up the Local Offer, and, importantly, the educational and social returns on these activities, re-configured as investments (McGimpsey, in press), that it oversees but does not control.

That the local state, through its manifestation of the demands of the Code, becomes responsible for the amelioration of future social and educational risks and returns highlights the context of the Code's production. That is, it is part of a suite of 'austerity' policy and legislation affecting education, children's and young people's services, health, criminal justice and local governance that inaugurates a new moment of policy and governance. 'Austerity' is seeing central government effect massive financial disinvestment in public services, notably in the form of major reductions in centrally controlled resources devolved to local government. Local government remains responsible for the effective 'solution' of a whole raft of 'problems' – from safeguarding children to managing waste to the SEND Local Offer – but must fulfil these responsibilities with far fewer resources. Evident in this policy ensemble are familiar moves to position the state as securer of services in a decentralised, deregulated and expanding and competitive 'public' service marketplace that includes many non-state players – such as we see in the local authority's responsibility for the on-going modulation of the Local Offer. What appears 'new' in this raft of policy, and evident in the Local Offer, is the vigorous promotion of a particular sort of 'localism' in which the local state is at once responsibilised and stripped of both autonomy to design or deliver and of resources to fund at the same time as it is 'opened up' to challenge and provision by non-state entities. In combination with austerity economics, these moves are transforming 'public' services (Youdell & McGimpsey, 2015). SEND provision may well be the next domain to see 'spin off', mutualisation, privatisation and straightforward closure while the private sector steps in or the (imaginary) community takes (imaginary) steps to 'co-produce' SEND services. This is the 'continuous control' that is 'delivering the school over to the corporation' (Deleuze, 1990, p. 5).

Flows

The Code of Practice produces a number of flows – the child or young person with special educational needs or disabilities, flowing temporally in the present and in imagined future possibilities as special, and outwards as the child becomes re-marked as a legally competent young person; educational provisions and the professionals associated with them; and resources. Each of these flows contribute to the consolidation of a control society, with its complex and constant domains of power that contain individuals as part of 'a field of collective improvisation' (Bogard, 2000, p. 290) and fix them in 'webs of alliances' (p. 290). At the same time, Deleuze and Guattari (1984, p. 139) remind us, there is a constant 'closing up' and re-establishment of interior limits so that flows are slowed or stymied.

The flowing child

The child or young person, who, as we have suggested, has been ghosted through a refusal to place them within diagnostic categories in the first part of the Code of Practice, is subsequently made to flow through processes of definition and granting membership of the domain of special educational needs and through predictions of their future risk of belonging to this domain. They are also made to flow into particular categories of need, and in so doing to acquire characteristics, traits and dangers that may affect other children and young people and therefore need to be 'managed'.

The naming of particular children as special and therefore qualifying for additional intervention within the educational setting or, where need is thought to be greater, for an 'Education, Health and Care' (EHC) assessment and plan, circulates and never settles.

In what might merely be a tautology, arising from language neglect, a child or young person, according to the Code 'has SEN' if they have a learning difficulty or disability that 'calls for 'special educational provision, namely provision different from or additional to that normally available to pupils of the same age' (p. 83). But the Code also refers to children 'with SEN *or* disabilities' (our emphasis) and cautiously claims 'a significant overlap between children and young people with SEN and those with disabilities'. It is never made clear what the difference between these 'types' of children and young people is, but there is a suggestion that they are covered by different legislation and that post-16 institutions use the term 'learning difficulties and disabilities'. The children and young people are sometimes caught in a flow of causation and sometimes in an over-spill. The Code announces its interaction with the Equality Act 2010 and its common concern for 'removing barriers to learning'.

A futuristic flow is made of children and young people in respect of their *potential* for having a learning difficulty or disability and this is both tautological and uncertain:

> They are considered to have a learning difficulty or disability if they would be likely to have a learning difficulty or disability when they are of compulsory school age if no special educational provision were made for them. (DfE/DoH, 2014, p. 117)

This 'additional precautionary consideration' (p. 117) implies an element of clairvoyance, or at least predictive skill, on the part of the professionals.

Children deemed worthy of entry into the domain of special educational needs are made, within the Code, to flow into specific categories, in spite of claims that 'the purpose of identification is to work out what action the school needs to take, not to fit a pupil into a category' (p. 86). The 'broad areas of need' (p. 86), 'communication and interaction', 'cognition and learning', 'social emotional and mental health difficulties' and 'sensory and/or physical needs' (pp. 86–87) are delineated and are accompanied by accounts of what these children typically struggle with. A different collation of children and their special education 'types' is given later in the document, distinguishing between the 'child with challenging behaviour' in a mainstream primary school, 'a child with autistic spectrum disorder who is distracting and constantly moves around' in a mainstream secondary school and a 'young person with a learning disability who does not use verbal communication' in an further education college. Here the concern is about reducing the 'incompatibility' of the individual's presence with the education of others within that provision, but in so doing the individual child with SEN is made into a 'dividual' (Deleuze, 1990, p. 5) and required to flow with his or her specific essences and characteristics.

This new form of subjectification creates, according to Deleuze, a physically embodied human subject who is endlessly divisible, reducible to data representation, massed, and open to the abstraction of capital. This is achieved by creating an obligation to mark (Bogard, 2000, p. 279) the child as special in such a way as to 'insure that differences do not exceed the limit beyond which elements … would no longer constitute a heterogeneous yet consistent mix of social surfaces'. These markings, or 'policy apparitions' (Webb & Gulson, 2012, p. 89), deploy fear to manipulate interpretations including specification of risks, dangers and potential distractions (of other – non special – children) and legitimate the Code's delineation of isolating special practices, training and support that are aimed at minimising these troubles.

A final flow of responsibility is exercised upon the child, who, on reaching the age of 16, becomes designated as a young person, deemed capable of exercising choice over his or her educational provision (unless he or she lacks mental capacity, in yet another qualifier). The Code asserts that the young person's choice must be upheld, but, of course, not if the choice is 'unsuitable' or 'incompatible' with the efficient education of others. Legally, according to the Code, the young person's choice prevails over that of the parents.

Passing provision and professionals

Flows of provisions associated with education, health and social care are created within the Code and while there have been many calls for 'joined up working' (Watson, 2010, p. 101) among professionals in children's services, what is distinctive here is the way in which the professionals are collected in a network of responsibilising desires. The professionals cited within the Code of Practice are subsequently written into a 'classic romance narrative' (Thomson, 2013, p. 173), in which their connectedness and obligation – to each other – is crucial to the delivery by the nation state of a 'better life for those deserving of rescue from the dreadful fate of not progressing' (p. 173). The children mentioned here are not just deserving but are 'entitled' (p. 68) to high aspirations and expectations for achievement of educational and other outcomes, for becoming confident and for making a successful transition into adulthood. The desires of professionals from education, health and social care to enact these high expectations are interpellated (Althusser, 1971) within the Code of Practice in the sense of hailing them into its discourses (Watson, 2010) and directing their desires.

The purpose of actions, such as assessments or the identification of strategies, being 'joint' (DfE/DoH, 2014, p. 27) is not specified beyond being said to 'promote wellbeing and improve the quality of provision for disabled young people and those with SEN' (p. 27) and local authorities are required to integrate education, health and social care provision only where they think it will lead to a promotion of well-being and improved quality of provision. The non-specific nature of the obligation, generated through the Code's empty architecture, is somewhat overtaken by the high level of prescription associated with the preparation, development, publishing and review of the Local Offer.

Moving money

Resources, in the form of the 'goods and services' paid for through direct payments, are made to circulate, pushing the 'product', the child or young person's special educational needs, through circuits of power. As a consequence, the child with SEND, whom as we have seen has been ghosted as the 'apparition of the inapparent' (Derrida, 1994, p. 195), simultaneously convoked and conjured away (Cixous, 2012), becomes valorised and exalted (Harwood & Allan, 2014). The child's special educational needs and disabilities are called up and made manifest through the debts and duties attributed to the various actors responsible for informing about and making provision. The requirement for continuous review and the potential recourse to litigation, complaint or mediation, makes these circuits unsteady and unpredictable. This consolidates the society as one of control rather than discipline by pushing the various actors, the purchasing parents and the compliant providers into a series of obligations to one another, or, in Deleuze's

(1990, p. 6) words, places them 'in debt'. The monetary cost associated with making particular kinds of special educational provision, calculated on the basis of 'floating rates of exchange' (p. 5), is never articulated and is never introduced as a consideration in decisions about placements. In the absence of any fiscal commitment within the Code, the reader is forced to introduce this particular flow – we, and the agencies called up in the Code, must be the ones to ask the uncomfortable question of what we can afford from a shrinking purse that is largely out of our control. At the same time, the new 'freedoms' to choose schools that are outside local authority control and financing open the door to possibilities of the 'conquests of the market' (p. 6). The operation of the market is, according to Deleuze, the most pertinent and effective instrument of social control.

The Code allows a parent or young person to request a 'Personal Budget' (p. 167), but there is a cautious encouragement to local authorities to introduce parents and young people to 'the idea of Personal Budgets'. This, together with the specification of a series of uncertain mechanisms – direct payments, notional budgets where the local authority holds the money and commissions the support, 'third party arrangements' (p. 168) where money is paid to an individual or organisation on behalf of the child's parent or the young person' – ensure a flow of resources, potentially away from the child or young person. Money is required to flow, not as payment but as a structure of finance, 'a pure movement of creation and destruction' (Smith, 2012, p. 12).

The Code generates a flow of responsibilisation towards the child's parent or young person in respect of the Personal Budget, where they are expected to exercise judgment, responsibility, including economic responsibility, and to accept the consequences. They are invited, having been given an indication of what funding might be required for particular provision, to make a decision about whether they want to take up a Personal Budget. Local authorities are also caught in this flow of responsibilisation through the requirement to 'be clear that any figure discussed at this stage is indicative and is a tool to support the planning process' (p. 168). Each of these actors is required to act as if their choice is of their own free will, while also assessing the costs and benefits of this action as opposed to any other and bearing the consequences of their decision. For families and local authorities alike, this is an investment in a future educational return (or cost saving) as much as a purchasing of a fixed educational product (Rose, 1996).

Thinking the near future

In this paper we have argued that the UK's Code of Practice for SEND marks at once a further expansion of the SEN industry (Tomlinson, 2012) and the inauguration of a series of new policy movements which we have characterised as ghostings, materialisations, and flows – all modulations of the empty architecture of the societies of control. We have found this way of engaging with the Code generative in that it has enabled us to approach and apprehend the workings of a policy text which will have far reaching effects for SEND provision in the UK but which feels simultaneously familiar and unfamiliar, and whose intentions and directives at times seem indecipherable. In this sense the Code's spectral elements might be thought of through Freud's uncanny, the return of the familiar that bothers the edges of consciousness (Freud, 1990; Youdell, 2010).

As EHC professionals as well as children, young people and parents/carers work to apprehend, make meaning from, furnish and navigate the empty architecture built by the Code, they are not simply constituted again as responsibilised neo-liberal professional and consumer subjects. These subjects continue to haunt the Code, but materialised in sharper focus and flowing through the Code's modulations are 'dividuals' (Deleuze, 1990, p. 7), whose fragile subjectivity rests on their effective self-production as citizen investors who can fill the empty space with which they are presented with unspecified investments in a future of risks and costs averted and educational and social outcomes returned.

As we read the Code we show how, in the societies of control, the corporation's modulations overlay and displace, rather than replace, disciplinary technologies and institutions that are not so much abandoned as diminished, repurposed or re-announced. This becoming thing, then, is layered with the spectres of inclusive education struggles and allied social movements, medicalised and psychopathologised subjects, and education quazi-markets. These modulations suggest not so much disintegration, as a conversion of the SEND assemblage. We hope that our reading of the Code begins to demonstrate the usefulness for analysis and critique of reading the 'new' and the emergent with assemblages and with the modulations of the societies of control.

Disclosure statement

No potential conflict of interest was reported by the authors.

References

Allan, J. (2008). *Rethinking inclusive education: The philosophers of difference in practice*. Dordrecht: Springer.
Allan, J. (2010). The sociology of disability and the struggle for inclusive education. *British Journal of Sociology of Education, 31*(5), 603–619.
Althusser, L. (1971). *Lenin and philosophy and other essays*. London: NLB.
Audit Commission (2002). *Special educational needs: A mainstream issue*. London: Audit Commission.
Bogard, W. (2000). Smoothing machines and the constitution of society. *Cultural Studies, 14*(2), 269–294.
Cixous, H. (2012). Shakespeare ghosting Derrida. *Oxford Literary Review, 34*(1), 1–24.
Deleuze, G. (1990). *Postscript on the societies of control. Pourparlers*. Paris: Editions Minuit.
Deleuze, G. (1992). What is a dispositif? Michel Foucault philosopher. In T. J. Armstrong (Ed.), *Michel Foucault philosopher* (pp. 159–168). London: Havester Wheatsheaf.
Deleuze, G. (1995) *Letter to a harsh critic. Negotiations*. (M. Joughin, Trans.). New York: Columbia University Press.
Deleuze, G. (1997). *Representation of Masoch. Essays critical and clinical*. (D Smith & B. Greco, Trans.). London: Verso.
Deleuze, G. (2007). *Capitalism, flows, the decoding of flows, capitalism and schizophrenia, psychoanalysis, Spinoza*. Lectures by Gilles Deleuze. Retrieved July 14, 2014, from http://deleuzelectures.blogspot.co.uk/2007/02/capitalism-flows-decoding-of-flows.html
Deleuze, G., & Guattari, F. (1984). *Anti-Oedipus: Capitalism and schizophrenia*. London: The Athlone Press.
Deleuze, G., & Guattari, F. (1987). *A thousand plateaus: Capitalism and schizophrenia*. London: The Athlone Press.
Department for Education/Department of Health. (2014). *Special educational needs and disability code of practice: 0–25 years. Statutory guidance for organisations who work with and support children and young people with special educational needs and disabilities*. London: DfE/DoH.

Department for Education and Science. (2001). *Special educational needs: Code of Practice*. London: DfEE.
Derrida, J. (1994). *Spectres of Marx*. (Peggy Kamuf, Trans.). London: Routledge.
Foucault, M. (1970). *The order of things: An archaeology of human sciences*. New York, NY: Random House.
Freud, S. (1990). *The uncanny. Art and literature*. London: Penguin.
Harwood, V., & Allan, J. (2014). *Psychopathology at school: Theorising mental disorders in education*. London: Routledge.
House of Commons Education and Skills Select Committee. (2006). *Special educational needs: Third report of session 2005, 2006 (Volume 1). Report, together with formal minutes*. London: Stationery Office.
McGimpsey, I. (in press). *Social investment and post-neoliberal policy: Diagnosing a new phasing of education policy making*. Unpublished paper, University of Birmingham.
Musser, A. (2012). Reading, writing and masochism: The arts of becoming. *Differences: A Journal of Feminist Cultural Studies, 23*(1). Retrieved July 14, from https://www.dukeupress.edu/differences/index.html
Office for Standards in Education. (2004). *Special educational needs and disability: Towards inclusive schools*. London: Author. Retrieved December 16, 2004, from http:image.guardian.co.uk/sys-files/Education/documents/2004/10/12/Ofsted.pdf
Rose, N. (1996). Governing 'advanced' liberal democracies. In A. Barry, T. Osborne, & N. Rose (Eds.), *Foucault and political reason. Liberalism, neo-liberalism and rationalities of government* (pp. 37–64). London: UCL Press.
Smith, D. (2012). *Essays on Deleuze*. Edinburgh: Edinburgh University Press.
Thomson, P. (2013). Romancing the market: Narrativising equity in globalizing times. *Discourse: Studies in the Cultural Politics in Education, 34*(2), 170–184.
Tomlinson, S. (2012). The irresistible rise of the SEN industry. *Oxford Review of Education, 38*(3), 267–286.
Watson, C. (2010). Education policy in Scotland: Inclusion and the control society. *Discourse: Studies in the Cultural Politics in Education, 31*(1), 93–104.
Webb, R. T., & Gulson, K. N. (2012). Policy prolepsis in education: Encounters, becomings, and phantasms. *Discourse: Studies in the Cultural Politics in Education, 33*(1), 87–99.
Youdell, D. (2010). Queer outings: Uncomfortable stories about the subjects of post-structural school ethnography. *International Journal of Qualitative Studies in Education, 23*(1), 87–100.
Youdell, D. (2011). *School trouble: Identity, power and politics in education*. New York, NY: Routledge.
Youdell, D., & McGimpsey, I. (2015). Assembling, disassembling and reassembling youth services in austerity Britain. *Critical Studies in Education, 56*(1), 116–130.

◌ OPEN ACCESS

Blaming the victim: assessment, examinations, and the responsibilisation of students and teachers in neo-liberal governance

Harry Torrance

ABSTRACT
Historically, for a period of a hundred years or more from the 1860s to the 1960s, assessment developed as an educational technology for selecting and certificating small numbers of individual students. This process was largely focused on excluding the majority. Over the last 30–40 years, the focus and purpose of assessment has changed. The emphasis is now on education for all and the development of a fit-for-purpose assessment system *as a system*, that is, as part of an integrated approach to national human resource development. These changes have been both driven by, and contributed to, the development of the knowledge economy and neo-liberalism. Students and teachers have been 'responsibilised' for the quality and outcomes of education, with assessment and examinations providing the quintessential vehicle for individualising and responsibilising success and failure in relation to achievement and social mobility.

Introduction

This paper explores the role of assessment in relation to issues of social and political governance. The paper draws largely on evidence from the UK (especially, and more recently, England) but with obvious resonances with experience elsewhere. Examinations are intended, in principle, to measure and report the outcomes of education, but have always exerted a controlling influence over the school curriculum and, through processes of selection and certification, operated as a key intermediary mechanism between school, tertiary education, and employment, that is, between education and the economy (Bowles & Gintis, 1976; Broadfoot, 1979, 1984). Assessment and examinations have always been with us, or at least since the origins of what we might term modern schooling in the late nineteenth and early twentieth centuries. But the argument in this paper is that their role, reach and discursive influence have expanded as education systems have expanded, and vastly increased numbers of students are exposed to the processes and consequences of assessment. The paper brings together the normally fairly hermetically sealed literature of educational assessment, including empirical studies of assessment processes

This is an Open Access article distributed under the terms of the Creative Commons Attribution License (http://creativecommons.org/licenses/by/4.0/), which permits unrestricted use, distribution, and reproduction in any medium, provided the original work is properly cited.

and practices, with discussions of the knowledge economy and Foucauldian governance. In some respects key elements of the argument can be traced back to *Discipline and Punish* itself (Foucault, 1977, pp. 186–192). But they are extended here in the context of a much more widespread and voluntaristic use of assessment and examinations in modern education systems. Students submit willingly, if reluctantly, to taking examinations, and they are not simply imposed upon them in direct disciplinary fashion. Thus the argument is that empirical experience of both the cognitive and affective impacts of assessment is as important, if not more so, as the ideological impact.

Historically, perhaps for a period of 100 years or more from the 1860s to the 1960s, assessment developed as an educational technology for selecting and certificating individual students. This process was largely focused on small minorities of students. Assessment, particularly in the form of selection tests and school examinations, was used to identify and select small numbers of students for elite education and subsequently to record their academic achievements. Different forms of assessment, sometimes known as mental measurement or intelligence tests, were used to identify and direct small numbers of the supposedly 'feeble minded' to special institutional provision. Such tests were also developed and used more widely in the selection and allocation processes noted above, but still their use was limited. Education was a scarce good, access to educational opportunities was restricted, and educational assessment was largely concerned with selecting individuals for those restricted opportunities: for access to an elite secondary education and access to university (Broadfoot, 1984, 1996; Sutherland, 1984). So the focus of assessment was on identifying individual achievement, and selecting and certificating individuals. In so doing, this process functioned to identify, and legitimate on grounds of educational merit, the identification of the next cohort of suitably qualified and socialised personnel for economic and social leadership roles in society.

Thus assessment systems in general, school leaving examinations in particular, have always constituted a key mediation point in the articulation of schooling with the economy. At one and the same time, key individual identities of being an educational 'success' or 'failure' were constructed and used to legitimate the distribution of economic and social advantage. Success was individually merited and failure was individually inscribed – most students were designated as simply not clever enough to succeed. Responsibility for educational outcomes was produced by particular institutional arrangements underpinned by a particular psychological theory of innate intelligence distributed across a population. Assessment developed as a *technology of exclusion*.

Over the last 30–40 years, the focus and purpose of assessment has changed, particularly to involve far larger numbers of the school population. We now live in a world of intense global economic competition and mass movements of capital and labour. Unskilled mass production and employment opportunities have virtually vanished from the UK and other similar economies, and the emphasis now is on education for the so-called knowledge economy and as a form of investment in human capital (Brown & Lauder, 1992; Lauder, Brown, Dillabough, & Halsey, 2006; Lauder, Brown, & Tholen, 2012). Both the technological development of assessment and the policy context of educational standards and qualifications now assume that all, or at least the overwhelming majority of the population, can and should be educated to the highest level possible. The focus is now on education for all and the development of a fit-for-purpose assessment system *as a system*, that is, as part of an integrated approach to national human resource development. Instead of needing a legitimate reason to dispense with the intellectual capabilities of most of the population, governments now need to cultivate these capabilities. The imperative is to treat education as an economic investment, both on the part of the individual student, and on the part of government, and in turn to develop assessment as a *technology of inclusion*.

There is not a single determining driver of this change. Rather, such change reflects developments in the social and economic aspirations which we hold for education systems, and what it is that assessment is designed to accomplish. Changes in assessment reflect a combination of socio-economic and educational factors. These factors are clearly influenced by, and are responsive to, the neo-liberal analysis of the role of schooling in a knowledge economy (Lauder et al., 2012; Torrance, 2011). But change has also derived from debates about:

- criterion referencing, clarity of outcomes and the development of 'curriculum content standards' – the 'standards' agenda;
- social justice and educational inclusion – making objectives and assessment criteria explicit for all students in order to render the system fairer; and
- the role of summative and formative assessment – providing feedback to students on criteria, objectives and the ways in which they might improve their achievement.

There is not space here to review all these factors in more detail and to rehearse their interaction (see Torrance, 2011, for a longer exploration) though I will return to some aspects later in the paper. One element that is of particular interest at this point, however, is the social justice agenda and how it dovetails with neo-liberal arguments about human resource development. Advocates argue that the majority of the school population should not be abandoned to comparative, selective, norm-referenced, failure. Rather, we need our assessment systems to identify and report what students can do, rather than what they cannot. Thus curriculum objectives and assessment criteria should be made as explicit as possible so that they are accessible for all students (Broadfoot, Nuttall, James, & Stierer, 1988; Butterfield, 1995; Inner London Education Authority (ILEA) Hargreaves Report, 1984). The inclusion agenda also argues that these objectives should embrace the many social and attitudinal outcomes of education which are just as important as academic outcomes: we should value achievements in other domains, including social and political understanding, and ensure that students can contribution to civil society (Pole, 1993). In tandem with such general arguments about widening the scope and inclusiveness of assessment, have come specific technical developments incorporating the modularisation of the curriculum, the development of graded modular tests, and the possibility of accumulating better final results though the assessment of coursework and even re-sits of examination modules to improve grades (Hayward & McNicholl, 2007; Murphy & Torrance, 1988; Torrance, 1995). Thus neo-liberal economic arguments about changing and extending educational provision overlap with social justice arguments about expanding educational inclusion, and call forth specific technical and procedural innovations in assessment theory and practice.

In turn, these developments carry profound implications for the way in which assessment articulates not just with the economy, and the allocation of opportunity, but with neo-liberal governance and the ways in which students (and indeed teachers and parents) come to think about themselves. Previously, educational 'failure' was the assumed norm, and the limited progression of the majority of the school population was the default position of the system. Now however the opportunity to progress through the school system and onto university is claimed to be available to all and for all. All that is required to access these opportunities is hard work – from both students and teachers.

The knowledge economy, neo-liberalism and responsibilisation

As noted above, the terms of trade have changed very significantly for Western industrial societies over recent decades. The argument of economists and policy-makers is now that innovation, creativity and flexibility will drive economic growth through the provision of intellectual and personal goods and services, rather than large-scale manufacturing. Knowledge is the new capital that nation-states and individuals need to pursue and accumulate – being both the raw material and the product of a knowledge-based economy – rather than the mass unskilled production processes of primary extraction and manufacture (Drucker, 1993; Friedman, 2006). In turn, the school system must produce higher and broader educational standards for far larger cohorts of students than hitherto. Higher standards in basic academic subjects are demanded – maths, science, languages and so forth – but also the capacity to put them to good use. Thus problem-solving, data analysis, report writing, teamwork, etc. are similarly demanded. Whether or not such skills and capacities are fostered by narrow testing regimes is a matter to which we will return. The key point to note for the moment is that higher standards of education are being demanded for all.

In parallel with such demands, however, which are located in the relatively narrow arena of education policy, the way policy can and should have an impact on practice has also been reconfigured over recent years. Increased investment in education and the expansion of educational provision could have continued to be undertaken through well-established social democratic state processes. In the UK, for example, the expansion of educational provision and opportunity was achieved by moving to a comprehensive, rather than a selective, system of secondary education (beginning in 1964) and raising the school leaving age from 15 to 16 years in 1974. This process of providing a single system of comprehensive education for the whole school cohort, rather than a selective academic education for a few, could be said to have been finally completed with the implementation of a single system of secondary school examinations and the introduction of a national curriculum in 1988. Almost as soon as this process was complete, however, arguments about how public provision needed to become more efficient and effective, through mechanisms of differentiation and competition, were gaining traction – and not just in the education sector. The argument became one which was much more fundamentally about the nature of state provision and the role of competition in promoting innovation, quality and efficiency.

Classical political liberalism arose out of a critique of absolutist states, so that the 'liberal' social democratic state comes to justify and legitimate itself through guaranteeing fundamental freedoms, including the freedom of the individual, the rule of law, regulation of markets and so forth. Neo-liberalism reverses this process of legitimation. Rather than subjecting the market to regulation by what it argues is an overbearing and inefficient state, neo-liberalism subjects the state to the regulation of the market:

> The state no longer defines and supervises the freedom of the market; rather the market itself represents the organising and regulatory principle of the state. (Lemke, 2012, p. 16)

As Lemke further notes, Foucault was particularly insightful in pointing out that under neo-liberalism the market 'is a sort of permanent economic tribunal confronting government' (quoted in Lemke, 2012, p. 16).

Some recent manifestations of neo-liberalism have involved a greater role for government than others. In the UK, for example, under successive governments since the 1980s, policy assumed that government still had a role to play in creating and supporting markets, to make them 'work' properly. Nevertheless markets are still thought to be the most efficient way of producing and supplying high-quality goods and services, including public services, such as education. Creating and supporting markets has included producing appropriately skilled and socialised personnel to operate them (i.e. school leavers and graduates). Thus 'raising standards in education' not only responds to the direct call for a skilled workforce to compete globally, but also creates the idea of a skilled workforce, and what constitutes such an entity, in the first place – including the 'soft skills' of flexibility, creativity and so forth, in addition to straightforward academic achievement. As Lemke (1999) reminds us, following Marx and Foucault, 'labour power must first be constituted as labour power before it can be exploited' (p. 59).

In tandem with such developments, and indeed deeply implicated in them, are arguments about the management of social and economic risk in advanced and post-industrial societies. Historically, during much of the twentieth century and particularly during the 50 years after the Second World War, risk was largely socialised in many industrial and manufacturing economies. Various forms of social security – public health provision, pensions, unemployment pay and so forth – were introduced to manage job transitioning in the labour market and the threats to a healthy and productive workforce. Education was developed as one of these socialised investments to benefit not only the individual but also, more particularly, the needs of the nation-state for an educated workforce. Neo-liberalism sees such investment both as too expensive for nation-states to sustain, let alone develop further, and as corrosive of personal responsibility. Again, the argument is that it will be far more efficient and effective for individuals to choose what investment to make in themselves, and for markets to provide such personal and public services. Equally, however, individuals are not simply left to their own devices, governments still seek to shape the objects of and desire for their choices. As Peeters (2013) notes, such new forms of governance involve 'the view that citizens have their own responsibility in preventing social harms' (p. 584). Thus a key characteristic of what he terms 'new welfare' is the state's role in enabling, persuading, enticing or nudging citizens to 'take responsibility' for their lives and communities (p. 584).

Similarly Lemke (2001) observes:

> The strategy of rendering individual subjects 'responsible' ... entails shifting the responsibility for social risks such as illness, unemployment, poverty etc. ... into the domain ... of 'self care' ... [achieving] congruence ... between a responsible and moral individual and an economic-rational actor ... wage labourers [become] ... autonomous entrepreneurs with full responsibility for their own [human capital] investment decisions ... they are the entrepreneurs of themselves. (Lemke, 2001, pp. 199, 201)

As with wage labourers, so it is with so-called 'at risk' youth (Kelly, 2001), parents of young children (Dahlstedt & Fejes, 2013), recipients of health care (Liebenberg, Ungar, & Ikeda, 2013), and indeed school and university students, particularly as manifested through the pursuit of test results and examination passes. We are all now responsible for the management of our own economic welfare and career trajectories. Nor is this simply as it was always so. The idea of personal responsibility has become both more significant and more pre-emptively conceived. As Peeters (2013) further observes:

> This conceptual leap transforms 'individual responsibility' from its traditional liberal understanding as *ex post* accountability for one's actions [i.e. after the fact]... into an *ex ante* virtue, which emphasises acting in the present and preventing undesirable situations and events. (p. 588)

Assessment and examinations in an age of responsibilisation

Governments around the world are now looking to produce integrated curriculum and assessment systems to drive up educational standards for all. Content, including knowledge and skills, is defined, subject by subject, and assessment methods are then aligned with such content. Teaching the content is policed by the assessment system and, in turn, the effectiveness of the teaching is measured. Individual students pursue their individual interests with respect to examination passes and career opportunities, while schools and teachers are held to account by the same mechanism at the aggregate level – percentages of students passing certain national targets or benchmarks of expected achievement and progression through the system. Similarly such systems produce quasi-markets for schools via league tables reporting to what extent schools meet, do not meet, or indeed exceed, the targets.

Perhaps the two most visible examples of such changes are the National Curriculum and Assessment system in England (Dearing, 1993; Department of Education and Science (DES), 1987; Department for Education (DfE), 2015), and the No Child Left Behind legislation in the United States (NCLB, 2001). This has more recently been developed into the standards-oriented 'Race to the Top' programme and the State-level Common Core Standards Initiative (Common Core Standards (CCS), 2015; Obama, 2009). Other countries are adopting similar programmes, including New Zealand, which has been developing national standards linked to a testing system since 2002 (New Zealand Qualification Authority (NZQA), 2011), and Australia (cf. Wyatt-Smith, Klenowski, & Gunn, 2010). The choice of 'Race to the Top' as the brand name of the US government's most recent manifestation of these policy pressures seems particularly illuminating as to how the pressures are perceived and understood by policy-makers:

> America will not succeed in the twenty-first century unless we do a far better job of educating our sons and daughters... And the race starts today. I am issuing a challenge to our nation's governors and school boards, principals and teachers... if you set and enforce rigorous and challenging standards and assessments... if you turn around failing schools – your state can win a Race to the Top grant. (Obama, 2009)

In England, results at the national level have certainly improved significantly over the last 30–40 years. Around 70% of the school cohort now pass at least five GCSEs at grades A* – C (considered passing grades) compared to 20% in the mid-1970s[1] (Torrance,

2011). Thus the apparent productivity and effectiveness of the system has been transformed, in exactly the way that advocates of the move to a knowledge economy would argue is necessary. But whether or not this has resulted from a 'genuine' rise in educational standards, or grade inflation, or some combination of the two, is highly contested. There is considerable debate about whether rising test scores might actually mean that educational standards are falling rather than rising, as teachers and students simply focus on passing tests (Sykes Review, 2010; Torrance, 2011). Such arguments can also be observed internationally (Hamilton et al., 2007).

Of equal concern in England, if not more so, is that a significant minority of students (approximately 30%) do not achieve even this minimally acceptable level of secondary school achievement, and only around 40% of the cohort eventually progress to university-level higher education. Furthermore, and not surprisingly, given all we know about the relationship of educational achievement with economic status, it is still working-class children that do least well at school, and white working-class boys that do least well of all (Cassen & Kingdon, 2007; Perry & Francis, 2010). Yet the policy rhetoric of the system is that everyone *can* succeed, so responsibility for failure now lies with the students themselves, in combination with poor parenting and poor teaching. Working-class children may no longer be categorised as incapable, but they (and their parents and teachers) are categorised as disorganised and lacking in endeavour and ambition. (Lack of) responsibility has replaced (lack of) intelligence as the key explanatory variable in educational success and failure.

Moreover, even supposedly successful students who do indeed progress to higher education and graduation do not necessarily progress to the 'graduate level' professional jobs that the move to a knowledge economy might assume and indeed promise. By 2011, 31% of the UK adult workforce had a degree (Lindley & Machin, 2012, p. 269). Yet, while employers might support the general rhetoric of needing a large highly educated workforce for the knowledge economy, including many of the soft skills and new courses in design, media, computing and so forth, what they actually seek in practice are applicants with straightforward academic qualifications from the most prestigious global universities (Lauder et al., 2012). Similarly, given the growth in qualified applicants, universities now seek higher and higher entrance grades. Thus employers seek the 'best' graduates from the supposedly 'better' universities (i.e. students with good degrees from those universities which are the hardest to get into in the first place). In turn, students seek places in precisely these universities – making them even harder to get into. The gradient of the 'Race to the Top' is getting steeper and disappointment is often as real for those who succeed as those who do not. Lauder et al. (2012) further note that this is producing an increasingly differentiated version of the globalised knowledge economy. High-speed, high-volume information and communications technology (ICT) not only renders manufacturing jobs obsolete, but also previously high-quality professional jobs. Many forms of professional analysis and judgement are now ensconced in computer programmes and require little in the way of human interpretation and intervention. The creation and management of knowledge systems is increasingly separated from their operational execution, through a process which Lauder et al. (2012) term 'digital taylorism':

> Digital Taylorism ... [translates] knowledge work into working knowledge ... codified and routinised ... making it generally available to the company rather than the 'property' of the

individual worker ... creative work ... has been separated from ... routine 'analytics' .... (pp. 46–47)

Thus while elite graduates might be recruited from elite universities to work in elite, globalised management roles, the vast majority of graduates are recruited to routine processing and administration, or 'grunt work' as the employers themselves put it (p. 47), if indeed they even get recruited to this level of organisational activity. Lindley and Machin (2012) further report that differentiation at the graduate level is now increasingly at the level of a Master's degree rather than an undergraduate degree.

Subjectification and responsibilisation

Passing and failing examinations not only defines individuals as educational successes and failures, but also establishes the legitimacy of the idea of being an educational success or an educational failure and all that flows from this in terms of life chances. Examinations render legitimate the idea that there are extant bodies of knowledge that must be mastered and that such knowledge is external to the knower. Examinations define both the 'subject' (history, geography, etc.) and the 'knowing subject' (the certified individual). Examinations organise and legitimate knowledge *qua* knowledge, in testable form, and at one and the same time produce/endorse the fact that knowledge can be and should be tested. Furthermore, examinations also legitimate the idea of subjecting oneself to scrutiny – to examination by others who are more powerful than oneself. As Foucault (1977) notes, 'The success of disciplinary power derives ... from the use of hierarchical observation, normalising judgement and their combination in a procedure that is specific to it, the examination' (p. 170). In this Foucault was not just restricting himself to educational examinations, medical examinations and indeed other forms of professional scrutiny would also fit within this analysis, but it is clear that measurement and comparison are crucial to the effectiveness of the process:

> The art of punishing, in the regime of disciplinary power, is aimed [not] ... at repression ... it refers to a whole that is at once a field of comparison, a space of differentiation ... the constraint of a conformity that must be achieved .... (Foucault, 1977, pp. 182–183)

And with respect to schooling in particular, the power of such processes will be especially formative of subjectivities when they are encountered as probably the first proceduralised experience we have of the power of the generalised other:

> The school became a sort of apparatus of uninterrupted examination ... it is the examination which, by combining hierarchical surveillance and normalising judgement, assumes the great disciplinary functions of distribution and classification .... (Foucault, 1977, pp. 186, 192)

However, as discussed previously, while examinations may manifest and realise the idea of educational success and failure and the legitimacy of being subject to examination, the actuality has only been directly experienced by the majority of the school population relatively recently – over the last 30 years or so. At one and the same time this experience has been amplified in intensity, as the consequences of passing and failing examinations has become ever more severe. Subjectification is now produced through much wider empirical experience of examinations as well as general exposure to their ideological role and status. This is now combined with responsibilisation through the emphasis on social mobility achieved through personal endeavour.

There is more to this process of subjectification and responsibilisation than simply the encounter with tests and examinations however. Tests and examinations have themselves also changed over recent years, partly in response to calls for new and different skills and knowledge to be included in the curriculum (problem-solving, data analysis, report writing and so forth), partly as a result of different views about the role of assessment in promoting learning (formative assessment). Thus, there is more coursework, practical work and extended project work included in assessment systems than once was the case – 'authentic assessment' as it is sometimes known (Torrance, 1995); and there is far more feedback about progress to students from teachers, and far more discussion of assessment criteria and how they can be met, including via peer assessment. As such, the detail of the examination process is insinuated into the day-to-day relationship between teachers and students, and students and students, such that 'surveillance and normalising judgement' are absolutely central to the educational process. Such developments have been accommodated within traditional examination grading systems but have also included the development of 'portfolio assessment' or the reporting of profiles of achievement. Such developments can also be seen as part of the move towards 'lifelong learning' and the accumulation of a changing portfolio of skills and capabilities, as each stage of one's educational and employment career demands it (cf. O'Brien, Osbaldiston, & Kendall, 2014). Thus we can see these developments as both making visible the detailed criteria for educational success and inserting discussion of them into the curriculum, and in so doing making their appropriation in the pursuit of the entrepreneurial self ever more available. Elsewhere I have termed such appropriation the replacement of learning by 'criteria compliance' (Torrance, 2007) and noted that it may be one explanation for why, as test scores rise, educational standards and the quality of learning do not necessarily seem to improve. Rather teachers are simply 'teaching to the test', or indeed the portfolio criteria, and most students are content to accumulate grades in this way. Equally however, if such criteria and grades are not duly appropriated and accumulated, responsibility either lies with the reluctant learner – it has all been laid out in great detail for them – or the teacher – they have not laid it out in enough detail.

Even for the successful, however, responsibility for achieving and sustaining that success is similarly located in their willingness to comply with the process and compete for the rewards. In the 'Race to the Top', or even to the relatively secure middle, all are victims of the increasing intensity of the competition. What is intriguing is that this process of responsibilisation has been produced precisely because it is understood as necessary and even desirable. Examinations are not 'imposed' on schools or teachers or students, though some versions of particular testing regimes are more specifically designed and imposed by government than others. But examinations in general are engaged with voluntarily. People (teachers, examiners) create them and other people (students/candidates) submit to them because of the rewards they may bring. Equally, the moves towards a more inclusive mass system of education, and to the use of more coursework, more formative feedback, and more transparency of educational objectives and assessment criteria are located in developments in psychology and pedagogy (Torrance, 2012), not governmentality, yet the congruence with governmentality is clear. Similarly, designing and administering examinations is a multi-million dollar international business – many (vested) material interests have developed from the social necessity of certifying practical competence and educational achievement.

A key fulcrum in this articulation of examinations, governmentality and responsibilisation is the possibility of getting left behind in the race. Lemke (2012) alights upon the Foucault's notion of the 'fear of fear ... [being] one of the preconditions of the working of a security state' (quoted on p. 48). He then expands on this in the context of neo-liberal governmentality:

> The vision of an enterprising self promises manifold options and opportunities ... but it also necessitates the permanent calculation and estimation of risks, thus establishing a fear of failure. (Lemke, 2012, p. 49)

This fear of failure is nowhere more apparent than in students' fears about failing exams – along with the fears of their parents, their teachers, and even of governments themselves as they strive to keep ahead in the global race for a 'knowledge-ready' workforce. Lemke continues:

> Fear fulfils an important moral function in neo-liberal government. The constant threat of unemployment and poverty, and anxiety about the future ... stimulates a consciousness of economic risks and uncertainties that accompany the ... expected entrepreneurship. (p. 49)

We are all implicated/co-opted in this endeavour. We all, from different positions within the educational system, have an 'interest' in examinations continuing to exist in one form or another – teachers for purposes of student motivation and classroom control; students and parents for purposes of credentialism and social mobility; governments to measure educational performance and control teachers.

Thus examinations are produced to mediate and manage the effects of social and economic competition while, at one and the same time, contributing to the legitimacy of such competition. Their use underwrites the legitimacy of the process of measurement, comparison and individual responsibility for success and failure. The very fact that we allow ourselves to be subjected to examinations, or subject others to them, validates and endorses the power relationships inherent in such practices, and the construction of identity through discourses of 'passing and failing', 'knowing and not knowing', defining who becomes one sort of person and who another. Recent developments have further intensified the process of competition and the further individualisation of responsibility for educational success and failure, rendering individual students and teachers ever more liable for their own abject subjectivity and alienation, pursuing the indicators of educational quality and achievement – grades, grades and more grades – rather than educational quality itself. Thus assessment processes and examinations provide the quintessential vehicle for individualising and responsibilising success and failure for both students and teachers – with respect to achievement, social mobility and school accountability.

Could assessment be organised differently?

We seem to have moved from using assessment to identify and certify the actual practical skills, competences and educational achievements of (a minority of) individual students, to a mass system of assessment and testing which focuses on the indicators of achievement (grades and test scores) rather than achievement itself. Moreover this movement has been accompanied by an increasing emphasis on the personal responsibility to engage with the system and maximise outcomes. One issue is the scale of the endeavour – the larger the student cohorts included in the system the simpler the assessments are likely to have to be and thus the narrower the educational experience is likely to be. Another issue is the intensity of the consequences – as more students are included in the possibility of succeeding, the more the bar must be raised with respect to what counts as success – since ultimately assessment does not just identify achievement in any absolute sense, it also regulates social and economic competition through validating selection processes. Higher grades must be continuously pursed.

Yet neo-liberalism does also require higher educational standards in the most general sense of the phrase. Narrow testing regimes, reliant on coaching and practice to produce higher and higher grades, which actually signify less and less in terms of educational achievement, are unlikely to produce flexible and creative individuals over the longer term. Currently the broader educational outcomes of investigation, data analysis, report writing and so forth are being pursued in the context of grade accumulation which is as likely to detract from their development as ensure it. Meanwhile the 'soft skills' of collaboration, teamwork and creativity, which so often feature in employers' lists of 'twenty-first century skills' (Assessment and Teaching of 21st Century Skills (ATCS), 2010) are hardly addressed at all in current testing regimes. So, neo-liberalism produces responsibilisation, but not necessarily higher educational standards. It is apparent that a broader range of knowledge, skills and competencies must be included in accountability systems if they are to develop in tandem with improving educational standards. Considerable international interest is focused on such possibilities, including developing broader approaches to assessment to support knowledge development (Scardamalia, Bransford, Kozma, & Quellmalz, 2012) and culturally responsive forms of evaluation (Hopson, 2009; Hopson, Kirkhart, & Bledsoe, 2012). Elements of such discussions hark back to the development of records of achievement in the 1980s in the UK (Broadfoot et al., 1988; Pole, 1993) and portfolio assessment in the 1990s in the USA (Koretz, 1998), both of which sought to broaden the reporting of a wider range of educational outcomes. It may be that with the widespread use of hand-held personal devices, and the almost ubiquitous use of interactive media by young people, creating and posting one's own 'record of achievement' online may be one way of countering the narrowing impact of system accountability measures.

However, this would not necessarily address the issue of responsibilisation, indeed, it may further exacerbate it. Thus it is also necessary to re-think responsibilisation at the level of the collective, rather than the individual (cf. Stiegler, 2003, 2015). Educational encounters have always involved collaborative and reciprocal responsibility. Understanding the idea of responsibility and obligation and becoming a responsible citizen are not inappropriate goals for an education system to pursue. But such understandings must be recognised as collective responsibilities. Neo-liberal processes of responsibilisation, far over-emphasise the individual nature of responsibility and far underplay the collective element, thereby producing a very inefficient and ineffective form of social and educational investment in the future.

Much research tells us that learning is a social process and that achievement is co-produced in context even as it is attributed to individuals (cf. Lave & Wenger, 1991; Filer, 2000). If these insights were to be taken seriously in the organisation of curriculum, teaching and assessment, it might be possible to produce a system that really did pursue teamwork and the co-production of collaborative outcomes. While subjectification and responsibilisation are hardly avoidable in the operation of governmentality, the focus of this process could be significantly different, with much more emphasis being placed on the collective responsibility of teachers, students and their peers to understand that educational encounters are a collaborative endeavour which should produce outcomes that benefit communities as well as individuals. And outcomes, moreover, which must self-consciously look to the sustenance and long-term development of collective knowledge and culture, not simply to short-term utility and market advantage. What might assessment involve if it focused on the development and identification of collective understanding, collaboratively produced through educational experiences? If it valued difference, the need to identify and report a variety of complex, contingent and uncertain outcomes, and acknowledged that success and failure are inherently unstable and equally required for the development of curiosity, flexibility and resilience? Responsibilisation at the level of the individual will not be easily reversed, but education, and its attendant assessment processes and procedures, must be seen as a collective responsibility, maximising success and minimising failure, but above all recognising that both are co-produced as part of a collaborative process in context, and may change over time as circumstances and the nature of the educational encounter change.

Note

1. General Certificate of Secondary Education – a subject-based examination generally taken at 16 years of age.

Disclosure statement

No potential conflict of interest was reported by the author.

References

Assessment and Teaching of 21st Century Skills (ATCS). (2010). Draft white paper 1: Defining 21st century skills. Retrieved July, 28, 2014, from http://atc21s.org/wp-content/uploads/2011/11/1-Defining-21st-Century-Skills.pdf.
Bowles, S., & Gintis, H. (1976). *Schooling in capitalist America*. London: Routledge.
Broadfoot, P. (1979). *Assessment, schools and society*. London: Methuen.
Broadfoot, P. (Ed.) (1984). *Selection, certification and control*. London: Falmer Press.
Broadfoot, P. (1996). *Education, assessment and society*. Buckingham: Open University Press.
Broadfoot, P., Nuttall, D., James, M., & Stierer, B. (1988). *Records of achievement*. London: Department of Education.
Brown, P., & Lauder, H. (1992). *Education for economic survival*. London: Routledge.
Butterfield, S. (1995). *Educational objectives and national assessment*. Buckingham: Open University Press.
Cassen, R., & Kingdon, G. (2007). *Tackling low educational achievement*. York: Joseph Rowntree Foundation.
Common Core Standards (CCS). (2015). Retrieved June 22, 2015, from http://www.corestandards.org/.
Dahlstedt, M., & Fejes, A. (2013). Family makeover: Coaching, confession and parental responsibilisation. *Pedagogy, Culture and Society*, iFirst2013.
Dearing, R. (1993). *The national curriculum and its assessment: Final Report*. London: School Curriculum and Assessment Authority.

Department of Education and Science (DES). (1987). *Task group on assessment and testing: A report*. London: DES.
Department for Education (DfE). (2015). The national curriculum. Retrieved June 22, 2015, from https://www.gov.uk/national-curriculum/overview.
Drucker, P. (1993). *Post-capitalist society*. London: Heinemann.
Filer, A. (Ed.) (2000). *Assessment: Social process and social product*. London: Routledge.
Foucault, M. (1977). *Discipline and punish*. London: Allen Lane.
Friedman, T. (2006). *The world is flat*. New York, NY: Penguin.
Hamilton, L., Stecher, B., Marsh, J., McCombs, J., Robyn, A., Russell, J., Naftel, S., & Barney, H. (2007). *Standards-based accountability under No Child Left Behind*. Santa Monica, CA: Rand Education.
Hayward, G., & McNicholl, J. (2007). Modular mayhem? A case study of the development of the A-level science curriculum in England. *Assessment in Education: Principles, Policy & Practice, 14*(3), 335–351.
Hopson, R. (2009). Reclaiming knowledge at the margins: Culturally responsive evaluation in the current evaluation moment. In K. Ryan & B. Cousins (Eds.), *International handbook on evaluation* (pp. 429–447). Thousand Oaks, CA: Sage.
Hopson, R. K., Kirkhart, K. E., & Bledsoe, K. L. (2012). Decolonizing evaluation in a developing world: Implications and cautions for equity-focused evaluations. In M. Segone (Ed.), *Evaluation for equitable development results* (pp. 59–82). New York: UNICEF.
Inner London Education Authority (ILEA). (1984). *Improving secondary schools* (The Hargreaves Report). London: ILEA.
Kelly, P. (2001). Youth at risk: Processes of individualisation and responsibilisation in the risk society. *Discourse: Studies in the Cultural Politics of Education, 22*(1), 23–33.
Koretz, D. (1998). Large-scale portfolio assessments in the US: Evidence pertaining to the quality of measurement. *Assessment in Education: Principles, Policy & Practice, 5*(3), 309–334.
Lauder, H., Brown, P., Dillabough, J-A., & Halsey, A. H. (Eds.) (2006). *Education, globalisation and social change*. Oxford: Oxford University Press.
Lauder, H., Brown, P., & Tholen, G. (2012). The global auction model, skill bias theory and graduate incomes. In H. Lauder, M. Young, H. Daniels, M. Balarin, & J. Lowe (Eds.), *Educating for the knowledge economy? Critical perspectives* (pp. 43–65). London: Routledge.
Lave, J., & Wenger, E. (1991). *Situated learning: Legitimate peripheral participation*. Cambridge: Cambridge University Press.
Lemke, T. (1999). The critique of political economy of organisation as a genealogy of power. *International Journal of Political Economy, 29*(3), 55–75.
Lemke, T. (2001). The birth of bio-politics: Michel Foucault's lecture at the college de France on neo-liberal governmentality. *Economy and Society, 30*(2), 190–207.
Lemke, T. (2012). *Foucault, governmentality and critique*. Boulder, CO: Paradigm.
Liebenberg, L., Ungar, M., & Ikeda, J. (2013). Neo-liberalism and responsibilisation in the discourse of social services workers. *British Journal of Social Work*, iFirst 2013.
Lindley, J., & Machin, S. (2012). The quest for more and more education: Implications for social mobility. *Fiscal Studies, 33*(2), 265–286.
Murphy, R., & Torrance, H. (1988). *The changing face of educational assessment*. Buckingham: Open University Press.
New Zealand Qualification Authority (NZQA). (2011). History of NCE. Retrieved July 28, 2014, from http://www.nzqa.govt.nz/qualifications-standards/qualifications/ncea/understanding-ncea/history-of-ncea/.
No Child Left Behind Act (NCLB). (2001). Public Law 107–110. Retrieved July 28, 2014, from http://www.ed.gov/nclb/landing.jhtml.
Obama, B. (2009). *The race to the top*. Retrieved July 24, 2014, from http://www.whitehouse.gov/the-press-office/fact-sheet-race-top.
O'Brien, P., Osbaldiston, N. M., & Kendall, G. (2014). ePortfolios and eGovernment: From technology to entrepreneurial self. *Educational Philosophy and Theory, 46*(3), 284–295.
Peeters, R. (2013). Responsibilisation on government's terms: New welfare and the governance of responsibility and solidarity. *Social Policy and Society, 12*(4), 583–595.

Perry, E., & Francis, B. (2010). *The social class gap for educational achievement: A review of the literature*. Retrieved July 26, 2014, from http://www.thersa.org/__data/assets/pdf_file/0019/367003/RSA-Social-Justice-paper.pdf.

Pole, C. (1993). *Assessing and recording achievement*. Buckingham: Open University Press.

Scardamalia, M., Bransford, J., Kozma, R., & Quellmalz, E. (2012). New assessments and environments for knowledge building. In P. Griffin, B. McGaw, & E. Care (Eds.), *Assessment and learning of 21st century skills* (pp. 231–300). Dordrecht: Springer Science+Business Media B.V.

Stiegler, B. (2003). Our ailing educational institutions. *Culture Machine*, 5. Retrieved January 19, 2015, from http://www.culturemachine.net/index.php/cm/article/viewArticle/258/243.

Stiegler, B. (2015). Biopower, psychopower and the logic of the scapegoat. *Ars Industrialis*. Retrieved January 19, 2015, from http://www.arsindustrialis.org/node/2924.

Sutherland, G. (1984). *Ability, merit and measurement: Mental testing and English education 1880–1940*. Oxford: Oxford University Press.

Sykes Review. (2010). *The Sir Richard sykes review of the future of English qualifications and assessment system*. Retrieved July 28, 2014, from http://www.conservatives.com/~/media/files/downloadable%20files/sir%20richard%20sykes_review.ashx?dl=true.

Torrance, H. (1995). *Evaluating authentic assessment: Issues, problems and future possibilities*. Buckingham: Open University Press.

Torrance, H. (2007). Assessment as learning? How the use of explicit learning objectives, assessment criteria and feedback in post-secondary education and training can come to dominate learning. *Assessment in Education: Principles, Policy & Practice*, 14(3), 281–294.

Torrance, H. (2011). Using assessment to drive the reform of schooling: Time to stop pursuing the chimera? *British Journal of Educational Studies*, 59(4), 459–485.

Torrance, H. (2012). Formative assessment at the crossroads: Conformative, deformative and transformative assessment. *Oxford Review of Education*, 38(3), 323–342.

Wyatt-Smith, C., Klenowski, V., & Gunn, S. (2010). The centrality of teachers' judgment practice in assessment: A study of standards in moderation. *Assessment in Education: Principles, policy & practice*, 17(1), 59–75.

Academic responsibility: toward a cultural politics of integrity

William G. Tierney and Daniel J. Almeida

ABSTRACT
The authors consider how globalisation has fundamentally reshaped education. The assumption that in a knowledge economy workers need to be better educated has led to the belief that education is a private good. What the authors define as 'responsibilisation' frames a radically different vision of public life from that of the past. The pressures of globalisation, privatisation, and changes in communications technology have led to educational reforms consistent with the neoliberal suggestion that all individuals can succeed; if they do not, then it is their failure rather than that of the state. The authors suggest that ideas such as 'grit' and a culture of assessment are by-products of globalisation and responsibilisation, and argue that the educator's role is to engage in an analysis of the overall cultural politics that defines the era and proffer ways for social engagement aimed at the elimination of injustice and the promotion of democracy.

Introduction

Although education has been a central concern of industrialised nations for several hundred years, what has been meant by education is constantly a matter for debate. In the early nineteenth century in the United States, for example, Horace Mann made the point that children should receive free education offered by the state. Such a belief took hold throughout the country and by the turn of the twentieth century universal public education existed for all children. By the 1950s the expectation was that children would receive a free public education until they graduated from secondary school. The state funded and oversaw the school. If students dropped out or failed, the state bore the responsibility for the failure.

The advent of globalisation has continued this trend insofar as education has become a prominent factor in how analysts view the prosperity of a nation. The expansion of tertiary education in China, for example, and the associated costs to the federal budget have been significant; many countries, such as Malaysia and Turkey, aspire to have 'world-class' universities (Altbach, 2004; Mok, 2003; Salmi, 2009). The result is that the need for education has only increased in import. To get jobs, students apparently need not only to graduate from secondary school but also receive some form of a tertiary education. Countries with a better educated citizenry are more likely to prosper; those that do not focus their resources on schooling will fall further behind in the 'knowledge economy' (Peters, 2001). Who pays for education, however, has become a key topic of debate. In Australia, for example, the government has continued to privatise its tertiary system such that the consumer (aka student) will now be expected to pay more, whereas an education was once considered a public good (Vidovich & Currie, 2014).

For over 200 years industrialised nations, whether democratic or socialist, have said that more education is good for the country. The assumption has been that the individual and society benefits with a better-educated workforce. Educated individuals earn more income which in turn contributes to the tax base and civic infrastructure. The more education individuals have the more likely they will vote in elections, do volunteer work, and undertake a host of other tasks that contribute to the welfare of a democratic state (McMahon, 1999). Education, then, has been seen as a central building block of the modern state.

However, how one interprets education in the age of globalisation has two significant differences with regard to previous definitions of education that we will explore in this essay. First, education generally has been seen as a public good. As such the school and university have been public institutions supported by the taxpayer. Second, the assumption has been that both the individual and society benefit from a better-educated citizenry.

Globalisation, however, and its neoliberal supporters, has turned these ideas upside down. Education in the industrialised world, as best exemplified by the United States and Australia, increasingly is becoming privatised. Rather than assume that education benefits society, the argument has become that education largely benefits the individual. The fallout from such an assumption is twofold. On the one hand, if only the individual benefits, then the individual should pay education. Rather than public schooling for all, globalisation's supporters have put forward an array of private and for-profit providers that cater to individual preferences and restructure who decides issues such as teacher hiring, pedagogy, and educational philosophy.

On the other hand, if an individual encounters difficulty as a student, the responsibility for the student's success or failure rests with the individual. From this perspective student achievement depends upon the individual. Society is merely the field where action happens, and schools are simply parochial locales in that field. Fiscal support by the state, the existence of teacher unions, a concern for democratic pedagogy and the like are seen as impediments to successful reform efforts. Competition is good, and dramatic reforms are needed. Assessment and the monitoring of individual achievement become paramount objectives for the state. The state's role has transformed from one of the developer and deliverer of a public good to that of an evaluator of whether the individual has succeeded. If the student has not succeeded, the responsibility lies with the individual.

Our goal here is to consider how what we shall call 'responsibilisation' frames a radically different vision of public life from that of the past. We define responsibilisation as assigning the burden of managing one's risk in society solely with the autonomous individual rather than the state (Kelly, 2001; Liebenberg, Ungar, & Ikeda, 2013). Such an analysis of education follows others (e.g. Liebenberg et al., 2013; Skinns, 2003) who have examined how responsibilisation functions in other public arenas such as crime, health, and child welfare. We shall suggest that the pressures of globalisation, privatisation, and changes in communications technology and social media have presaged calls for significant educational reform.

As we elaborate below, this idea of responsibilisation has led to the emphasis on students' self-discipline, determination, and grit – a character trait defined as 'perseverance and passion for long-term goals' (Duckworth, Peterson, Matthews, & Kelly, 2007, p. 1087) – in educational discourse and practice (see U.S. Department of Education, Office of Technology, 2013). The education reforms that stem from ideas such as grit and responsibilisation depart from a view of education as a public good and instead offer the neoliberal suggestion that all individuals can succeed; if they do not, then it is their failure rather than that of the state. Although grit is most often discussed in the psychology literature with little regard for differences in race, class, gender, etc., we maintain that grit be considered from a sociocultural perspective. We ultimately argue that the role of the academic is not simply to acquiesce but instead to engage in an analysis of the overall cultural politics that defines the era and proffer ways for social engagement.

Considering globalisation and its impact on education

One of the challenges of globalisation is settling on a definition about what it is, and what it is not. Our usage of globalisation largely relies on the work of those who have critiqued it from a neoliberal vantage point (e.g. Burbules & Torres, 2000; Gulson & Fataar, 2011; Rizvi & Lingard, 2000, 2009). As with any emerging theoretical term, globalisation often stands as a proxy for other terms: capitalism, American culture, and Westernisation are the most common synonyms. Of course, if globalisation is nothing more than a synonym for one or another term then there is no need for its analysis. To be sure, globalisation has something to do with capitalism, and with American values, and with Westernisation, but globalisation is also much more than simply the transmutation of economic or social values from one country to the next.

McGrew and Held (2002) suggest that globalisation is the 'widening, deepening and speeding up of world-wide interconnectedness in all aspects of contemporary social life, from the cultural to the criminal, the financial to the spiritual' (p. 2). Although human societies always have interacted with one another through trade, war, religion, and culture, globalisation goes beyond such easy observations and extends interconnectedness in multiple ways. The nation-state is, by and large, an artefact of the twentieth century. Globalisation is, if not breaking down the idea of a nation with impermeable boundaries, at least helping us realise that borders are porous rather than rigid, ideological rather than geographic.

Clifford Geertz (1998) observed that the world 'is growing both more global and divided, more thoroughly interconnected and more intricately partitioned at the same time' (p. 107). The interconnections of which Geertz wrote are not mirrors of one another. Individuals and groups combine and recombine based on a myriad of cultural processes and histories, such that interpretive heterogeneity occurs at the same time that homogenisation occurs. While the expectation grows in developing countries and in the industrial world, for example, that all individuals ought to be able to have access to particular kinds of goods and services, how one utilises those goods and services varies.

We work from the assumption that none of these presumably instrumental actions, such as trade policy or technology transfer, are a de-cultured medium that merely drive transnational development. People still interpret and reinterpret those larger processes in some fashion that bear down on them. These micro-interpretations have larger consequences.

Such a viewpoint stands in contradistinction from what Sklair (2006) and others (e.g. Rizvi & Lingard, 2009) have labelled those who speak of globalisation 'suffused with a good deal of fatalism, popularly known as the TINA (there is no alternative) philosophy' (p. 101). We are suggesting that the idea of human agency exists such that individuals are capable of leading lives that they have helped determine, but globalisation forces these same individuals to think about their lives in a manner that did not exist only a generation ago. The result is that major crises and daily interactions erupt in ways that no one could have envisioned. Individuals are able to interact with one another in a much more sustained and immediate basis because of advances in technology and social media. YouTube, Twitter, and other social media outlets were instrumental for activists and organisers during the Arab Spring, for example. These same changes in communications technology have simultaneously created unprecedented ways of thinking of privacy in general and identity in particular.

Globalisation, then, refers to practices that extend beyond national borders even though they are frequently enacted in local and national contexts. Globalisation has come about and is spread by capital, migration, and technology. The result is greater integration across sectors and countries and an increase in cross-border goods, services, and capital. Because globalisation refers to transnational actions it is often difficult to see how local practices are impacted. We concur with Gutek (2006), however, that globalisation 'as a general process needs to be considered in terms of contextual settings' (p. 100), particularly when we are discussing education. The nation-state frames processes and goals.

Education is a useful example of the breadth of globalisation insofar as education's reach transcends one or another category. Education not only is transformed by globalisation, but as knowledge-producing organisations schools and universities also transform our understanding of globalisation and how a country performs in a globalised world. At one point the impact of globalisation on education was in dispute, but as Mok (2005) notes in the twenty-first century it has become clear how far-reaching globalisation's reach is, and how much it has impacted education. Discussions often centre around, for example, globalisation's impact on economics, trade, or culture. Education cuts across all of these categories. The result is that education is undergoing as significant changes as at any time in the last century, in large part because globalisation assumes a knowledge-based economy informed by technological change (Brown, Lauder, & Ashton, 2008; Peters, 2001; Peters & Roberts, 2000).

The assumption has been that in part because of globalisation countries need a better-educated workforce (Brown et al., 2008). If an industrialised country is to remain competitive then it needs more people participating in education. In the United States, for example, the Obama administration has called for a million more people a year to be added to tertiary education for the next decade. Tertiary education's 'product' gets defined as equipping individuals with the skills necessary to compete in a global economy. Numerous reports such as that done by McKinsey (see Auguste, Cota, Jayaram, &Laboissière, 2010) highlight that the United States faces an achievement gap in comparison to other industrialised countries and there will be a severe economic impact if nothing is done. The result is a renewed focus on improving primary and secondary education, increasing participation in tertiary education, and decreasing the length of time it takes students to earn degrees in all educational sectors.

All of these changes, or talked-about changes, go to the core of how an industrialised democracy such as the United States is to define a public good. Until recently the country has had a quite traditional definition of what is meant by a public good. As Kaul, Grunberg, and Stern (1999) have pointed out, a private good is excludable and rival in consumption whereas a common good has benefits that are non-rivalrous in consumption and non-excludable. The typical example of a common good is a traffic light or lighthouse. The use by one individual of the traffic light or the lighthouse does not detract from the use by others, and the cost and benefit is similar for all.

Education has been thought of as a public good and as such, the 'public' has created organisations where everyone can be educated. In the United States if a parent wanted his or her child to attend a private institution (such as a Catholic school) then the parent received no public support to attend the school. The parent also needed to continue to pay taxes toward the public good. As with other public goods in the United States – national defence, potable water, fire prevention, and the like – the provider was a taxpayer-supported public entity. If individuals wanted their own security or a private road on private land, then that was within their rights, but they had to pay for it – and they still had to pay taxes toward the public good.

A central derivative of globalisation has been a rethinking of what we mean by a public good and who is responsible for its provision (Peters & Roberts, 2000). As noted earlier, education always has been seen as important. In the nineteenth and early twentieth centuries, however, the obligation for educating the citizenry was the state's. Globalisation has shifted the responsibility from a public obligation to a private need. To be sure, any review of how capital has functioned will see the coercive nature of the state in an earlier era, but over the last half-century the Keynesian welfare state had assumed a more direct role in education than is seen now.

The globalised self and its consequences

The culture of assessment

One by-product of globalisation is a movement away from the idea that education should be a liberatory process based on communal goals about citizenship. Instead, education has been reduced to the skills one needs to perform in the workplace. The primary goal of the state is to assess those goals in order to see if the individual has learned what has been taught. Such a focus has multiple ramifications. The role of the teacher is reduced insofar as curriculum needs to be standardised if it is to be tested. The student's focus is on outcomes in order to do well on the examinations. The worth of a school can be determined by how well students do on tests.

The culture of assessment (Tierney & Rhoads, 1995) underscores who is in control and who is not. Outside evaluators and authorities have asserted more authority about what counts as knowledge and in doing so the state has asserted its power to define knowledge. Education, then, becomes the training ground for corporate and economic development. The locus of control is not the educator or school, but the evaluator and state. The assumption is that the evaluator is able to demonstrate how much students learn. The responsibility for learning falls on the student, a relatively new premise. Obviously, students ultimately learn material, but previously the responsibility for learning was a shared undertaking; student failure was viewed as a societal and individual failure. If students failed, then schools needed to be improved. Given recent rulings about teachers'-behaviour (e.g. *Vergara v. California*), the responsibilisation of individual teachers over the state comes into play. In the new environment success primarily turns on students' individual determination and hard work, or on 'grit', which we shall elaborate below.

The result is that a focus on what critical theorists (Tierney, 1992) have called dispositional knowledge, such as the values and ethics that guide life in a community, becomes irrelevant. What it means to be a member of a democracy, or to work for social justice, is of little use because it cannot be evaluated and assessed for jobs in the marketplace. Standardised assessment criteria give priority to factual information that demonstrates thinking skills. Ironically, educational institutions have long been thought of as cultural sites where knowledge gets defined.

The result is that rather than argue about the meaning of knowledge the assumption is that knowledge is static and preordained. Such a notion has its epistemological roots in the positivist belief that reality exists, and society exists by way of shared moral values. Such an assumption does not bring into question how values get defined, or how to become critically engaged citizens. Further, as we turn to now, if the individual does not internalise these shared pieces of knowledge then the failure lies with the student.

Youth, grit, and responsibilisation

Although hard work and determination are not new concepts in education, the specific construct called 'grit' was situated in the psychology literature in 2007 as a stable character trait deemed important to and predictive of educational success (Duckworth et al., 2007). Having the capability of sustaining effort and interest in assignments over long periods of time is seen as characteristic of a gritty student, one who is likely to succeed in the school environment (Duckworth & Quinn, 2009). Grit has also been described as a 'commitment to a single mission and an unswerving dedication to achieve that mission' and 'self-discipline wedded to a dedicated pursuit of a goal' (Tough, 2012, pp. 74, 136). Although these depictions may be instructive a more critical examination of grit is necessary given its increased prevalence in educational discourse. We raise the question about responsibilisation: who is responsible for learning, or for academic success and failure?

If we assume as the Grit Scale (Duckworth & Quinn, 2009) suggests that grit is a function of: (1) consistency of interest and (2) perseverance of effort, then it begs the question: who is responsible for these two goals? Is a student always to blame for not continually exerting effort despite teachers' instructions to do so? The neoliberal trend of responsibilising students suggests that the burden rests with the students themselves rather than the state.

Although issues of race, class, or gender are not often examined extensively in the literature on grit in psychology, considering grit from a sociocultural perspective is useful especially in educational contexts, and has direct ties to work of authors such as Anna Yeatman. Yeatman (2000) writes of mutual obligations where individual actors need to determine their future rather than remain passive participants in the welfare state. This new paternalism intertwined with neoliberal philosophy is focused on the concept of self-reliance (Schram, Soss, Houser, & Fording, 2010; Yeatman, 2000). Moving away from the Keynesian welfare state, individuals now become responsible for their future. To be sure, over a century ago philosophers extolled the virtues of self-reliance, and such a notion has linkages to those ideas. But as noted above, what differs in the twenty-first century is the idea that failure resides within the individual and that the state has little obligation to aid in the success of its citizenry.

The ideas of neo-paternalistic mutual obligation and contractualism (Rawolle, 2013; Yeatman, 1996) in education are grounded in Vygotsky's (1978) sociocultural theory, which acknowledges that learning is dependent upon social interactions and historical, institutional, and cultural contexts. Hence, a sociocultural perspective of grit accounts for myriad factors such as students' race, class, ethnic heritage, gender, age, geographic location, economic conditions, school environment, community, religion, values, social norms, etc. (Farrington et al., 2013; Gauvain, 2005; Kozulin, 2003; Lemke, 2001). Who is responsible for the sociocultural contexts of the homes and schools in which students are situated? Much of the differences in students' environments and circumstances are out of their own or even their families' control. And even though many admit that these uncontrollable sociocultural factors are constraining, individual students still are responsibilised with regard to their ultimate success or failure in school.

As with Yeatman's ideas of mutual responsibility and self-reliance, a focus on grit at this moment in history is not merely serendipity but rather ties into the idea that individuals are responsible for their success. If one has 'grit', one succeeds; if one does not, he or she does not. The role of society is largely absent in the discourse on grit and youth. As Kelly (2001) has noted, the youth-at-risk literature is extensive, and rarely problematises how society conceptualises youth. We are suggesting that the need for such formulations has only increased with the advent of globalisation, with the responsibilisation of youth becoming a central focus.

This observation is different from the conservative rhetoric of traditional family values. Conservative commentary still highlights that learning is mediated by numerous constituencies (e.g. teachers, parents, church). The governmentality literature, however, and with it, the idea of responsibilisation, atomises identity. As Lemke (2001) has observed, 'Governmentality is introduced by Foucault to study the "autonomous" individual's capacity for self-control and how this is linked to forms of political rule and economic exploitation' (p. 4). Rather than a state that takes overt actions of control, the responsibilisation of the individual comes into focus. The state's responsibility is not to educate, but rather to enable individuals to be responsible for their education (Lemke, 2001). The result is that when negative actions occur – illness, unemployment, displacement – the responsibility lies not with the policies of the state but the individual. What needs to be explored, then, are how the technologies of self and domination function in a synthetic manner that coerces individuals to do the job that the state once did. As Lemke (2001) has pointed out:

> This theoretical stance allows for a more complex analysis of neoliberal forms of government that feature not only direct intervention by means of empowered and specialised state apparatuses, but also characteristically develop indirect techniques for leading and controlling individuals. The strategy of rendering individual subjects 'responsible' (and also collectives, such as families, associations, etc.) entails shifting the responsibility for social risks such as illness, unemployment, poverty, etc. and for life in society into the domain for which the individual is responsible and transforming it into a problem of 'self-care'. (p. 12)

Such an observation is important because it highlights how responsibilisation makes it appear that the individual is acting out of a rational mind-set and that the choices he or she makes are self-evident. As with grit, the assumption is that if students work hard enough they will succeed. Because what counts for knowledge is presumably known, then everyone is on a level playing field making choices that presumably benefit their advancement. Neoliberalism in a globalised world has centralised state power in a manner that requires an authoritarian approach preoccupied with analysis and examination where the responsibility resides with the individual. As Liebenberg et al. (2013) point out: '[t]hese mandates have led to the development of systems that evaluate, manage and track citizens, particularly those who are "at risk" or whose behavior is "risky" '(p. 3).

Responsibilisation essentially requires people to be accountable for managing their own risk in society (Kelly, 2001). As such, notions of autonomy and individualism are coupled with extremely authoritarian ways of viewing individuals in general and students in particular (Liebenberg et al., 2013). By 'responsibilising' learning in individuals the government averts focus from a regime of power. How is it, at this particular historical juncture that the rise of a culture of assessment coincides with a literature demonstrating the import of individual determination and grit?

Methodologically the desirability of understanding the personal stories of students has become irrelevant. Testing and assessment blurs individual identities and rather than trying to understand rich histories of youth through life histories, cultural portraits, and the like, instead the state enquires whether students have passed a particular exam, and if not, which remedies may be prescribed. A methodological framework in accordance with governmentality and responsibilisation of the individual marginalises the voices of those very same individuals (Hope, 2014). The voices and concerns of individuals become irrelevant; what matters is how individuals perform or react to proffered remedies. And after these remedies are provided then ultimately individuals have demonstrated that they lack grit and are failures in the modern economy of the twenty-first century.

Such an outcome paints a society of winners and losers, or as Gulson and Fataar (2011) claim, 'neoliberalism constructs policies and practices that enable and embody the entrepreneurial educational and urban self as the ideal citizen' (p. 277). The state has moved, then, from a focus on the welfare of all citizenry to a consumerist model where one's success gets determined in singular fashion. We are arguing that the pattern that exists, although certainly having lineaments to a conservative discourse surrounding the individual, the family, and the nation, is also new in large part because of the rise of neoliberal globalisation, and the rapid expansion of social media connecting individuals globally. Foucault (1991) accurately predicted the pervasive force of governmentality, and Bourdieu's (1994) notions of cultural and social capital have shown how those who are marginalised stay on the margins by the invisible force of capital. But what they could not have predicted is how the individual has become atomised in the twenty-first century. The state regulates not by force, regulation, or policies. Instead, globalisation has enabled the market to reign supreme. The interpretation of that with regard to schools and universities, we have argued, can be seen by a desire for tests and assessments that have multiple ramifications. Curricula get translated as instrumentalities to be learned. Pedagogy gets developed by external agents that teachers present without interpretation or deviation. Schools and universities are sites for the transmission of an unquestioned knowledge rather than locales where individuals construct knowledge. Testing supplants qualitative methodologies as ways to determine outcomes.

Cultural politics and the engaged intellectual

Grahame Thompson (2007) has observed: '[t]he issue of "responsibility" has increasingly become a defining feature of the current era of neoliberal globalisation' (p. 1). Indeed, the concept of responsibilisation might be criticised not only for implying a degree of passivity of those being responsibilised (Skinns, 2003), but also for denying agency to individuals. The point, of course, is not to deny individual responsibility but to problematise the actions of individuals, schools, and the state (Foucault, 1985, 1991). In doing so, one needs to acknowledge the issues raised previously regarding globalisation and its ramifications for education concerning assessment and the like, but then consider what an engaged intellectual might do to reinsert a sense of democracy not only in the curriculum and educational organisations but also with regard to a country's citizens and students.

Our concern here is that the enormous force of the neoliberal agenda has not been met with counter-narratives pointing out how educational institutions are cultural sites where knowledge not merely gets transmitted, but also defined. As McLaren (1991) noted over a generation ago, 'the culture of schooling is fundamentally a struggle over meanings and about meanings. It is a struggle over events, representations, and meanings' (p. 237). Advocates of assessment, grit, and responsibilisation, however, assume knowledge as static and preordained. Relatedly, as Braverman (1974) noted, it is equally important to think about how academic labour is being reorganised, which in turn, changes the nature of social relations. The neoliberal agenda, then, reorganises education and its constituents in order to meet globalisation's needs in the marketplace. The reproduction of already existing power relationships circumscribes action such that at times an alternative politics seems not simply difficult to achieve, but impossible to conceive.

However, rather than assume that the nature of social relations is preordained such that issues such as assessment or grit are givens, we are suggesting that a transformation is possible. The role of the academic moves away from a transmitter of knowledge and toward one that enables, foments, ideological dialogues and resistances. As Giroux (1988) has noted, 'ideology becomes useful for understanding not only how schools sustain and produce meanings, but also how individuals and groups produce, negotiate, modify or resist them' (p. 5). The transformative academic, then, is someone who rejects overriding assumptions and struggles to isolate and interrogate beliefs and interpretations that globalisation's proponents have made to appear as self-evident and necessary.

The responsibility of the academic, then, is to help focus dialogue on the reconstruction of the social imagination in order to advance a cultural politics of democracy that honours diverse voices rather than subscribes to notions of responsibilisation. Such a stance stands in contradistinction to what we have described above as governmentality where the state's power becomes vast and invisible and the individual's voice mute and homogenous. Clearly, then, we are concerned with how those of us in educational organisations might be more engaged in promoting democracy and empowering those who are most at risk of being responsiblised for failures that are not of their own making. Concentrating on the cultures, ideologies, and discourses that enable them provides the potential not for submission or adherence to norms but instead disrupts them and in doing so advances democratic organisations.

The struggle to understand how responsibilisation functions, then, is a key responsibility of the engaged academic. However, a simple understanding of how a coercive force operates is not enough. To be sure, one well-intended strategy is to develop ways that those who are on the margins develop strategies to gain control of their lives. Strategies to develop grit in children, for example, may be well intended and may succeed for one or another child. But the point suggested here is that responsibilised strategies may work for someone but nevertheless function in a way that does not allow systemic reform. Our assumption is that when an educational organisation's discursive strategies are about common goals to enable diverse voices rather than homogenise them by way of standardised assessments that students, faculty and staff will move closer to creating bonds of reciprocal obligation.

Some may suggest that moving against standardised curricula and assessments or responsibilised strategies that atomise the individual is wishful intent rather than strategic. From this perspective complete understandings of how governmentality functions and how to overcome it is impossible. But as Denneny (1989) has pointed out, if the answer to ideology 'cannot be solved, (it) can be thought about; one can strive to reach not an answer but perhaps greater clarity about the issue, and in the process better locate oneself in the contemporary world' (p. 16). The responsibility, then, of the academic is aimed not at fitting into the agenda that has been defined in a globalised world but instead focused on creating a society without injustice. One's project becomes transformative rather than maintaining the status quo. The cultural politics of academic staff struggles to create the conditions for a better world. Methodology becomes a project aimed not as scientific understanding but enabling the voices of those who are silenced to be heard.

Such a stance may seem utopian or a liberal's lament from a modernist age. But we remain wedded to Giroux's (1983) notion that 'human beings not only make history, but also make the constraints; and needless to say, they also unmake them. It needs to be remembered that power is both an enabling as well as a constraining force' (p. 38). Ideas such as responsibilisation, standardised assessment measures, and grit are not created whole cloth by an invisible force impervious to change. Academics' challenge is to develop a democratic public philosophy that works against homogenisation and instead honours difference as a way to enact a common struggle that is emancipatory both as process and outcome. We need a multiplication of democratic practices that enable diverse social relations based on a multitude of subject positions fraught with issues pertaining to power and privilege. The challenge is not to provide the skills for those who are powerless in a zero sum game so that the structural relations of power remain the same. Rather, our collective responsibility to one another and especially to our students is to create the conditions for a reconfigured democratic public sphere that enables voice and a diversity of public stances formed by a renewed sense of obligation to one another and the responsibility of the state for changing those structural conditions that privilege some and disable others.

Disclosure statement

No potential conflict of interest was reported by the authors.

References

Altbach, P. G. (2004). The costs and benefits of world-class universities. *Academe*, *90*(1), 20–23. doi:10.2307/40252583

Auguste, B. G., Cota, A., Jayaram, K., & Laboissière, M. C. A. (2010). *Winning by degrees: The strategies of highly productive higher-education institutions*. New York, NY: McKinsey & Company. Retrieved from http://mckinseyonsociety.com/winning-by-degrees/

Bourdieu, P. (1994). Rethinking the state: Genesis and structure of the bureaucratic field. *Sociological Theory, 12*(1), 1–18. doi:10.2307/202032

Braverman, H. (1974). *Labor and monopoly capital*. New York, NY: Monthly Review Press.

Brown, P., Lauder, H., & Ashton, D. (2008). Education, globalisation and the future of the knowledge economy. *European Educational Research Journal, 7*(2), 131–156. doi:10.2304/eerj.2008.7.2.131

Burbules, N. C., & Torres, C. A. (Eds.). (2000). *Globalization and education: Critical perspectives*. London: Psychology Press.

Denneny, M. (1989). Chasing the crossover audience. *Out/look, 1*(4), 16–21.

Duckworth, A., & Quinn, P. (2009). Development and validation of the short grit scale (Grit-S). *Journal of Personality Assessment, 91*(2), 166–174. doi:10.1080/00223890802634290

Duckworth, A. L., Peterson, C., Matthews, M. D., & Kelly, D. R. (2007). Grit: Perseverance and passion for long-term goals. *Journal of Personality and Social Psychology, 92*(6), 1087–1101. doi:10.1037/0022-3514.92.6.1087

Farrington, C. A., Roderick, M., Allensworth, E., Nagaoka, J., Keyes, T. S., Johnson, D. W., & Beechum, N. O. (2013). *Teaching adolescents to become learners: The role of noncognitive factors in shaping school performance—A critical literature review*. Chicago, IL: Consortium on Chicago School Research. Retrieved from http://ccsr.uchicago.edu/sites/default/files/publications/Noncognitive%20Report.pdf

Foucault, M. (1985). *Discourse and truth: The problematization of Parrhesia*. Evanston, IL: Northwestern University.

Foucault, M. (1991). Politics and the study of discourse. In G. Burchell, C. Gordon, & P. Miller (Eds.), *The Foucault effect: Studies in governmental rationality* (pp. 53–72). Chicago, IL: The University of Chicago Press.

Gauvain, M. (2005). Sociocultural contexts of learning. In A. Maynard & M. Martini (Eds.), *Learning in cultural context* (pp. 11–40). New York, NY: Springer.

Geertz, C. (1998). The world in pieces: Culture and politics at the end of the century. *Focaal: Tijdschrift voor Antropologie, 32*, 91–117. Retrieved from http://ayman980.com/class/Readings/Clifford%20Geertz%20-The%20World%20in%20Pieces.pdf

Giroux, H. A. (1983). *Theory and resistance in education: A pedagogy for the opposition*. South Hadley, MA: Bergin & Garvey.

Giroux, H. A. (1988). *Teachers as intellectuals: Toward a critical pedagogy of learning*. Gradby, MA: Bergin & Garvey.

Gulson, K. N., & Fataar, A. (2011). Neoliberal governmentality, schooling and the city: Conceptual and empirical notes on and from the global south. *Discourse: Studies in the Cultural Politics of Education, 32*(2), 269–283. doi:10.1080/01596306.2011.562672

Gutek, G. (2006). *American education in a global society: International and comparative perspectives*. Long Grove, IL: Waveland Press.

Hope, A. (2014). Schoolchildren, governmentality and national e-safety policy discourse. *Discourse: Studies in the Cultural Politics of Education, 36*(3), 1–11. Advance online publication. doi:10.1080/01596306.2013.871237

Kaul, I., Grunberg, I., & Stern, M. A. (1999). *Global public goods: International co-operation in the 21st century*. Oxford, UK: Oxford University Press.

Kelly, P. (2001). Youth at risk: Processes of individualisation and responsabilisation in the risk society. *Discourse: Studies in the Cultural Politics of Education, 22*(1), 23–33. doi:10.1080/01596300120039731

Kozulin, A. (2003). *Vygotsky's educational theory in cultural context*. New York, NY: Cambridge University Press.

Lemke, J. L. (2001). Articulating communities: Sociocultural perspectives on science education. *Journal of Research in Science Teaching, 38*(3), 296–316. doi:10.1002/1098-2736(200103)38:3<296::AID-TEA1007>3.0.CO;2-R

Liebenberg, L., Ungar, M., & Ikeda, J. (2013). Neo-liberalism and responsibilisation in the discourse of social service workers. *British Journal of Social Work, 45*(3), 1–16. doi:10.1093/bjsw/bct172

McGrew, A., & Held, D. (2002). *Governing globalisation: Power, authority and global governance.* Cambridge, UK: Polity Press.

McLaren, P. (1991). Decentering culture: Postmodernism, resistance, and critical pedagogy. In N. B. Wyner (Ed.), *Current perspectives on the culture of schools* (pp. 231–257). Boston, MA: Brookline.

McMahon, W. W. (1999). *Education and development: Measuring the social benefits.* Oxford; New York: Oxford University Press.

Mok, K. H. (2003). Globalisation and higher education restructuring in Hong Kong, Taiwan and Mainland China. *Higher Education Research and Development, 22*(2), 117–129. doi:10.1080/07294360304111

Mok, K. H. (2005). The quest for world class university: Quality assurance and international benchmarking in Hong Kong. *Quality Assurance in Education, 13*(4), 277–304. doi:10.1108/09684880510626575

Peters, M. (2001). National education policy constructions of the 'knowledge economy': Towards a critique. *The Journal of Educational Enquiry, 2*(1), 1–22.

Peters, M., & Roberts, P. (2000). Universities, futurologies, and globalisation. *Discourse: Studies in the Cultural Politics of Education, 21*(2), 125–139. doi:10.1080/713661155

Rawolle, S. (2013). Understanding equity as an asset to national interest: Developing a social contract analysis of policy. *Discourse: Studies in the Cultural Politics of Education, 34*(2), 231–244. doi:10.1080/01596306.2013.770249

Rizvi, F., & Lingard, B. (2000). Globalization and education: Complexities and contingencies. *Educational Theory, 50*(4), 419–426. doi:10.1111/j.1741-5446.2000.00419.x

Rizvi, F., & Lingard, B. (2009). *Globalizing education policy.* London: Routledge.

Salmi, J. (2009). *The challenge of establishing world-class universities.* Washington, DC: World Bank.

Schram, S. F., Soss, J., Houser, L., & Fording, R. C. (2010). The third level of US welfare reform: Governmentality under neoliberal paternalism. *Citizenship Studies, 14*(6), 739–754.

Skinns, L. (2003). Responsibility, rhetoric and reality: Practitioners' views on their responsibility for crime and disorder in the community safety partnerships. *British Society of Criminology Conference Proceedings, 6*, 1–18. Retrieved from http://www.britsoccrim.org/volume6/007.pdf

Sklair, L. (2006). A transitional framework for theory and research in the study of globalisation. In I. Rossi (Ed.), *Frontiers of globalisation research: Theoretical and methodological approaches* (pp. 93–108). New York, NY: Springer.

Thompson, G. (2007, July 31). Responsibility and neo-liberalism. *Open Democracy, 31*. Retrieved from http://www.opendemocracy.net/article/responsibility_and_neo_liberalism

Tierney, W. G. (1992). *Official encouragement, institutional discouragement: Minorities in academe – the Native American experience.* Norwood, NJ: Praeger.

Tierney, W. G., & Rhoads, R. A. (1995). The culture of assessment. In J. Smyth (Ed.), *Academic work: The changing labour process in higher education* (pp. 99–111). Bristol, PA: Society for Research into Higher Education & Open University Press.

Tough, P. (2012). *How children succeed: Grit, curiosity, and the hidden power of character.* Boston, MA: Houghton Mifflin Harcourt.

U.S. Department of Education, Office of Technology. (2013). *Promoting grit, tenacity, and perseverance: Critical factors for success in the 21st century.* Washington, DC: SRI International. Center for Technology in Learning. Retrieved from http://www.ed.gov/edblogs/technology/research/

Vidovich, L., & Currie, J. (2014). Aspiring to 'world class' universities in Australia: A global trend with intended and unintended consequences. In A. M. Maldonado & R. M. Bassett (Eds.), *The forefront of international higher education* (pp. 295–307). Netherlands: Springer Verlag.

Vygotsky, L. (1978). *Mind in society.* London: Harvard University Press.

Yeatman, A. (1996). Interpreting contemporary contractualism. *Australian Journal of Social Issues, 31*(1), 39–54.

Yeatman, A. (2000). Mutual obligation: What kind of contract is this? In P. Saunders (Ed.), *Reforming the Australian welfare state* (pp. 156–176). Melbourne: Australian Institute of Family Studies.

The implications of contractualism for the responsibilisation of higher education

Shaun Rawolle, Julie Rowlands and Jill Blackmore

ABSTRACT
Within the context of heightened perceptions of risk within the higher education sector worldwide, responsibility for outcomes is increasingly required not only of universities but, also, of individual academics. In turn, contracts have become a key form of governance for institutions in mediating and modulating this risk and responsibility. While much writing around the use of contracts in higher education has focused on market-based, competitive neoliberal conceptions of contractualism, this article argues that there are, in fact, two largely antagonistic new modes of contractualism – market contractualism and relational contractualism – and a third, residual mode, paternal contractualism. These three modes of contractualism coexist within universities, in tension. The article draws on two Australian exemplars to highlight how these tensions play out and to highlight the potential for contractualism to create spaces for shared goals and projects and shared risks resulting from the ways in which responsibility and individual agency are negotiated.

Introduction

Universities are in crisis, we are told in recent reports. Around the globe, nations from the United Kingdom, the United States and Australia have looked to universities as government face unprecedented risks in the wake of the Global Financial Crisis and global pressures on national economies. In Australia, the Ernst & Young[1] (2012) report on the higher education sector identifies numerous risks that if not addressed will lead to the demise of the public university. They identify five key trends, namely democratisation of access to knowledge, contestabililty of markets and funding, digital technology, global mobility and integration with industry. As a solution, Ernst & Young propose that universities should become more businesslike. They identify three 'business' models, each leading to increased privatisation of costs to students, and more contractual academic labour.

In similar vein, another financial multinational network, Deloitte (2011) highlight challenges including funding and financial analysis and management, competition for students, access and affordability, the employment prospects of graduates and increased regulatory, accountability and information management requirements. Other global trend reports are more sensitive to the complexity of, and ambiguity arising from, university responsibilities to multiple stakeholders, yet also express concerns about the 'enormous challenge ahead' (Altbach, Reisberg, & Rumbley, 2010, p. 161).

Despite the urgency of such reports, studies of leadership in higher education found that most university executives consider Australian universities to be highly responsive and resilient (Blackmore, 2014a; Blackmore & Sawers, 2015). Trends already coexist within more corporate frames in universities, intensified in speed, scale and scope of change over the past decade in response to greater deregulation. Foregrounded by Altbach et al. (2010) is the tension between the role of the university with regard to the public and private good, and the differing obligations and responsibilities to their respective stakeholders (students, governments, industry) in higher education (Marginson, 2011).

Higher education debates and research emphasise that universities, academics and students are experiencing higher levels of risk, but there is little discussion about the responsibilities of the higher education sector. Education is now a more precarious business. Individual universities and the sector are subject to increased risk arising from events such as the global financial crisis, fluxes in recruitment from threats to the safety of international students or rapid shifts in policy with regard to migration, visas and fees. Such factors have caused a significant drop in international fee-paying student enrolments upon which Australian universities are so dependent (Gribble & Blackmore, 2012). Governments see risks in university reputations, and acknowledge that higher education is central to the balance of trade and exports and balancing government budgets.

The response of the Australian coalition conservative government in 2014 to responsibilisation focused on the costs of universities to the public purse rather than the benefits. This ignores the OECD's (2009) emphases on, and contemporary global discourses about, knowledge economies (Rawolle & Lingard, 2014), instead requiring greater individual investment in education as a private good. For students, higher education is equally risky, with credentials no longer holding the same value as in the twentieth century and no longer guaranteeing employment. In this article, we refer to responsibilisation as a process by which citizens or categories of citizens are shaped by pressures to be 'responsible'.

Neglected in analyses and reports are shifts in governance that have also occurred due to changing relations between the individual (student and academic), the university, and the nation-state. For universities, a trend has been for greater institutional autonomy, leading universities to an ongoing process of 'responsibilisation' to orient academics and departments, and to achieve accountability targets (Stensaker & Harvey, 2010). Accountability is important to university managers and government, as the discourse and mechanisms of accountability signify legitimacy for both in being effective and efficient. At the same time, markets pressure universities, particularly as funding decreases, to be distinctive and to develop a brand.

Governments want a high-quality higher education sector and individual world class universities. These objectives are claimed to be achieved through national standards, qualification frameworks and quality assurance measures such as Excellence in Research in Australia (ERA) or its equivalent in other nations, and student evaluations of teaching (Blackmore, 2014b). Within self-managing universities, such accountability frameworks include contract-like mechanisms that facilitate comparing and judging institutions. Industry–university research partnerships, another form of contract, also shape the nature of research in knowledge-based economies. Accountability mechanisms have transformed the nature of academic work, what research gets done, how it gets done, who teaches and what they teach, informing academic identities due to the focus on the performative (Blackmore & Sachs, 2007).

The spread of contracts in education has fostered interest in their emerging role in governance in higher education in the form of contractualism. Yeatman (1997), for example, views the spread of contracts into social services as ushering in a *new contractualism* that involves an 'ethos of contractualism', which has the potential to produce 'contractual personhood' that accommodates 'within individuality both what we have called voice and the various kinds of dependency individuals have with regard to each other' (p. 51). The focus of this article is on shifts in the deployment of contractual relations within and relating to universities (Rawolle, 2013; Rawolle, Rowlands, & Blackmore, 2014). We use 'contracts' and 'contract-like mechanisms' to point to agreements made between people in universities, while we use 'contractualism' to talk about different modes of governance that are drawn on to modulate the use of contracts. Hence, one contract might be employed in different ways depending on the mode of contractualism in which it is embedded and deployed. The argument is developed from an ongoing empirical research project on contractualism in education. This article is theoretical in nature, dealing with the theory which underpins our research. The context is one of heightened risk and uncertainty for the sector nationally and internationally.

We argue that responsibilisation is now centrally connected to contractualism as contracts become a governance mechanism for mediating manufactured risks and apportioning responsibility. Contracts mediate responsibilities from higher education policy through to education practice. Theorizing needs to help explore and explain overlapping experiences of responsibilisation that relate to individuals in higher education. In particular, higher education is an exemplary site for exploring different kinds of manufactured risk, and contracts are central as a mechanism for managing this risk, and for the communication of responsibility. Contractualism theorises the relationships signified by contracts and involves considering the way that risk and responsibility are anticipated and responded to in universities. To advance this argument, we draw on Bauman (2001), Beck (1992) and Giddens (1999) on risk and responsibilisation, and Yeatman's account of new contractualism (Rawolle, Rowlands & Blackmore, 2014; Yeatman, 1997), which are used to explore two specific exemplars drawn from the Australian higher education sector.

Responsibilisation

Theories of risk and responsibilisation are interwoven within writings around late modernity (Giddens, 1999, p. 16) where, for both Beck and Giddens, risk refers to things that *might* happen as opposed to things that *have* happened. Ulrich Beck's (1992) theory of the risk society speaks of society's efforts to prevent, minimise or control 'the various unintended consequences of radicalized modernization' (Beck, 1999, p. 3). The risk society is a response to what Giddens has described as manufactured risk: new, unpredictable and even invisible areas of risk created by human development, particularly in areas of science and technology (Giddens, 1999, p. 4). A key feature of the risk society is individualisation, the 'variation and differentiation of lifestyles and forms of life, opposing the thinking behind the traditional categories of large-scale group societies' (Beck, 1992, p. 88). Beck argues that, 'for the sake of their own material survival', individualisation requires people to 'make themselves the center of their own planning and conduct of life' (p. 88). Risks force people to:

> ... decide for themselves: What is still tolerable and what is no longer? They require decisions about whether or not, when, and where to protest even if this only takes the form of an organized, intercultural consumer boycott. These issues raise questions about the authority of the public, cultural definitions, the citizenry, parliaments, politicians, ethics and self-organization. (Beck, 2000, p. 218)

Individualised decision-making relates to both the perception of risk and responses to it. For Bauman (2001), individualisation provides 'a new level of freedom and autonomy' (Atkinson, 2008, p. 8), Beck's writing around forced choices allows for a much less emancipatory individualised environment.

Individualisation is connected to responsibilisation, where individuals and not governments or institutions are responsible for their own welfare and the consequences of decisions they make (or not, as the case may be) (Bauman, 2001; Beck, 2000; Giddens, 1999; Rose, 1999). Processes of individualisation and responsibilisation characteristic of contemporary times contrast with the post-1945 welfare state, which served as a form of collective protection against largely external and visible risks such as poverty and ill health (Giddens, 1999; Mythen, 2004). Academic discussions around the responsibilisation of citizens became prominent from the 1980s when, in response to perceived financial crises and pressures related globalisation and the knowledge economy, individual citizens and state agencies were encouraged to become entrepreneurial and take risks (Giddens, 2000). Clarke has described this as the shift from classic liberalism to competitive and market-based neoliberalism, characterised by 'self-regulating subjects' (Clarke, 2005, p. 452; see also Lemke, 2001).

As might be expected, Beck, Giddens, Rose and others have each written extensively about responsibilisation but do not all share the same view or express it in the same way. For example, Giddens writes about the:

> ... core importance of active government and the public sphere. The public sphere does not coincide with the domain of the state. State institutions can diminish or discredit the realm of the public when they become oversized, bureaucratic or otherwise unresponsive to citizen's needs. The neoliberals were right to criticize the state in these respects, but wrong to suppose that the public good can be better supplied by markets. (Giddens, 2000, pp. 163–164)

Giddens argues here that the responsibilisation of citizens is not in and of itself an enactment of neoliberalism but is instead about agency, empowerment and participation. This is consistent with his role as an advisor to the UK's Blair government in the 1990s (O'Malley, 2004) on its Third Way policies which sought to forge a path in between the extremes of the Keynesian welfare state on the left and neoliberalist economic policy on the right with what Clarke describes as 'choice' and 'voice' (2005, p. 450). In a similar vein, Trnka and Trundle (2014) differentiate between neoliberal notions of responsibilisation and broader conceptions of responsibility that encompass autonomy, self-care and enablement (p. 142).

Beck argues that a 'power game of risk politics' has supplanted consideration of factors such class, race and gender, despite global risks exacerbating inequalities where, for example, *'pollution follows the poor'* (Beck, 1999, p. 5, original emphasis). Rather than responsible citizens being empowered agents, Beck sees them as experiencing the consequences of a 'structural transformation process' within wider society (Mascini, Achterberg, & Houtman, 2013, p. 1211). He argues that responsibility for bearing the burden of risk is not shared equally: '[t]here is a basic power structure within world risk society, dividing those who produce and profit from risks and the many who are afflicted with the same risks' (Beck, 1999, p. 16). For this latter group, responsibility is not freedom of choice but forced choice, 'where [d]ecisions on education, profession, job, place of residence, spouse, number of children and so forth ... must be made' (Beck, 1992, p. 135). While everyone chooses between alternatives, information about the advantages of some and the disadvantages of others is not shared equally. The range of alternatives from which to choose is wider and more advantageous for some and narrower and more hazardous for others.

Rose (1996a) also writes on responsibilisation from a genealogical, Foucauldian governmentality perspective rather than from the historical sociological standpoint that he argues Beck and others have adopted. Rose asserts that 'complex social and governmental phenomena' such as risk cannot be reduced to sociological causes at particular points in time (Rose, O'Malley, & Valverde, 2006, p. 96) and that individualisation and the associated responsibilisation of subjects are neither recent or exclusive to neoliberal political regimes but are, instead, common to a number of political perspectives (Rose, 1996b). He also takes the arguments about the effects of responsibilisation upon the marginalised further than either Beck or Giddens, asserting that:

> ... from a variety of directions, the disadvantaged individual has come to be seen as potentially and ideally an active agent in the fabrication of their own existence ... And, thus it follows, that they are to be assisted not through the ministrations of solicitous experts proffering support and benefit cheques, but through their engagement in a whole array of programmes for their ethical reconstruction as active citizens .... (Rose, 1996b, p. 60)

Rose posits that individuals are expected not only to provide for their security through the expenditure of their own funds, but that provision of welfare to those who cannot or will not be responsible for themselves is seen as damaging (Rose, 1999). As Sulkunen (2007) states, '[j]ustice requires reciprocity, not dependence, and the weak should be educated to understand this' (p. 328). In contrast to Beck, Rose argues that those who are marginalised are not forced to choose between undesirable or hazardous alternatives but are, instead, excluded from the regime of choice by their own unwillingness or inability to participate (Rose, 1999, p. 89).

Higher education is an exemplary site to explore manufactured risk through a focus on the use of different kinds of contracts. There are risks attached to negotiations over enterprise bargaining, academic workload allocations and doctoral supervision, for example. These include cost over-runs, unintended consequences such as stress leave, or non-completion of doctoral research. These are manufactured risks contingent largely on their construction in individual universities, but also on the broader political landscape that increasingly devolves risk through insufficient funding to cover costs. Drawing from the conceptualisations of risk and responsibilisation by Beck, Bauman and Rose, responsibilisation is understood as playing out in three potentially overlapping ways, as freedom, autonomy and empowerment, as forced choice and unequal burdens, and finally as exclusion from choice.

Contractualism

Higher education institutions draw on contracts as part of their strategies of governance (Yeatman, 1997). Contractualism points to a turn in policy in which both formal contracts and contract-like mechanisms are used as means of governing, mediating and modulating risk and responsibility. Contracts are drawn on by governments and institutions as a tool to help meet accountability requirements for funding and simultaneously shape individuals towards desired ends and outcomes. In this section, we explore the links between contractualism and responsibilisation in higher education, and talk specifically about how three different forms of contractualism (market, relational and paternal) work with risk and responsibilisation.

Writing on contractualism assumes that service providers are connected with their clients through contracts and contract-like mechanisms, in terms that are agreed upon, negotiated and accompanied by different forms of accountability (Yeatman, Dowsett, Fine, & Gursansky, 2008). Yeatman's influential account of contractualism outlines three broad principles that underpin the use of contracts:

(1) informed consent between those connected in the contract;
(2) regular points of renegotiation at specific times while the terms of contract are in place and
(3) reciprocal accountability for each party to obligations that they have agreed upon. (Rawolle, 2013; Yeatman, 1997)

As a mode of governance, the purpose and use of contracts is altered and modified to a variety of different means and ends.

Research on contractualism follows contracts and considers how these principles are represented and taken up in practice. One argument about contractualism is that there is a growing spread of contracts throughout *all fields* including higher education. Contractualism is closely linked with a meta-process involving the contractualisation of society (Lallement, 2006), connected with other meta-processes such as globalisation, mediatisation, responsibilisation and individualisation. This spread raises questions about how contractualisation and contractualism are expressed in policies and settlements (Rawolle, 2013).

A contention about contractualism is over the prevalence and impact of two new, antagonistic versions of contractualism that have emerged. The first position argues that contractualism represents an extension of the logic of business, the logic of neoliberalism, and the language and words of markets (White, 2007). The assertion is that the way contracts have been taken up and employed in higher education is closely connected with the manner of contracting in the business community, and that the modes of relating in business are embedded within this form of governance. The relationship between universities and students is refashioned and reinterpreted as producer–consumer relationship, with a reduced expectation about the obligations that both share to one another. Complications emerge in the expectations that accompany international students, whose experiences are shaped by different national traditions. As extension of this position is that contractualism in universities always represents an enactment of managerialist practices that are established on the basis of neoliberal philosophy (see, for example, Peters, 2013).

In this account of contractualism, the focus is on *representations* of meeting the principles of contractualism, on ensuring that there is the appearance of informed consent, renegotiation and accountability to meet legal obligations whilst at the same time fostering market-like behaviours such as accepting personal responsibility for risk. The extension of contracts and contract-like mechanisms within higher education represent a kind of colonisation, and an erosion of its distinctive forms of governance. Contracts relay risks associated with the provision of educational services that an institution is obliged to manage as part of its broader compact with society and government. Risks are relayed to the endpoints of service delivery. In contrast, the core is obliged to manage and evaluate through contracts and accountability mechanisms. The social commitments in individual higher education institutions' compacts (Krause, 2013) and risks associated with commitments and obligations, which are social, are divided, individualised and relayed to lecturers, supervisors and ultimately to students. The risk is presumed to be balanced and mitigated by providing individual consumers with choice among different support options, and points of renegotiation for these choices, who then take responsibility for their selection. In this account of contractualism, responsibilisation is understood as forced choice and unequal burdens.

Alternate views of contractualism emphasise that not all contracts and contract-like mechanisms have their origin in markets, and as strategic tools for adversarial relationships (Yeatman & Owler, 2001). Contracts have been drawn on in policy fields related to services for persons with a disability, as a way of supporting the autonomy and individuality of clients towards mutually desired goals, such as attainment of education, skills or employment and equity policies which involve targets. The emphasis is on providing a *variety of practices* (including representation) that foster and revisit informed consent, renegotiation and reciprocal accountability in the pursuit of a relational space. This second view of contractualism rejects the market-based alternative as a form of patrimonial governance (Yeatman, 2000). New contractualism views contracts as having the potential to realise post-patrimonial relationships in service delivery, in which risk and responsibility for outcomes are shared by those involved in the contract towards a mutually negotiated outcome or set of goals. This involves a complex reading of individuality in educational relationships as being located within and expressed though relational spaces, such as espoused by Bauman (2001), as opposed to self-centred and competitive enactments of individualisation described (but not necessarily advocated) by Beck and others (Beck, 1992; Yeatman et al., 2008). In new contractualism, both parties are implicated in asserting their individuality by identifying contributions they will make to the shared goal (e.g. the completion of a PhD thesis). There are different risks attached to these goals, yet parties are held responsible for meeting their own distinctive contribution to these goals, and for outlining the need for new supports or the obsolescence of current supports. Contracts and contract-like mechanisms provide a relational space in which the goals, individual needs or project develops. In this account of contractualism, responsibilisation is understood as freedom, autonomy and empowerment.

Arising out of this debate between new forms of contractualism is acceptance that both offer an alternative to older, residual forms of contractualism. Yeatman (2000) argues that these older forms are patrimonial, in which people in more powerful positions are assumed to know more and be more informed to make decisions about what is best for those in less powerful positions, which is outlined in the form of a contract. In higher education, this is seen in decisions that are made on behalf of students about the course of study they must undertake to complete a degree. In this account of contractualism, responsibilisation is understood as exclusion from choice.

We now provide an account of the complex interplay between what we will discuss as modes of contractualism through a focus on two examples of contracts and contract-like mechanisms in higher education. Based on our discussion above, and reflecting on contractualism in higher education, we refer to these modes of contractualism as *market contractualism*, *relational contractualism* and *paternal contractualism*. This will help us to consider how modes of contractualism link to responsibilisation and risk in higher education.

Enterprise bargaining and academic workload allocations

Since 2011, the governance of Australian universities has been driven through individual institutional mission-based compacts with the federal government, a contractual text, to determine the parameters of each university's funding, projected growth and contribution within the broader community. These texts mirror similar contractual texts linking universities to governments in other nation states. Universities then devolve – through modes of contractualism – risk and responsibility down to organisational units, academics and students. The responsibility for compacts has been experienced within universities in a variety of ways, as freedom, autonomy and empowerment, as forced choice, unequal burdens, and as exclusion from choice. There have been university sector level trends. The context since 1989 has been that of a shifting industrial relations regime, with the introduction of enterprise agreements that devolved all bargaining down to the individual university levels rather than across the sector nationally, allowing academics in more established elite universities to leverage higher salaries, particularly for executives on contracts, for example, vice chancellors. These formal collective contracts negotiated and signed off by university executives and National Tertiary Education Union representatives define key aspects such as what constitutes an active researcher, whether there are teaching-only positions, the hours of work for academics. In return, academics receive annual pay increments and in some instances improved security and benefits, for example, for casual staff, and flexibility to undertake caring responsibilities. Moves towards enterprise agreements have resulted in forced choice and the necessary distribution of unequal burdens.

From formal, legal university-level enterprise agreements, academic workload models are developed at the faculty level. Workload models shape the nature and amount of academic labour, identify what is expected through targets and hierarchical point systems and determine what activities are allocated under the headings of teaching, research and service (Bexley, James, & Arkoudis, 2011). Most workload models across the sector in Australia have a notional apportionment of 40% teaching, 40% research and 20% service for those employed in teaching and research, although the numbers of staff in teaching-only and research-only positions have increased in the past decade (Universities Australia, 2013). As with all contracts, while providing specific statements about the total numbers of hours worked over a year (e.g. 37.5 hours per week on average in Australia), there are implicit contractual obligations. For example, workload models ignore strong evidence that most academics work significant unpaid overtime (between 10 and 20 hours per week in some cases; Coates, Dobson, Goedegebuure, & Meek, 2010). In particular, research output (e.g. publications) is achieved by writing up during leisure and leave time. The informal agreement is that academics gain relative autonomy and flexibility as to where and when they do this work provided they meet their expected output targets (Blackmore, 2014b). They are endowed with responsibility as freedom and autonomy for their own productivity.

Academic workload models remain open to re/interpretation at faculty and school level. Under this model, academic managers such as deans or heads of school are able to define how particular activities are understood and measured, what individual academics are expected to achieve and criteria for how certain academic work is defined. For example, the number of publications required per year in listed journals and with commercial publishers to gain points necessary for a 40% allocation for research, or the time span allowed post-PhD to build a research profile (e.g. 2 or 5 years). It then becomes the responsibility of individual academics to achieve required points in order to gain a balanced research/teaching/service load. This is despite Australian academics experiencing a trebling of their workload in the past 10 years while subject to ongoing student evaluations, pressure to increase quality and quantity of research output measured by research assessments such as ERA, which focus on quality outputs and research quantums that pay universities on the basis of quantity, to expedite supervision of doctoral students within minimum time and to raise external research income (often to pay for their salaries; Universities Australia, 2013). It also ignores additional labour obligations relayed to individual academics by administrative quality assurance and financial audit demands, multimodal pedagogies and online teaching, amongst other matters. These invisible labour obligations have been experienced as responsibilisation as an exclusion from choice.

This exemplar indicates a relay of contractual obligations, from formal to informal, from collective to individual, and indicates links between individualisation, responsibilisation and contractualism. It is indicative of tension between Beck's and Bauman's notions of how processes of individualisation are characterised by increased capacity to exercise agency in ways that recognise social and relational aspects of greater interdependence evident in modern societies and neoliberalism's notion of competitive individualism where individuals seek only to maximise their own outcomes in pursuit of their own interests. This specific exemplar is illustrative of *market contractualism*, and its spread in one setting as universities draw on neoliberal philosophies and practices to individualise risk and responsibility.

Individualisation of responsibility renders invisible the asymmetry of power relations, which exist as contractual relations become more informal and private. One-on-one meetings with a head of school where more assertive individuals are able to negotiate better deals and where bullying can occur, in particular, disadvantage women who are less likely to negotiate deals favourable to themselves other than gaining greater flexibility to undertake caring responsibilities, and which do not necessarily improve their promotion possibilities, and early career researchers who rely on the goodwill of managers.

Individualisation (and by extrapolation the responsibilisation) of academic work runs counter to collegiality, traditionally understood as being enacted through disciplinary communities of academics (Middlehurst, 1993). In turn, collegial governance is deeply embedded in Western democratic notions of what it means to be a university (Rowlands,

2013) and is associated with self-regulatory, autonomous academics operating as a 'republic of scholars' (Bleiklie & Kogan, 2007, p. 477). Pressures for greater accountability and mechanisms with which they are associated are premised upon claims that transparency made evident, for example, in explicit contractual agreements, will achieve quality and efficiency (value for money). Evidence suggests that such mechanisms, while providing legitimacy for governments under pressure in high-risk times, do not necessarily produce quality (Shore, 2008). Increased demands for accountability can infuse university cultures with a loss of trust, impacting on the affective economy, which in turn can damage those collegial relations so important for research and innovation (Blackmore & Sachs, 2007).

Doctoral supervision

While relays of *market contractualism* in enterprise bargaining and academic workload allocations highlight the use of contracts and contract-like mechanisms as a neoliberal form of responsibilisation, spaces also exist in universities that encompass other modes of contractualism. One space that acts as a site of potentially both *paternal contractualism* and *relational contractualism* is doctoral supervision, which also serves as a key connection between research development and teaching. Doctoral supervision is also linked to a range of institutional targets outlined in university compacts and funding. We draw on doctoral supervision to highlight possible overlaying of different modes of contractualism in relation to the same contract, and to illustrate that it need not lead to individualism. As an extensive commitment between academics and candidates, doctoral supervision is accompanied by a range of contracts and contract-like mechanisms.

Doctorates in a variety of OECD nations such as Australia, UK and US are initiated through negotiations around suitable supervision relationships, formalised through explicit candidature agreements. Such agreements set specific roles for ongoing relationships between supervisors and candidates, and identify commitments made to supervision meetings, production of writing and feedback. These commitments are oriented towards an overall shared project – be this a singular doctoral text, or a performance and exegesis – and targeted milestones towards completion of doctoral research projects. Some commitments are decided in a paternal manner, where the risk of some choices is made by the university on behalf of the doctoral student. The obligation to revisit the original agreement accompanies doctoral supervision, regardless of need, with separate feedback on progress requested from all parties to the candidature agreement as an ongoing form of accountability. This allows for the reshaping of projects as research develops, revising of timelines as events impact on progress or for altering the structure and nature of supervision support. The practice of candidature agreements may be experienced as explicit exclusion from choice attached to a specific form of *paternal contractualism*.

Drawing on Yeatman's (1997) arguments, doctoral supervision is also guided by a broader ethos where the target is the development of a doctoral text, sets of dispositions and strategic positioning in academic or other fields. While contracts emphasise specific responsibilities and accountability measures, this broader ethos suggests that the relational space that accompanies supervision also demands an acknowledgment of active and changing responsibilities between supervision teams and candidates. The relationship is built not only on goals related to candidates producing a dissertation or thesis but also to pursuing publishing opportunities, both scholarly and engagement oriented, presenting at conferences, developing research experience and work opportunities. Accountability and renegotiation are then a central and ongoing part of this relational space. Doctoral supervision, as a relational space, enables pursuit of shared interests and goals that benefit not only individuals and research teams but also the university more broadly. In these practices, we see revisiting of informed consent, renegotiation and reciprocal accountability as a way of weighting their importance to both the doctoral project and to broader goals. The responsibilisation of aspects of doctoral supervision is then positioned as a collective freedom, autonomy and empowerment.

Practices of doctoral supervision are located between competing modes of contractualism. Traditionally, *relational contractualism* takes precedence as a result of carrying out a contract underpinned by an ethos of mutual relations and an emerging relational space. This is supported at an institutional level by reaching successful agreed outcomes, positive feedback on annual reviews and timely completion of the thesis. *Market contractualism* would sit to the side, as a kind of state of exception, in which the university would intervene if accountability measures or proposed goals were not met, or if feedback at regular intervals indicated that problems had arisen. In such instances, and in line with the original candidate agreement, a range of increasingly intrusive oversight practices are put in place to ensure that progress resumed, that a new contract is negotiated, or that the contract is terminated.

Conclusion

Responsibilisation connects and emerges from residual and new modes of contractualism as an outcome of a complex system of contractual relays and layers in higher education institutions. These links form a hierarchical network of contracts that relay obligations from broad education policies through higher education institutions, and potentially beyond these institutions for some obligations. Hence, university-level contractual texts outline institutional obligations, which are connected to employment contracts covering work conditions of academics and support staff, academic workloads and then to students through academic contracts or contract-like mechanisms, such as subject guides or candidate agreements. But responsibilisation also emerges from relational spaces enabled by contracts and contract-like mechanisms where academics and students engage in shared projects and goals such as research grants and doctoral research, where responsibility shifts and is negotiated organically and according to emerging needs.

Contractualism is linked to both individualisation and responsibilisation in universities, but that this process, while broadly juridical, operates in at least three distinctive modes: paternal, market and relational. As explored in relation to doctoral supervision, the same contract is located within more than one mode of contractualism. In a conventional way, contractualism is utilised in both a paternal and a market form. In its paternal form, contractualism represents the relay of obligation to less powerfully placed people in asymmetrical relations. This mode nominally works through informed consent, but in practice limits renegotiation and reciprocal accountability, and relies on dominant agents in contracts taking risks for choices while relaying responsibility. In its market form, contractualism represents the spread of market logic into higher education, in which obligations are relayed to the periphery of institutions as a way to manage both risk and individualise responsibility. Market contractualism also relays responsibility onto individuals, encourages competitiveness rather than cooperation and undermines rather than nurtures research and teaching cultures. Underlying strong external accountabilities between individual academics and their employers also produces, for the former, a loss of autonomy and lack of trust, expunging the 'social' in the social contract upon which much of public education is based.

Contractualism is utilised in a relational form as a way to create a space where shared goals or projects are pursued openly, and where there is shared risk in meeting these goals. In relational contractualism, responsibilisation emerges as one necessary consequence of the process of carrying out and enacting a specific contract, and involves a revisiting of informed consent, renegotiation and reciprocal accountability in relation to different practices. The form of responsibilisation enacted is dependent largely on the way that contracts are taken up and used to connect people together around specific obligations and responsibilities in each specific field, and of changing dynamics of obligations within relational spaces.

One view of contractualism holds that the use of contracts builds on and reinforces asymmetrical relations as the basis for negotiation, renegotiation and accountability between people named in the contracts. Viewed in this way, contractualism is inherently conservative and reinforces inequalities of pre-existing and unequal relationships that are not adequately considered when people commit to these contracts. A full account of contractualism must explain both its potential use as a means of developing autonomy and individuality of persons involved in service relationships, and its potential to act as a specific and sharp instrument to ensure compliance with accountability targets and as an implement for authorisation of consequences. The potential of contractualism for understanding responsibilisation and risk lies in the seemingly contradictory relationships that it authorises. Within higher education, the tension and potential that arises lies in how these three modes, market, relational and paternal contractualism, are negotiated and enacted.

Note

1. Both Ernst & Young and Deloitte are multinational networks of auditing firms.

Disclosure statement

No potential conflict of interest was reported by the authors.

References

Altbach, P. G., Reisberg, L., & Rumbley, L. E. (2010). *Trends in global higher education: Tracking an academic revolution*. Rotterdam: UNESCO and Sense.
Atkinson, W. (2008). Not all that was solid has melted into air (or liquid): A critique of Bauman on individualization and class in liquid modernity. *The Sociological Review, 56*(1), 1–17.
Bauman, Z. (2001). *The individualized society*. Cambridge: Polity.
Beck, U. (1992). *Risk society: Towards a new modernity*. London: Sage.
Beck, U. (1999). *World risk society*. Cambridge: Polity.

Beck, U. (2000). Risk society revisitied: Theory, politics and research programmes. In B. Adam, U. Beck, & J. Van Loon (Eds.), *The risk society and beyond: Critical issues for social theory* (pp. 211–227). London: Sage.

Bexley, E., James, R., & Arkoudis, S. (2011). *The Australian academic profession in transition: Addressing the challenge of reconceptualising academic work and regenerating the academic workforce.* University of Melbourne: Centre for the Study of Higher Education.

Blackmore, J. (2014a). Disciplining academic women: Gender restructuring and the labour of research in entrepreneurial universities. In M. Thornton & G. Withers (Eds.), *Markets, managers and mandarins: The modern university and the social sciences* (pp. 171–194). Canberra: ANU Press.

Blackmore, J. (2014b). Wasting talent? Gender and the problematics of academic disenchantment and disengagement with leadership. *Higher Education Research & Development, 33*(1), 86–99. doi:10.1080/07294360.2013.864616

Blackmore, J., & Sachs, J. (2007). *Performing and reforming leaders: Gender, education restructuring, and organisational change.* Albany: State University of New York Press.

Blackmore, J., & Sawers, N. (2015). Executive power and scaled-up gender subtexts in Australian entrepreneurial universities. *Gender and Education, 27*(3), 320–337.

Bleiklie, I., & Kogan, M. (2007). Organization and governance of universities. *Higher Education Policy, 20*(4), 477–493.

Clarke, J. (2005). New labour's citizens: Activated, empowered, responsibilized, abandoned? *Critical Social Policy, 25*(4), 447–463.

Coates, H., Dobson, I. R., Goedegebuure, L., & Meek, L. (2010). Across the great divide: What do Australian academics think of university leadership? Advice from the CAP survey. *Journal of Higher Education Policy and Management, 32*(4), 379–387.

Deloitte. (2011). *Making the grade: Strategies for addressing the top challenges facing higher education institutions.*

Ernst & Young. (2012). *University of the future: A thousand year old industry on the cusp of profound change.* Sydney. Retrieved from http://www.ey.com/Publication/vwLUAssets/University_of_the_future/$FILE/University_of_the_future_2012.pdf

Giddens, A. (1999). Risk and responsibility. *The Modern Law Review, 62*(1), 1–10.

Giddens, A. (2000). *The third way and its critics.* Cambridge: Polity.

Gribble, C., & Blackmore, J. (2012). Re-positioning Australia's international education in global knowledge economies: Implications of shifts in skilled migration policies for universities. *Journal of Higher Education Policy and Management, 34*(4), 341–354.

Krause, K.-L. (2013). Quality enhancement the Australian scene. In R. Land, & G. Gordon (Eds.), *Enhancing quality in higher education: International perspectives* (pp. 129–140). New York: Routledge.

Lallement, M. (2006). *New patterns of industrial relations and political action since the 1980s. Changing France: The politics that markets make.* London: Palgrave Macmillan.

Lemke, T. (2001). The birth of bio-politics: Michel Foucault's lecture at the college de France on neoliberal governmentality. *Economy and Society, 30*(2), 190–207.

Marginson, S. (2011). Higher education and public good. *Higher Education Quarterly, 65*(4), 411–433.

Mascini, P., Achterberg, P., & Houtman, D. (2013). Neoliberalism and work-related risks: Individual or collective responsibilization? *Journal of Risk Research, 16*(10), 1209–1224. doi:10.1080/13669877.2012.761274

Middlehurst, R. (1993). *Leading academics.* Buckingham: The Society for Research into Higher Education and Open University Press.

Mythen, G. (2004). *Ulrich Beck: A critical introduction to the risk society.* London: Pluto.

OECD. (2009). *Higher education to 2030, volume 2, globalisation.* Paris: OECD Publishing.

O'Malley, P. (2004). *Risk, uncertainty and government.* London: Glasshouse.

Peters, M. (2013). Managerialism and the neoliberal university: Prospects for new forms of 'open management' in higher education. *Contemporary Readings in Law and Social Justice, 5*(1), 11–26.

Rawolle, S. (2013). Understanding equity as an asset to national interest: Developing a social contract analysis of policy. *Discourse: Studies in the Cultural Politics of Education, 34*(2), 231–244. doi:10.1080/01596306.2013.770249

Rawolle, S., & Lingard, B. (2014). Mediatization and education: A sociological account. In K. Lundby (Ed.), *Mediatization of communication* (pp. 595–614). Berlin: De Gruyter Mouton.

Rawolle, S., Rowlands, J., & Blackmore, J. (2014). Education in contract: Theorising contractualism in education. Paper presented at 2014 ECER Conference, Portugal, 4 September 2014.

Rose, N. (1996a). The death of the social? Re-figuring the territory of government. *Economy and Society, 25*(3), 327–356.

Rose, N. (1996b). Governing 'advanced' liberal democracies. In A. Barry, T. Osborne, & N. Rose (Eds.), *Foucault and political reason* (pp. 37–65). London: UCL Press.

Rose, N. (1999). *Powers of freedom: Reframing political thought*. Cambridge: Cambridge University Press.

Rose, N., O'Malley, P., & Valverde, M. (2006). Governmentality. *Annual review of Law and Social Science, 2*, 83–104.

Rowlands, J. (2013). Academic boards: Less intellectual and more academic capital in higher education governance? *Studies in Higher Education, 38*(9), 1274–1289. doi:10.1080/03075079.2011.619655

Shore, C. (2008). Audit culture and illiberal governance universities and the politics of accountability. *Anthropological Theory, 8*(3), 278–298.

Stensaker, B., & Harvey, L. (2010). *Accountability in higher education*. New York: Routledge.

Sulkunen, P. (2007). Re-inventing the social contract. *Acta Sociologica, 50*(3), 325–333.

Trnka, S., & Trundle, C. (2014). Competing responsibilities: Moving beyond neoliberal responsibilisation. *Anthropological Forum: A Journal of Social Anthropology and Comparative Sociology, 24*(2), 136–153.

Universities Australia. (2013). *A smarter Australia: An agenda for Australian higher education 2013–2016*. Canberra: Universities Australia. Retrieved from http://universitiesaustralia.s3.amazonaws.com/wp-content/uploads/2013/02/Universities-Australia-A-Smarter-Australia.pdf

White, N. R. (2007). 'The customer is always right?': Student discourse about higher education in Australia. *Higher Education, 54*(4), 593–604.

Yeatman, A. (1997). Contract, status and personhood. In G. Davis, B. Sullivan, & A. Yeatman (Eds.), *The new contractualism?* (pp. 39–56). Melbourne: Macmillan.

Yeatman, A. (2000). The politics of postpatrimonial governance [online]. In T. Seddon, L. Angus (Eds.), *Beyond nostalgia: Reshaping Australian education* (pp. 170–185). Camberwell: ACER Press.

Yeatman, A., Dowsett, G. W., Fine, M., & Gursansky, D. (2008). *Individualization and the delivery of welfare services: Contestation and complexity*. London: Palgrave Macmillan.

Yeatman, A., & Owler, K. (2001). The role of contract in the democratisation of service delivery. *Law in Context, 18*(2), 34–57.

Responsibilisation and leadership in the neoliberal university: a New Zealand perspective

Mark Amsler and Cris Shore

ABSTRACT
We examine how discourses of leadership and responsibilisation are used in contemporary universities to deepen neoliberal administration and further the corporate university's business plan by restructuring and redescribing academic work. Strategically, responsibilisation discourse, promoted as 'distributed leadership', is a technology of indirect management. Responsibilisation language stipulates 'expectations' for workers and integrates academic work (teaching, learning, research, service) into an administered regime recognising and rewarding successful conduct ('leadership') in the university. We intervene in this responsibilisation discourse by critically analysing texts about distributed leadership in one New Zealand university context. Linking Foucault's analysis of earlier forms of liberal governmentality with critical discourse analysis, we explore how administrative structures, power relations, and regulating management discourse seek to reshape employee behaviour in the neoliberalised, post-democratic university. We present a case study of one university's 'Leadership Framework', which exemplifies a new form of 'post-neoliberal governmentality' in higher education, embedding self-governance within increasingly instrumentalising centralisation.

Introduction: ambiguities of being responsible

The call to 'responsibility' is loaded and heterogeneous. So are the word's roots and derivatives. In English and French, *responsibility*, from *response* (n.), *respond* (v.), implies openness, accessibility, accountability, as well as 'self-care', self-determination, maturity. Legally, *responsibility* calls forth liability, the guilty subject, but also the authority to speak, act, or decide on another's behalf. The antonym, *irresponsibility*, implies dangerous risk-taking behaviour, neglect, lack of care, or fanaticism. Curiously, the legal negation *not responsible* suggests something more positive: release from blame or obligation.

Yet we sometimes lose track of *responsibility*'s link to recognition, agency, personhood, cooperation, and social being. How do we be *responsible to*, not just *for*, another? What ethical gaps and political consequences emerge when we shift *responsibility* from response and recognition to guilt or consequences? How do *responsible citizens* act? When corporations declare their policies for *social responsibility*, whose interests are served?

These paradoxes embedded in *responsibility*'s semantic network are amplified in the term *responsibilisation*. As Foucauldian scholars and governmentality theorists have noted (Miller, 2001; Rose & Miller, 1992), 'responsibilisation' has become a key strategy in contemporary capitalism. In neoliberal discourses of responsibilisation, the derived noun operationalises the condition of rational, autonomous 'self-care' as the objective or standard for civilised, law-governed, rational society and as the behaviour 'expected' by government, institutions, or society of citizens, employees, and persons.

We argue this latter mode of *responsibilisation* discourse conflates positive and negative meanings of *responsibility* in a managerial language of entrepreneurial selfhood, thereby conflating responsibility as free choice, personal initiative, innovation, meritorious conduct with responsibility as liability, blame, jurisdiction. What happens when these conflated positive and negative meanings are discursively deployed to control and re-regulate conduct in the contemporary university? Building on the work of critical education and curriculum theorists (Ball, 2012; Olssen & Peters, 2005, pp. 323–324; Peters, 2001, p. 61), we show how responsibilisation works as a strategy for deepening neoliberal administration and carrying out the corporate university's business plan by restructuring and redescribing academic work. The discourse of responsibilisation – sometimes euphemised as 'distributed leadership' – is a technology of indirect management. The language of responsibilisation addresses academic and administrative staff as functions within a production system and stipulates what is 'expected' of each worker in order to integrate academic work into an administered schema for recognising and rewarding *responsible*, successful conduct ('leadership') in the university.

We ground our critical inquiry of this responsibilisation discourse by analysing texts about distributed leadership in a contemporary university setting. Our argument develops in three steps. First, we situate responsibilisation discourse by discussing Foucault's 1978–1979 Collège de France lectures on liberal models, biopolitics, and governmentality. Second, we rework Foucault's (1991) analysis of earlier forms of liberal governmentality to explore how contemporary administrative structures and management discourse are seeking to reshape employee behaviour in the neoliberalised university. Finally, we refine this analysis in a case study of the *Leadership Framework* developed by senior managers at a large New Zealand university. The *Leadership Framework* is an administrative imperative exemplifying a new form of governmentality intended to restructure academic work. We argue the Leadership Framework also represents a new phase in the neoliberal model of responsibilisation, combining the mobilisation of agency by responsibilised yet highly managed workers with increasing emphasis on top-down managerial control and redescription of university work as primarily production serving a business plan. Rather than 'governing at a distance' (Rose & Miller, 1992), this conflation of responsibilisation and managerial surveillance is the calculative effect of a command and control mentality that uses economic models to organise university workers' activities in an increasingly low trust institutional environment.

Biopolitics and responsibilisation

In 1979, Michel Foucault delivered a Collège de France lecture course entitled 'The Birth of Biopolitics'. His lectures focused on the historical origins and intellectual contexts for post-WW2 western liberalism: Adam Smith, German social liberalism articulated by

Ordoliberalism, and US free market liberalism exemplified by the Chicago school. Foucault shows how these postwar liberal models take different positions on the role of the state. In both the liberal and neoliberal systems, '*homo œconomicus*' is constructed not as a partner in an economic exchange but as the exemplary citizen, employee, or person. The enterprise of self-care is the primary activity of the economised person: '*Homo œconomicus* is an entrepreneur of himself, being for himself his own capital, … his own producer … the source of [his] earnings' (Foucault, 2008, p. 226). The postwar German social state was established to intervene when necessary to correct the inevitable distortions created by competitive capitalism. US liberalism, contra the New Deal, advocated a more anarchic form of capitalism with minimum state regulation and intervention. Moreover, US liberalism applied the calculative model of *laissez faire* to social areas traditionally not susceptible to economic or commercial framing, including healthcare, education, justice system, and family life. US liberals defined rational choice as a socio-economic calculus: What is cost effective and economically advantageous will be socially beneficial. All social behaviours can be 'managed'. As Foucault (2008) stated:

> … *homo œconomicus*, that is to say, the person who accepts reality or who responds systematically to modifications in the variables of the environment, appears precisely as someone manageable … *Homo œconomicus* is someone who is eminently governable. (p. 270)

Foucault's lectures on biopolitics and a new governmental reason identified with a plurality of interests seeking advantage in the market have turned out to be astonishingly prescient. The state as end in itself (*raison d'État*) was long ago replaced by an economic system of interests that establish objectives, standards, performance targets, and administrative procedures to compete with one another for limited resources. According to this new governmental logic, liberal government's role is reshaped and re-legislated to protect and enable entrepreneurial capitalism, populated with tangible goods, intellectual property, performance-pegged salaries, and 'flexible' workforces. Individuals are 'free' to act within this system, but their behaviours are evaluated and generally recognised almost exclusively with respect to economic and/or institutional interests. Individuals, not collectives, are the units of the neoliberal workforce. A person's education, skills, demeanour, dress, conversational interaction, workspace, and energies are organised to enhance the bottom line. The person is defined by his or her self-care and 'engagement', aka entrepreneurial effort and economic contributions. In US-style liberalism, social behaviours (family, community, politics, education) are reframed in terms of market competition. Subjects become responsibilised when they are internally persuaded that social risks such as illness, unemployment, poverty, and lack of education or job training or career progression are problems whose solutions are the personal responsibility of the individual subject, not something the state is responsible for remedying by creating better conditions or support. Personal responsibility, a heterogeneous value with a long history, is transformed into a problem of 'self-care' best handled by economic 'rational' decision-making enacted by individuals for their 'best interests' (cf. Lemke, 2001, 2011, 2012). Responsibilisation quickens the folding together of the economic and social spheres while it narrows the criteria for rationality and conduct to what is economically advantageous within a competitive market ideologically imagined to be perfect and creating equal opportunity for all.

Of course, Foucault cannot be faulted for not taking into account developments after 1985. To understand the current globalised landscape of advanced liberalism we must recognise how the neoliberal model of social action Foucault described is being reworked through new forms of managerial discipline and regulation. These regulatory practices, rather than correcting market distortions as in the German social state model, often intensify the market model for state or institutional productivities, with mixed results worldwide. The discourse of responsibilisation has become a key practice within this combination of self-care and regulation, especially in higher education.

The language of entrepreneurial subjectivity and responsibilisation appears to empower individuals to take charge of their own circumstances ('self-care') in order to benefit themselves ('self-interest') and, according to the neoliberal imaginary, society at large. In neoliberal responsibilisation discourse individuals are autonomous agents, whose freedom is made possible primarily by the open economic field. The vocabulary of responsibilisation ('responsibility', 'initiative', 'innovation', 'opportunity', 'results', 'improvement') interpellates individuals as autonomous selves with decision-making power, while foreclosing opportunities for shared, collegial decision-making and cooperative work and integrating public and private domains in a totalising economic calculus preordained by government or institutional senior management on behalf of productivity targets.

Responsibilisation discourse organises the conduct of conduct by replacing both hierarchies of direct governance and horizontal, collaborative decision-making with benchmarks, standards, and targets established by a strategic plan, implemented by administrative authorities, and realised by persons who are monitored and audited for performance and results – the 'audit culture' (Power, 1999; Shore & Wright, 1999). Responsibilisation thus functions as a meta-discourse for constructing and interpellating 'responsible' subjects suited to the liberal socio-economic domain.

Recently, this liberal model of the economic person has morphed in many universities, corporate workplaces, and government bureaucracies into a 'neoliberalism in overdrive' with a strong authoritarian bent in low trust settings. Outcomes must be planned for, predicted, and risk managed. Employees cannot be trusted to decide, deliver, and evaluate on their own. Managers must reach their targets. In education, business, and the public sphere, rhetorics of enterprise and accountability import the discourse of responsibilisation to bring people into line. One effect of increasing responsibilisation criteria is increasing performance anxiety.

Much has happened since Foucault's lectures: Thatcherism, Reaganomics, Clinton and Blair's versions of neoliberalism; 9/11, the 'War on Terror', the 2008 Global Financial Crisis; state bailouts of private banks 'too big to fail'; the rise of Corporate Social Responsibility (CSR) programmes; more regulatory financial policies and austerity programmes imposed by the IMF, Eurozone, and other world financial organisations. Worldwide, universities compete for position in the 'education market' by increasing research 'productivity' ('outputs'), attracting more international students, creating a positive brand, and generating 'impact'. Schools and universities are more micro-managed with teacher-proof curriculums, high stakes assessment tools controlled at the state level, and increasing employment of instrumentalised teachers on non-tenure track, fixed-term, or part time contracts – the new 'flexible' academic workforce (Amsler & Amsler, 2014). Universities are increasingly subordinated by state funding schemes and some corporate and private donors to channel students into particular subjects. Administrations stimulate entrepreneurial researchers to secure external funding and commercialise research, 'seize opportunities', and 'achieve results'. For many research-intensive universities, commercialisation, external contracts, and generating new revenue streams from research or international student enrolment are the principal means for creating and sustaining an 'autonomous university', even though the rhetoric of 'research-informed teaching' maintains the image of the university as a site for teaching and learning based on creating new knowledge and helping students aspire and achieve.

For some, these post-1980 developments are welcome improvements on earlier liberal models. For instance, the idea of CSR puts a new spin on the discourse of responsibilisation and complicates the critique. Ronen Shamir (2008) defines responsibilisation positively as 'expecting and assuming the reflexive moral capacities of various social actors' (p. 7). He argues 'the moralization of markets' sustains, rather than undermines, 'neo-liberal visions of civil society, citizenship, and responsible social action' (p. 1). Shamir is optimistic about how embedding social activities in the market creates the possibility for civic responsibilisation. CSR policies provide incentives for commercial enterprises to behave in morally responsible and socially beneficial ways, even if citizens can't: 'democratic politics, addressing structural conditions and redistributive arrangements, is in decline. Instead, we are ushered into "politics via markets"' (pp. 13–14).

Not everyone agrees with Shamir's assessment of corporate social responsibility as commercially incentivised public social action controlled by business for business on behalf of society. For many, post-1980 neoliberal developments continue to whittle away any sense of shared responsibility, collective knowledge creation, collegiality, and humane planned state government. Shortly after Foucault's 1979 lectures, Michael Walzer (1983) argued we need a more 'decentralized democratic socialism' in state structures to foster and sustain 'communitarian values' beyond economic competition (p. 318). Democracy demands 'distributed decision-making'. Thomas Piketty (2014) and Joseph Stiglitz (2012) demonstrate how 300 years of western econo-political practices have exponentially increased wealth inequalities in societies in favour of the entrepreneurial few and their heirs. Pierre Bourdieu (1998) calls out neoliberal discourse more directly, pointing to the real and symbolic violence enacted by neoliberal policies on workers and families. Neoliberal discourse is a strong discourse maintained and supported by

> … all the powers of a world of power relations which it helps to make as it is, in particular by orienting the economic choices of those who dominate economic relations and so adding its own – specifically symbolic – force to those power relations. (p. 95)

Neoliberal discourse supports its 'arbitrary decisions' by hypocritically coopting key value words such as *trust, cooperation,* and *loyalty* at a time 'when the worker's unremitting commitment is obtained by sweeping away all temporal guarantees' in favour of casualisation, short-term hiring, corporate conformism, and responsibilisation (Bourdieu, 1998, pp. 98–99).

As many national governments reduce support for higher education or target programmes and research 'worth' investing in for institutional positioning, how is this neoliberal responsibilisation discourse and rationality being enacted in contemporary universities?

Responsibilising academics in the neoliberal university: The *Leadership Framework*

To address these questions, we present a case study where responsibilisation discourse is being mobilised to reshape academic work. The University of Auckland's *Leadership Framework* (hereafter 'LF') articulates an especially bold version of responsibilisation discourse. Using critical discourse analysis concepts and strategies, we unpack the said and unsaid in the LF documents and their contexts to show how the texts and paratexts function in a wider university discourse of responsibilisation.

Critical discourse analysis goes beyond description to critique the socio-political power relations produced or contested in text and talk. We unravel the language of the text (vocabulary, grammar), its texture and form (layout, formal features, local coherence), intertextualities (genre, style, echoes of other texts), and frame (how the text is situated in a domain). Critical discourse analysis explores the connections between what is said and what is implied in a text and the strategies for expressing or concealing meaning. It also interrogates text and talk to understand how they construct social relations, power, and dissent and create subjectivities (Fairclough, 1992; Gee, 2011; Van Dijk, 1993).

In July 2013 the University of Auckland, following similar actions among other 'World Ranked' universities, launched a new policy document called *Guide to The University of Auckland Leadership Framework* (hereafter 'GLF'), claiming the LF 'provides clarity and a shared vision of what leadership looks like at The University of Auckland' (UoA, 2013a, p. 3). By redefining all academic and administrative work, including research and publication, as part of 'leadership', the policy document seeks to mobilise staff, especially academic staff, 'to contribute their leadership skills to taking the University forward' (UoA, 2013a, p. 3). To these ends, the Vice-Chancellor announced he would make the LF a key feature of the university's 'Strategic Plan 2013–2020'. The LF would be 'incorporated into all new position descriptions during 2013/2014' and thereafter would become part of Academic Performance Reviews (UoA, 2013a, p. 5). The Leadership Framework and its discourse of responsibilisation thus sit squarely within the University administration's redescription and evaluation of academic work. Although the initial focus of the LF was professional staff and administrators, the Vice-Chancellor declared that the LF's performance matrix would become a totalising assessment tool for evaluating all university staff performance, academics, and non-academics (UoA, 2013a, p. 4).

How does the GLF document describe leader subjectivity? According to the GLF, 'personal leadership is at the heart of every role within our organization and is key to our success'. The LF's stated goal is to foster 'a culture of distributive leadership' in which 'all staff play a leadership role' (UoA, 2013a, pp. 4, 6), but the inclusive quantifier ('all') promises more widespread, horizontal staff engagement than is likely to occur.

The GLF document identifies five higher-level dimensions of leadership: *Exhibiting Personal Leadership, Setting Direction, Innovating and Engaging, Enabling People*, and *Achieving Results*. These benchmarks are presented in verbal phrases emphasising their operational imperatives. Each benchmark is also assigned a Māori-themed logo and name, supposedly demonstrating the university's commitment to inclusivity and New Zealand's official policy of biculturalism. The bilingual labelling implies, but without explicit support, that the leadership standards are consistent with Māori social norms, epistemology, and community goals (see Bargh, 2007).

'Exhibiting Personal Leadership' (Māori *Rangatiratanga*, 'chief + power/responsibility/ sovereignty') is symbolised by a koru (not yet unfurled as a silver fern), an image almost synonymous with Māroi iconography and New Zealand national identity. The document's key attributes of personal leadership epitomise the rhetoric of self-care and manageable entrepreneurship we have identified: 'displays integrity and professionalism', 'builds and demonstrates self-insight', 'adapts to change', 'shows personal courage', and 'demonstrates university citizenship' (UoA, 2013a, p. 7).

The second dimension, 'Setting Direction' (*Mana Tohu*, 'control of direction', also the Māori title of the *New Zealand Qualifications Authority* [NZQA], which governs school curriculum standards) is represented by the Southern Cross constellation, also depicted on the New Zealand flag. *Setting Direction* idealises the individual who 'displays an understanding of the international and commercial context in which the University operates' (UoA, 2013a, p. 8). The 'capabilities' of senior leaders are translated here primarily into the language of global commercial expectations. While mention is made of 'deliver[ing] programmes, teaching and learning, research and service', those core academic activities are buried deep within a global, commercial discourse of responsibilisation. Word counts matter discursively. In the GLF, *strategy/strategic* occurs 27 times; *research* 11 times; *commercial* 4 times (3 times in headlines or rubrics, 2 times collocated with *acumen*); *teaching* 3 times; *political* 1 time; *citizenship* 1 time; *social* 1 time; *society* 0 times.

The ideal 'senior professor-as-leader' must exhibit additional qualities and action on an institutional or international scale, including: 'demonstrates an understanding of the competitive global environment and key market drivers … and uses this understanding to create and seize opportunities, expand into new markets and deliver programmes … '; 'displays behaviours of a leader who demonstrates global and commercial acumen'; 'leads and inspires innovation'; 'pursues ambitious ventures'; 'advocates and clearly articulates the University's aspirations, objectives and values' (UoA, 2013a, p. 8).

The LF's third dimension of leadership is 'Innovating and Engaging' (Māori *Whakamatara*, a polysemous verb that usually means 'loosen', 'put apart', or 'translate' but can mean antithetically 'weave together'), represented by the image of a woven flax mat. As icon, the completed mat invokes one of the verb's less frequent antithetical meanings. The innovating and engaging leader demonstrates interactional behaviours such as: 'Establishes and maintains effective working relationships with stakeholders'; 'us[es] an appropriate interpersonal style to advance the University's objectives'; [and for senior staff] 'identifies strategic opportunities, formulates action plans, and leverages own areas' expertise to add value elsewhere in the University'; 'facilitates and supports University changes needed to adapt to changing external/market demands'; 'addresses barriers to resistance' (UoA, 2013a, p. 9). What sort of institutional 'resistance' is meant remains undefined.

The fourth dimension, 'Enabling People' (Māori *Hapai*, 'handle, promote' [v.]) represented by the fantail (also a harbinger of death in Māori mythology), highlights the University's equity goals and aspirations, including collegiality, respect for others, and inclusiveness. These are important social, progressive, and nurturing values, but the GLF document aligns them with the more instrumental goal of 'developing self, others and teams so they can realise the University's strategy and values' (UoA, 2013a, p. 10). The institutional enterprise underpins and legitimates all individual and group behaviours. The document's persistent reference to 'the University' begs the question, *who* is 'the University'? For management, the institution is portrayed as unproblematically homogeneous, monolithic, and united around an uncontested, shared set of goals and values (Shore & Taitz, 2012). The idea of competing or contested policies or interests is foreclosed in the GLF document.

The fifth leadership dimension, 'Achieving Results' (Māori *haihua*, 'bloom' [v.]), symbolised by a traditional Māori watercraft (*waka*), emphasises accepting 'accountability for making decisions and taking action to deliver the University's strategy ... ', targeting opportunities, and establishing 'stretch objectives/goals'. The Achiever is someone who:

> Sets high objectives for personal/group accomplishment, uses measurement methods to monitor progress toward goals, tenaciously works to meet or exceed goals managing resources responsibly, seeks continuous improvement. (UoA, 2013a, p. 11)

The supplemental *Continuing Capability Development Guide* (hereafter 'LFG') embeds the LF in practice and provides staff with self-help instructions for making the LF part of their workplace toolkit: 'Consider the exploration of the guide as an on-going process rather than a one-off event'. It advises:

> Try cutting and pasting suggestions from the Guide into your Outlook calendar as a regular 5–15 minute appointment with yourself ... be sure to allow time to inspire yourself and to inspire and enable others. (UoA, 2013b, p. 4)

These documents conflate two different rationalities underpinning institutional managerial discourse. One is a neoliberal ethics of personal responsibility in which autonomous, self-disciplined, engaged individuals are expected to tailor their behaviours to a programme of continuous self-monitoring and improvement, similar to Foucault's 'self-care' or 'reflexive projects of the self' (Dean, 2010). However, individual empowerment is combined with institutional power through a system of monitoring that aligns institutional norms, expectations, and rewards with the self-monitoring of an individual's own performance. As Dean (2010) shows, such a regime works to increase the range of authoritarian dominance via responsibilisation. The second rationality is a commercially oriented, financialised vision of the academic 'leader' as a business-savvy, calculating entrepreneur, a dynamic innovator who displays the skills of an inspirational risk-taker and 'demonstrates global and commercial acumen'. Senior leaders are distinguished from junior leaders by the breadth and depth of their commercial and global productivity. At the top of the structure are Leaders of Leaders.

As noted earlier, the *Leadership Framework* rarely uses terms traditionally associated with core university activities: teaching, learning, scholarship, curriculum. Research is embedded within the University's strategic objectives and commercial acumen. Instead, the successful senior university leader:

> Translates strategic priorities into operational reality and drives high standards for own and others' accomplishment; creates alignment to ensure activities produce measurable and sustainable results; tenaciously works to meet or exceed challenging objectives; maintains fiscal responsibilities and seeks continuous improvements for all levels. (UoA, 2013a, p. 11)

The language of the document is referential at the level of managerial strategies and performance reports, not academic work. Nouns such as *activities, standards, objectives, responsibilities, improvements* become roadsigns for responsibilised behaviour. Fiscal 'responsibility' is linked with 'tenacious' efforts to 'achieve results'. But how do these benchmarks of 'excellence' map onto a humanities research project, a new ethics course in environmental studies, a multidisciplinary course exploring climate change, a student mentoring programme for nontraditional students in primary education, or a local arts programme driven by University staff? How are the nominated leadership behaviours concretised in academic teaching, research, service, and community engagement? Informally, many colleagues have told us their academic heads and directors have cajoled them not to get too involved with community activities, public engagement, or university governance because these distract from their job. The document's alleged 'clarity' lies in its idealised description of responsibilised leadership keyed to the University's strategic plan and restructuring of academic work.

Textually and paratextually, the GLF and LFG documents position official institutional discourse as assistance for users. The user is often addressed in the second person, even as the profile of the successful 'leader' is presented in the abstract third person. The GLF document is replete with bullet points, indigenous icons, a university-approved blue colour scheme, and a sleek online visual format, consistent with other University documents meant for staff. The GLF's gridsheet layout coordinates an individual's institutional position (junior, senior) with capabilities (*expectations*), behaviours (*seeks, encourages, achieves*), and attitudes (*tenaciously*) to encode a calculus of 'self-care' leading to institutional success.

How then does the *Leadership Framework* move beyond earlier neoliberal forms of governmentality? Our research found that the LF was modelled on initiatives developed in other major research universities, including the Universities of Sydney, Melbourne, Hong Kong, Bristol, Manchester, Toronto, University College London, University of California-Berkeley, and UCLA.[1] Some phrases and sentences in the LF appear to be taken wholesale without citation from other university HR websites.[2] The GLF document's intertextual echoes illustrate the dominance of managerial corporate discourse as a practice for restructuring academic work in contemporary research universities.

The GLF document is situated within a wider project to integrate all staff activities under the 'university leadership' rubric. The Senior Management Team ('SMT') – which recently changed its name to Senior Leadership Team ('SLT') – has used the implementation of neoliberal managerial principles and market ideology to radically reframe academic work. Even senior HR staff in the university are critical of the way in which the LF model, with its 'tick-box' approach to skills, competences, and expectations, has been implemented. As one senior HR official we interviewed noted, the explicit emphasis on commercialisation and entrepreneurship was something the Vice-Chancellor insisted upon, against the advice of others in the SLT at the time.[3]

The ideological subtext of the GLF and LFG documents emerges concretely when we compare them with one of their intertexts: the work of Professor Geoff Scott, Emeritus Professor of Higher Education and Sustainability and former Pro Vice-Chancellor for Quality at the University of Western Sydney. Following the publication of his influential report, 'Learning leaders in times of change' (Scott, Coates, & Anderson, 2008), Scott was brought to New Zealand in 2009 to run workshops on academic leadership and strategies for remaking university culture into a more managed corporate culture. His report recommends that universities identify the 'performance indicators and capabilities for effective performance', develop 'cost effective ways of assessing academic leadership potential and the capabilities that count', and ensure that 'change implementation in higher education be part of every orientation and development program' (2008, p. xix). Scott further advises university managers to 'listen in particular to "resistors"' in order to 'identify the "trip-wires" that must be overcome' (2008, p. xviii). This is risk management, not dialogue. Conspicuously, the LF documents omit any mention of Scott's other key argument, that 'emotional intelligence' and 'empathising' are the most critical competences for academic leadership (2008, pp. xv, 69).

Initially, the proposed project was entitled 'Academic Leadership Framework', but that was shortened to *Leadership Framework*. The Vice-Chancellor decided to adapt the LF to include academic as well as professional (administrative) staff and align it with the University Strategic Plan (2013–2020), particularly Objective 3: *'an environment in which distributed leadership is developed and valued'*. The University's Strategic Plan, although presented as a collaborative document shaped by the institution's constituent interests, was already embedding the ideationally dissonant concept of 'distributed leadership' as a prelude to the LF. This is an example of 'managerial synchronicity'. The Vice-Chancellor also wanted to incorporate the LF documents into his new, highly controversial Academic Standards regime for academic promotions. As the Vice-Chancellor was developing his *Leadership Framework* (2011–2012), University managers were involved in a difficult industrial dispute with academics employed under a collective agreement. The VC's new Academic Standards policy (which now included the LF) was implemented in 2013 for academic staff employed on individual contracts. However, when he attempted to apply these new Academic Standards to staff covered by the collective agreement, the academic union sued the Vice-Chancellor in the national Employment Relations Authority to retain their existing promotions procedures outlined in the collective agreement. After a decision in favour of the union, a further review of the promotions policy, and a second decision in favour of the Vice-Chancellor with respect to the conduct of the review, the dispute continues (as of August 2015), pending appeal. Nonetheless, the Vice-Chancellor went ahead and implemented the Academic Standards with the LF for all academic staff beginning in 2015.

We see the LF as exemplifying a 'post-neoliberal' responsibilisation discourse. By 'post-neoliberal' we do not mean transcending neoliberal market rationality; rather, the LF marks further entrenchment and institutional centralisation of that logic, with the addition of more authoritarian modes of governing to reshape academic behaviours (cf. Dean, 2010). The LF not only deploys responsibilisation as a 'reflexive project' of the self; it also seeks to produce responsibilised self-managing subjects by explicitly harnessing individual activities and roles to the institution's financial and managerial imperatives so that staff are rendered *responsible* for acting *tenaciously* to deliver the performance targets assigned to them and those they manage and *monitor*. The GLF document enjoins disciplinary technologies of the self with more authoritarian, instrumentalising modes of supervised production, managerial oversight, and audit.

This kind of stringent surveillance-based production system is not new. One version was developed more than 20 years ago in Britain and used extensively in private-sector corporations like British Telecom (MacKenzie, 2000). It reactivates a form of Taylorism and strict time-management organisation of private-sector production. Increasingly, such policies and models for delivering targeted outcomes are being introduced into the management of higher education, especially those universities with global public faces whose research activities are directly linked to their position in international university rankings. In the LF, university leaders, administrators, academics, and support staff, are held responsible for the activities of those under their charge as well as their own. Do they inspire people, or coerce them? Do they encourage others, or demand results? Do they seek out opportunities for engagement and research, or implement university-directed enterprises? The LF produces audited implementers more than empowered decision makers.

What concept of personhood does this model of academic leadership entail? The LF's responsibilising rhetoric interpellates a new academic subject, the responsible entrepreneur who must follow externally imposed targets and performance criteria legitimated by 'academic standards' and fulfil what is 'expected' by the managing authorities who speak in the name of the institution. The LF's gridsheet polices both the self *and* others. It institutes a language not for *recognising* but *prescribing* one's behaviours and attitudes in conformity with stated institutional objectives. The document encourages staff to align their behaviours to the commercial and managerial goals of 'the University' and define themselves as entrepreneurs with or without commercialisable outcomes.

The phrase 'the University', an agent noun in managerial discourse, has been disputed by University of Auckland academics since the 2011 industrial action (Shore & Taitz, 2012). It continues to be a contested phrase. In a November 2013 meeting of union academics and a deputy vice-chancellor to review academic policies, one lecturer challenged the administrator's use of the phrase by saying, 'The University is all of us', to which the administrator replied, 'I'm not so sure about that'.[4]

In the name of 'clarity', the GLF inscribes academics' professional behaviour as a set of expected outcomes headed by activity verbs and attitudinal adjectives and adverbs prescribed by top-down corporate management and instrumentalisation of the workforce. Neither Max Weber's 'iron cage' of bureaucracy nor the dead hand of rationalisation really describes what we read in the LF documents. Rather, the GLF document and the regime it structures read like a transparent 'glass prison' of accountability and punitive responsibilisation, a disciplinary strategy for governance that imagines its proactive, self-driven workforce simultaneously individualised, totalised, and permanently auditable against a set of externally imposed performance indicators benchmarked to mostly financial or market-driven objectives as determined by the SLT.

As we later discovered, the GLF document was drafted by an external management consultancy firm, Development Dimensions International, which may partly explain the document's managerial rhetoric and corporate tone.[5] However, the document's emphasis on verbalised entrepreneurial skills ('seize opportunities'), measurable competences ('achieve results'), and self-discipline ('tenaciously') was something the Vice-Chancellor reportedly insisted upon.[6]

The *Leadership Framework* is an institutional manifestation of a new form of neoliberal discourse, contradictory, high functioning, and relentless. In this model 'governing at a distance' is organised centrally through objectives, standards, norms, and evaluation, and then rationalised as responding to market forces and financial calculation in order to achieve institutional 'autonomy'. However, institutional *autonomy* seems to mean the university becoming as fully privatised and self-funded as possible.[7] At the same time, the LF documents describe academic work obliquely as the production of commodities ('outputs'), goods, and services (students, research outputs, external grants), which are monetised or assessed as the 'expected' outcomes from the distribution of institutional roles.

For such a discourse, the rhetorical challenge is to get employees to drink the KoolAid of responsibilisation in the name of enhancing the institution or state economy. The semantic force of value words such as 'initiative', 'responsibility', 'tenacious', 'higher', 'improve', 'encourage', and 'accountability' is pegged to actions which serve 'the University's strategy', 'improve and progress the University', 'realise the University's strategy and values', 'deliver the University's strategy and deliver excellent results' (UoA, 2013a, p. 6). The deputy vice-chancellor's questioning of the claim 'We all are the university' is consistent with the discourse ideology of the LF.

The GLF document reveals how the discourse of *responsibilisation* in managerial text and talk appropriates the vocabulary of empowerment, individual initiative, and accountability to rationalise structures and relations which empower some, usually institutional managers and employers, over others, mostly employees, academics, and administrative staff. Nonetheless, neither the verb *empower* nor the derived noun *empowerment* appear in the document, unlike other texts of responsibilisation discourse which do use the rhetoric of empowerment to describe their programmatic goals. For example, OECD and UN projects explicitly state they intend to *empower* underprivileged or disadvantaged groups, often women, in societies through microfinancing and other bottom-up social entrepreneurial schemes (Ilcan & Lacey, 2011).

The LF discourse avoids empowerment goals, often associated with progressivism, in favour of a more euphemistic rhetoric of 'leadership'. It constructs all University employees as 'leaders', while simultaneously itemising what is 'expected' of each staff member. The LF's discourse of responsibilisation is central to a new integrated regime for managing, prescribing, and measuring academic work, as reflected in the Vice-Chancellor's 2014 letter to successful applicants for promotion to Professor and Associate Professor. The final paragraph reads:

> I look forward to working with you as you assume greater leadership within your discipline and within the University. Please be assured that the University values deeply the service of its Associate Professors and Professors. As a community of scholars, we are reliant upon the contribution and leadership that those in the Professoriate are able to provide.[8]

Conclusions: responsibilised, entrepreneurial academics and the future of the university

In our critical analysis we have described how a particular discourse in higher education focused on leadership and responsibility is being developed in ways that both reproduce and transcend the rationality of neoliberal governmentality as analysed by Foucault. We believe critical discourse analysis provides us with a way to read against the said and expose the unsaid, to critique the ideologies inherent in official higher education texts and policies that aim to capture power and sustain dominance in the institution and public sphere. Based on our analysis we draw several key conclusions about the current and future trajectory of responsibilisation discourse and its effects on higher education.

1. Redefining academic work

Leadership is increasingly a code word for self-managed, *entrepreneurial* academics. The *Leadership Framework* and the discourse of responsibilisation it manifests participate in a wider set of institutional policies and practices seeking to monitor academic staff and redescribe professional intellectual work so they are more closely identified with values, technologies, and logics of entrepreneurial capitalism in the name of 'excellence', 'autonomy', and market position.

2. Eroding academic values

Our analysis of one particular responsibilisation regime exemplifies how this contemporary version of governmentality in free market overdrive fails, perhaps deliberately, to capture important aspects of academic work. The LF gridsheet of performance expectations does not, indeed cannot recognise or account for the diverse creative, empowering, and caring ways teachers, researchers, and support staff do the core business of academic work without ticking the boxes of leadership competences. Nor are the stipulated standards for academic 'leadership' adequate to academics' engagement with schools, communities, and nonprofit groups, their commitments to union, political, and community activism, or their contributions to government programmes, many kinds of non-governmental agencies, and various media conversations. Ignoring university governance and collegial dialogue as legitimate academic responsibilities, the GLF document refers to an ideologically imagined space of academic work based on the 'economic team player'. Where is the measuring stick for *tenacity*? Are all university contributions to be assessed against the institution's position in world rankings? How do academics' different life circumstances contribute to their effectiveness as teachers, researchers, and mentors? Where are shared governance and collaborative (distributed) responsibility and decision-making within a highly centralised, less than transparent regime of standards, competences, and targets?

3. Disciplinary technologies and responsibilised subjects

The GLF document seeks to operationalise a wider university discourse of responsibilisation as part of 'post-neoliberal governmentality'. It adapts and conflates self-responsibilisation with a coercive, non-democratically developed matrix of standards, strategies, and objectives that determine what is 'recognisable' (expected) academic activity. The GLF gridsheet integrated into a total management structure moves deceptively but simply from junior to senior academics in a series of widening concentric circles, from discipline, school, and faculty to institutional, national, and international 'impact', always with the university's 'position' and financial advantage as the ultimate goals. Texts, talk, and practices legitimated and prescribed by the LF render invisible and unrecognised many traditional and important aspects of academic intellectual work: strong critique and testing of received ideas, open and vigorous debate to ascertain truth, collegial pedagogy and research, shared governance, individual and collective empowerment at the local level, professional judgement, ideational innovation, independent and sometimes dissenting scholarship, and public intellectual and artistic engagement. The new responsibilised institutional environment makes it difficult for academics, teachers, and researchers to act as critics and conscience of society, which the New Zealand Education Act (1979) defines as a fundamental role of the university in society.

4. Imagining alternatives

Our critique suggests that alternatives to responsibilisation are not some nostalgic return to an imagined golden age of the university and academic freedom. Specifically, we endorse alternative models for a modern university committed to academic and philosophical, not just economic, autonomy, a university responsible to collective decision-making, committed to creating and disseminating publicly responsive and socially useful research and teaching, and motivated by an educational philosophy whose objectives are social empowerment, progressive knowledge creation, and the ongoing critique of received ideas. Unfortunately, the GLF document and its intertexts don't promise that kind of critical conversation. Democratic innovation, shared governance, and decentralised decision-making among university staff and management might. Is that irresponsible?[9]

Notes

1. See, *inter alia*, the following universities' Human Resources websites: http://www.hr.uq.edu.au/leadership-development: http://www.odlc.utoronto.ca/:nhttp://www.ucl.ac.uk/hr/osd/resources/competencies.php: http://hrweb.berkeley.edu/sites/default/files/attachments/LeadershipCompetencyModel.pdf: https://hr.unimelb.edu.au/__data/assets/pdf_file/0011/383717/hr-policy-framework.pdf: http://www.ucl.ac.uk/hr/osd/resources/competencies.php: http://map.ais.ucla.edu/portal/site/UCLA/menuitem.789d0eb6c76e7ef0d66b02ddf848344a/?vgnextoid=a728afba00c42010VgnVCM1000008f8443a4RCRD
2. Notably, the University of Berkeley, California. See http://hrweb.berkeley.edu/sites/default/files/attachments/LeadershipCompetencyModel.pdf. Retrieved 25 January 2015.
3. Interviews, University of Auckland, 28 August 2014.
4. M. Amsler, personal communication.
5. http://www.ddiworld.com/company#.VMRXB75BmfQ.
6. Interview, 28 August 2014.
7. Vice-Chancellor presentation, Head of Tāmaki Innovation Campus Seminar Series, 2 August 2013.
8. M. Amsler, personal communication, 9 December 2014.
9. Since research and writing for this essay were completed (January 2015), the University administration has revised the *Leadership Framework* and online supporting documents (www.auckland.ac.nz/leadershipframework; accessed 27 September 2015). At least one 2013 document (hr-38s) is no longer available. New versions of the LF documents specifically targeted to academics are titled '5D Leadership Capabilities for Lecturer, Senior Lecturer, Research Fellow, Professional Teaching Fellow and Senior Tutors' and '5D Leadership Capabilities for Senior Academic Leaders Associate Professor and Professor, Academic Head and Dean' (2015c = https://www.staff.auckland.ac.nz/assets/staff/HR/career-development/documents/5D%20Leadership%20for%20Academics.pdf). These new documents outline in micro detail the responsibilities and expectations for academic 'leadership' at each rank. Most of the structure, language, and format of the new documents or versions remain the same as in the two LF documents discussed here, but a few changes are worth mentioning. First, the new title of the LF reflects the University administration's increased reliance on commercial/corporate models and frameworks for organisation in higher education. The newly titled University of Auckland '5D Leadership' model may or may not be derived from Scott Campbell and Ellen Samiec's popular, business-directed text 5D *Leadership: Key Dimensions for Leading in the Real World* (2005). Second, the new gridsheets for '5D Leadership Capabilities' for junior and senior academics each identify 24 categories of capabilities and behaviours, two of which refer to 'Scholarship/Professional Development' and one to 'teaching and learning'.

References

Amsler, M., & Amsler, S. (2014). Imagining unthinkable spaces. *Argos Aotearoa: A Journal of Place/Politics, 1*(1), 102–109.
Ball, S. J. (2012). *Foucault, power, and education*. London: Routledge.
Bargh, M. (Ed.). (2007). *Resistance: An indigenous response to neoliberalism*. Wellington: Huia.
Bourdieu, P. (1998). *Acts of resistance: Against the new myths of our time*. (R. Nice, Trans.). Cambridge: Polity.
Dean, M. (2010). *Governmentality: Power and rule in modern society* (2nd rev. ed.). London, New York: Sage.
Fairclough, N. (1992). *Discourse and social change*. Cambridge: Polity.

Foucault, M. (1991). Governmentality. In G. Burchell, C. Gordon, & P. Miller (Eds.), *The Foucault effect: Studies in governmentality* (pp. 87–104). Chicago: University of Chicago Press.

Foucault, M. (2008). *Birth of biopolitics: Lectures at the Collège de France 1978–1979*. (M. Senellart and G. Burchell, Trans.). Houndsmill, Basingstoke: Palgrave.

Gee, J. P. (2011). *An introduction to discourse analysis* (3rd ed.). New York: Routledge.

Ilcan, S., & Lacey, A. (2011). *Governing the poor: Exercises of poverty reduction, practices of global aid*. Montreal and London: McGill-Queen's University Press.

Lemke, T. (2001). The birth of bio-politics: Michel Foucault's lecture at the Collège de France on neo-liberal governmentality. *Economy and Society*, 30(2), 190–207. doi:10.1080/03085140120042271

Lemke, T. (2011). *Biopolitics: An advanced introduction*. New York: New York University Press.

Lemke, T. (2012). *Foucault, governmentality, and critique*. Boulder, CO: Paradigm.

MacKenzie, R. (2000). Subcontracting and the reregulation of the employment relationship: A case study from the telecommunications industry. *Work Employment & Society*, 14(4), 707–726. doi:10.1177/09500170022118699

Miller, P. (2001). Governing by numbers: Why calculative practices matter. *Social research*, 68(2), 379–396.

Olssen, M., & Peters, M. (2005). Neoliberalism, higher education and the knowledge economy: From the free market to knowledge capitalism. *Journal of Education Policy*, 20(3), 313–345.

Peters, M. (2001). Education, enterprise culture and the entrepreneurial self: A Foucauldian perspective. *Journal of Educational Enquiry*, 2(2), 58–72.

Piketty, T. (2014). *Capital in the twenty-first century*. Cambridge, MA: Belknap Press.

Power, M. (1999). *The audit society: Rituals of verification* (2nd rev. ed.). Oxford: Oxford University Press.

Rose, N., & Miller, P. (1992). Political power beyond the state: Problematics of government. *British Journal of Sociology*, 43(2), 173–205.

Scott, G., Coates, H., & Anderson, M. (2008). *Learning leaders in times of change: Academic leadership capabilities for Australian higher education*. Sydney: Australian Council for Education Research. Retrieved January 15, 2015, from ACER website: http://research.acer.edu.au/higher_education

Shamir, R. (2008). The age of responsibilisation: On market-embedded morality. *Economy and Society*, 37(1), 1–19. doi:10.1080/03085140701760833

Shore, C., & Taitz, M. (2012). Who 'owns' the university? Institutional autonomy and academic freedom in an age of knowledge capitalism. *Globalisation, Societies and Education*, 10(2), 201–219.

Shore, C., & Wright, S. (1999). Audit culture and anthropology: Neo-liberalism in British higher education. *Journal of the Royal Anthropological Institute*, 5(4), 557–575.

Stiglitz, J. (2012). *The price of inequality*. New York: W.W. Norton.

University of Auckland (UoA). (2013a). *Guide to the University of Auckland leadership framework*. Auckland: University of Auckland. Retrieved April 1, 2015, from https://cdn.auckland.ac.nz/assets/staff/how-the-university-works/documents/Guide%20to%20the%20Leadership%20Framework%20-%20Capabilities%20Defined.pdf

University of Auckland (UoA). (2013b). *The leadership framework: Continuing capability development guide*. Auckland: University of Auckland. Retrieved April 1, 2015, from https://cdn.auckland.ac.nz/assets/staff/HR/career-development/documents/Continuing%20Capability%20Development%20Guide%20booklet%20layout%20March%202014.pdf

Van Dijk, T. (1993). Principles of critical discourse analysis. *Discourse and Society*, 4(2), 249–283. doi:10.1177/0957926593004002006

Walzer, M. (1983). *Spheres of justice: A defence of pluralism and equality*. New York: Basic Books.

From State responsibility for education and welfare to self-responsibilisation in the market

Michael A. Peters

The papers in this collection, each in their own way, express a concern for analysing and charting the effects of the process called 'responsibilisation' in the realm of education which, as the name implies, means 'making responsible'. Often, the use of the term is associated with Foucault's analysis of neoliberal governmentality, though not exclusively. Foucault provides a nuanced reading that comes from naturalising and historicising Kant. In doing so, he is also emphasising some continuity between liberalism, with its accent on individual autonomy, and neoliberalism that also stresses individuality and rationality from a perspective of self-interest where greater good is a result of the 'invisible hand'. Sometimes the term has also been used by others embracing Ulrich Beck's concept of the 'risk society' and an analysis of the neoliberal state. Such analysis critiques the state as privatising and individualising social provision with the use of market-like arrangements, through contracting-out, public–private partnerships, user-pays, and other parallel mechanisms for the privatisation of the social welfare state.

Using various theoretical approaches, the essays that constitute this collection tackle the question of responsibilisation in different ways, showing the diversity of its forms and the extent of its influence. Mark Amsler and Cris Shore examine the discourse of 'distributed leadership' as a form of responsibilisation that becomes a technology of indirect management in redescribing academic work in a neoliberal environment. Using Deleuze's work with control societies, Julie Allan and Deborah Youdell theorise the UK government's new approach to special educational needs and disability as 'emergent modulations of the societies of control'. William G. Tierney and Daniel J. Almeida develop a 'cultural politics of integrity' to reframe academic responsibility in the name of social engagement, and Harry Torrance examines the way that 'students and teachers have been "responsibilised" for the quality and outcomes of education', a process he describes as 'blaming the victim'. With a focus on young people, Peter Kelly explores the self as enterprise and the practice of freedom that carries with it the weight of responsibility that, since the Global Financial Crisis, leads to mortgaging an uncertain future. Julie McLeod, in her chapter 'Reframing responsibility in educational work in an era of self-responsibilisation', utilises feminist theories of care to reconsider teachers' work. In an interesting chapter full of nuances, Mary Lou Rasmussen examines the conflicts that young people experience in 'responding well' to homophobia and transphobia. Shaun Rawolle, Julie Rowlands, and Jill Blackmore examine the implications of different forms of contractualism for the responsibilisation of higher education in Australia, and Christine Halse examines the question of responsibility for racism in her discussion of the everyday talk of secondary students, wherein different modes of speech are discovered that reflect the weight of the past.

The collection, the first of its kind in education to my knowledge, demonstrates the analytical power of approaches that utilise the concept of responsibilisation to analyse the shift from state responsibility under the old, Keynesian, welfare state to a responsibilisation of teachers, students and associated forms of discourse, accountability, and assessment regimes. Each chapter also shows how market-like arrangements and a market rationality have been employed to responsibilise the individual and to naturalise regimes of self-care in neoliberal environments.

At the same time, one senses that the focus of the collection on the twin themes of responsibility and responsibilisation has been deliberately seditious: to disrupt the universalisation of responsibilisation as a practice and universal characterisation of education. This may well be the collection's key contribution. Many of the articles in this collection take a line that reflects the reponsibilisation literature and Foucault's influence. Yet, there is still room for further theoretical work here beyond its simple application, especially in relation to the construction of student identities (Keddie, 2016). Others in the collection – Rasmussen, McLeod, Halse, Rawolle, Hartung – rightly caution against conflating responsibility with responsibilisation. Of course, these are different concepts that originate in different 'moral' traditions. While responsibilisation aligns with a neoliberal technology of the self that forces an individualism on society and exports responsibility from state to individual, it has not been taken up by all players in education, particularly young people and teachers. They teach us that responsibility remains central to interpersonal relations – how could we possibly escape it? – and that the matter of *who* is responsible cannot be excised from history or social context.

There is some consensus on the way market-like structures and social provision delivered through the market leads to individualisation and privatisation of both welfare and the self. Shamir (2008) comments on the nature of market-embedded rationality:

> Generally recognized and referred to in terms of privatization, deregulation, structural adjustment and corporatization, the economization of the political transforms the very instruments of public authority, replacing laws with guidelines, relying on self- and reflexive regulation and treating normative prescriptions in general as commodities that are to be produced, distributed and consumed by a host of agencies, enterprises and non-profit organizations. (p. 1)

As he goes on to explain, commercial enterprises progressively take on tasks that 'were once considered to reside within the civic domain of moral entrepreneurship and the political domain of the caring welfare state, dispensing social goods other than profits to constituencies other than their shareholders' (p. 1). In this regard, we can cite the case of Serco, an international service company that operates in public service markets around the world with 100,000 employees in over 30 countries, a company that is active in both Australia and New Zealand especially in running private prisons at a profit.[1]

Shamir (2008) discusses the moralisation of markets that also 'entails the economisation of morality; a process which is compatible with the general neoliberal drive to ground social relations in the economic rationality of markets' (p. 3). Responsibilisation is one of the major strategies and practices of a neoliberal moralisation of markets that shifts responsibility from the state (the so-called welfare state) to the citizen – the user of social services, the citizen-consumer, the client such as students, pensioners, beneficiaries – and to professionals who are 'responsible' for providing the service.

In the new market environment, the figure of the entrepreneur becomes paramount in understanding the rise of a new individualism that strips away all collective value and responsibilises individuals to take care of themselves through enhanced choice-making in the market place. In these new arrangements, the state forces responsibility and responsibilisation on the individual, on families, and on professionals. It steps back from active social provision to devise juridical frameworks that set up the rules governing social distribution and set criteria for their continual monitoring and performativity.

The concept of 'responsibilisation' originally emerged out of the context of so-called Governmentality Studies. It is now widely used in various social sciences to describe a governing technology, particularly attuned to the challenge of neoliberalism, that is focused on the central question of how to govern free individuals and relies heavily on individual choice, freedom, and responsibility.

In the *Sage Dictionary of Policing*, O'Malley (2009), one of the leading Australian neo-Foucaudian theorists, defines responsibilisation as:

> … a term developed in the governmentality literature to refer to the process whereby subjects are rendered individually responsible for a task which previously would have been the duty of another – usually a state agency – or would not have been recognized as a responsibility at all. The process is strongly associated with neoliberal political discourses, where it takes on the implication that the subject being responsibilized has avoided this duty or the responsibility has been taken away from them in the welfare-state era and managed by an expert or government agency. (p. 276)

He explains that the term surfaces first in the 1990s governmentality literature to describe the neoliberal assumption that the old welfare state has robbed citizens of their independence and made them dependent on the state. The neoliberal strategy was used to reverse this process, to make subjects responsible for themselves and to take responsibility for governing themselves and their lives. This 'reversal' of responsibility is often dressed up in the catch words 'no rights without obligations'. He details the application of the responsibilisation strategy in the field of criminal justice by making subjects more cautious of becoming victims, by instituting government-community programmes like neighbourhood watch, turning the public into crime reporters, vigilantes, and surveillance operators, and holding offenders themselves responsible for their actions not only through tougher penalties but also through community consultations with their victims.

O'Malley (1992) reviews the critique of the neoliberal strategy as 'victim blaming' as the State devolves its responsibilities. He also points out that responsibilisation does find willing support from both the political Left and Right which criticise the state and look for greater citizen involvement, control, and responsibility (see also O'Malley & Palmer, 1996).

Neoliberal governmentality is a pragmatic, evolving form of post-welfare state politics in which the state systematically downscales its responsibilities, outsourcing 'well-being' and 'social security' to its citizen-subjects in the market, at the same time emphasising the concept of 'choice'. The subject, according to neoliberalism, is theorised as a rational, autonomous individual in all its behaviour – *Homo economicus* ('economic man') – that is expected to 'look after herself' modelled on assumptions of individuality, rationality, and self-interest. These highly abstract assumptions of *Homo economicus* reveal the limitations of a kind of economic rationality that does not take into account gender, collective dimensions, or cultural variation in the everyday economic management and decision-making of households and groups.

Somewhat curiously, in some ways this argument gels with arguments mounted in the 1960s and 1970s that were a critique of state power as exercised through big centralised institutions. Arguments concerning deinstitutionalisation, alongside arguments for community devolution and control, were being proposed by Ivan Illich, Michel Foucault, and David Cooper in fields of mental health, medicine, and education ('deschooling'). Under neoliberalism, state power and authority is rejigged in terms of the marketplace where the citizen subject is provided a kind of freedom through making consumer choices in the marketplace for all aspects of social welfare and provision.

The central aim of neoliberal governmentality ('the conduct of conduct') is the manufacture of social conditions that encourage and necessitate the production of *Homo economicus* as an historically specific form of subjectivity, constituted as a free and autonomous individual of self-interest. Such production is based on the following three assumptions: the classical liberal assumptions of individuality, and of rationality, and of free-interest, as developed through the work of Adam Smith. The neoliberal subject is, thus, an individual who is transparent to itself, and morally responsible for navigating the social realm using rational choice and cost–benefit calculations. This subjectivity is a new kind of prudentialism or actuarial rationality grounded on market-based principles to the exclusion of all other ethical values and social interests.

Homo economicus is no longer a partner in exchange but, as Foucault writes, 'Homo economicus is an entrepreneur, an entrepreneur of himself' (Foucault, 2008, p. 226). Hamann (2009) argues:

> the central aim of neoliberal governmentality is the strategic production of social conditions conducive to the constitution of *Homo economicus*, a specific form of subjectivity with historical roots in traditional liberalism. However, whereas liberalism posits 'economic man' as a 'man of exchange', neoliberalism strives to ensure that individuals are compelled to assume market-based values in all of their judgments and practices in order to amass sufficient quantities of 'human capital' and thereby become 'entrepreneurs of themselves'. Neoliberal Homo economicus is a free and autonomous 'atom' of self-interest who is fully responsible for navigating the social realm using rational choice and cost-benefit calculation to the express exclusion of all other values and interests. (p. 38)

The construction of *Homo economicus* leads to a double strategy. On the one hand, there is the economisation of state and civil society institutions. On the other hand, there is the moralisation of the market where the primary shift in responsibility is away from the state – a state-shedding of responsibility while retaining the power to strike norms of assessment and control – towards the private sector in all areas of social provision including pensions, welfare, health, and education. Responsibilisation thus functions as a technique for the self-management and self-regulation of social risks such as illness, unemployment, and poverty (Lemke, 2001).

There is, then, a 'new prudentialism' in education. Prudentialisation results when education is addressed to the entrepreneurial self, or the 'responsibilised' self who must make choices regarding his or her own welfare based on actuarial rationality (Peters, 2005). Such prudentialisation seeks to 'insure' the individual against risk in a context where the state has transferred risk to the individual. The role of social prudentialism in education has encouraged a shift in forms of social insurance through education away from a welfare regime. The promotion of the entrepreneurial self represents a shift away from a rights-based welfare model of the citizen to a citizen-consumer model. The citizen-consumer model is based on the rejuvenation of *Homo economicus*, where individuals calculate the risks and invest in themselves at critical points in the life cycle (see Peters, 2001).

The key elements of the risk-management programme grow out of the shift from the Keynesian welfare state and compulsory social insurance to neoliberalism (or the culture of consumption) and a form of private insurance constructed through choice. Within this new regime (re/de)regulation represents an intensive juridification, a legal liberation and optimism based upon confidence in rules. Under this model, the well-governed society is committed to the coherence of a framework of rules, a codification, which allows the government to step back more and more from actual involvement in state activities which are now devolved to agencies, institutions or regions.

Government assumes the metaposition of rule-maker. In this political environment, the economic, constitutional, and legal or juridical forms of advanced liberalism overlap to construct the citizen-consumer. Increasingly, alongside the empowerment of consumers – simultaneously their individualisation and their responsibilisation – is a belief in the efficacy of rules and a distrust of professionals. These knowledges and discourses grew up with the welfare state, a fact evident in the role of the nineteenth-century census as an instrument of governmentality that came to have an independent existence over time. Understood as a risk-management regime, neoliberalism involves the distrust of expert knowledges, especially those traditionally associated with the welfare state, such as the expertise of social workers and teachers. Under neoliberalism, the trend has been towards creating a uniform structure of expert knowledges that is based on the calculating sciences of actuarialism and accountancy (thus explaining the label 'the audit society'). 'The social' is promoted as that which is capable of being governed, for example, the regulation of 'the poor'. 'Work' and 'unemployment' have, in this way, become fundamental modern categories of social regulation. In this sense, neoliberalism can be seen as an intensification of moral regulation resulting from the radical withdrawal of government and the responsibilisation of individuals through economics. It emerges as an actuarial form of governance that promotes an actuarial rationality through encouraging a political regime of ethical self-constitution as consumer-citizens.

'Responsibilisation' refers to modern forms of self-government that require individuals to make choices about lifestyles, their bodies, their education, and their health at critical points in the life cycle, such as giving birth, starting school, going to university, taking a first job, getting married, and retiring. 'Choice' assumes a much wider role under neoliberalism: it is not simply 'consumer sovereignty' but, rather, a moralisation and responsibilisation, a regulated transfer of choice-making responsibility from the state to the individual in the social market.

This shift means we have passed from an ontology of the self as producer, which characterised the era of Left politics and the welfare state, to an ontology of *self as consumer*, which now characterises politics of the Right, the neoliberal market economy and the provision of public services. This shift can be characterised in terms of a symbolic economy of the self. This involves a set of related processes of self-capitalisation, self-presentation, self-promotion, self-branding, and self-virtualisation as market processes having political, ethical, and aesthetic elements. We might, here, follow Foucault's lead and focus on processes of political, ethical, and aesthetic self-constitution through making choices that involve the purchase of goods and services and, in some cases, longer-term investment decisions.

A genealogy of the entrepreneurial self-reveals that it is a relation that one establishes with oneself through forms of personal investment (including education, viewed as an investment) and insurance that become the central ethical and political components of a new individualised, customised, and privatised consumer welfare economy. In this novel form of governance, responsibilised individuals are called upon to apply certain managerial, economic, and actuarial techniques to themselves as citizen-consumer subjects, calculating the risks and returns on investment in such areas as education, health, employment, and retirement. This process is both self-constituting and self-consuming. It is self-constituting in the Foucauldian sense that the choices we make shape us as moral, economic, and political agents. It is self-consuming in the sense that the entrepreneurial self creates and constructs him- or herself through acts of consumption.

Neoliberalism uses models of line management to insert a hierarchical mode of authority by which the market and state pressures can be instituted. For teachers, this carries with it the effect of de-professionalisation, involving a shift from collegial or forms of democratic governance in flat structures, to hierarchical models based on dictated management *specifications* of job performance in chains of command. The implementation of restructuring initiatives in response to market and state demands involves increasing specifications by management over workloads and course content. Such hierarchically imposed specifications erode traditional conceptions of professional autonomy over work in relation to both teaching and research. Neoliberalism systematically deconstructs the space in which professional autonomy is exercised.

The essence of contractual models involves a *specification*, which is fundamentally at odds with the notion of *professionalism*. *Professionalism* conveys the idea of a subject-directed power based upon the liberal conceptions of rights, freedom, and autonomy. It conveys the idea of a power given to the subject, and of the subject's ability to make decisions in the workplace. Traditional conceptions of professionalism involved an ascription of rights and powers over work in line with classical liberal notions of freedom of the individual. Market pressures increasingly encroach on and redesign traditional understandings of rights, as educational institutions must adapt to market trends. For example, just as individual university departments and academics are being told of the necessity for acquiring external research grants, so they are also being told they must increase their work load and teach summer schools. No professional, whether doctor, lawyer, or teacher, has traditionally wanted to have the terms of their practice and conduct dictated by anyone else but their peers, or determined by groups or structural levers that are outside of their control. As a particular patterning of power, then, professionalism is systematically at odds with neoliberalism, for neoliberals see the professions as self-interested groups who indulge in rent-seeking behaviour. In neoliberalism, the patterning of power is established on contract, which in turn is premised upon a need for compliance, monitoring and accountability organised in a management line and established through a purchase contract based upon measurable outputs.

There are, roughly speaking, four different contemporary forms that accountability takes. We might call them accountability regimes. They are not mutually exclusive and may exist as hybrids. First, there is the state-mandated agency form that regulates activity or performance according to standards or criteria laid down at state or federal level. Typically, this form is often associated with devolution of management (though not necessarily governance) and the development of parallel privatisation and/or the quasi market in the delivery of public services. Second, there is professional accountability which tends to operate through the control of entry and codes of practice that are struck by professional associations, most often in occupations like law, accountancy, dentistry, and doctoring. This professional self-regulation often does not include occupations like teaching and nursing, although it may include counselling. Third, there is consumer accountability, that is, accountability through the market, especially where consumer organisations have been strengthened in relation to the development of public services delivered through markets or market-like arrangements. Fourth, there is a form of democratic accountability that has its home in democratic theory and is premised on the demand for both internal and external accountability, that is, typically, accountability of a politician to parliament or governing organisation and accountability to his/her electorate. The second form, or professional accountability, may be seen, in reality, to be a form of the fourth or democratic form. Both proceed from Kantian-like assumptions about autonomy, self-regulation, duty, and responsibility for one's actions, whether this be in institutional (e. g. parliament, university) or individual terms.

There has been an observable tendency in Western liberal states to emphasise both agency and consumer forms of accountability at the expense of professional and democratic forms, especially where countries are involved in large-scale shifts from traditional Keynesian welfare state regimes to more market-oriented and consumer-driven systems. Indeed, it could be argued that there are natural affinities by way of shared concepts, understandings, and operational procedures between these two couplets. One of the main criticisms to have emerged is that the agency/consumer couplet instrumentalises, individualises, standardises, marketises, and externalises accountability relationships at the expense of democratic values such as participation, self-regulation, collegiality, and collective deliberation that are said to enhance and thicken the relationships involved.

This collection amply provides a nuanced and sophisticated reading of forms of 'responsibilisation' taking place in education broadly conceived and the manufacture of different forms of subjectivity that are morally self-constituting through the mechanism of choice within current neoliberal environments. It has to be said that State responsibilisation for welfare was a political achievement based on the power of trade unions and working people. It did not 'devolve' all power to the state to encourage an overweening sense of dependency but, at its best, emphasised a citizen's active participation within state-provided social and public infrastructures that led to, what we might call today, the co-creation and co-production of social goods. The dependency story beat-up is part of a neoliberal take that emphasises the way that the welfare state robbed economic liberalism of its vitality. By substituting the market and employing the moral vocabulary of individual choice-making, neoliberals have reinvented subjectivity and the market in moral terms. This allows a shrinking state and a kind of parallel privatisation that, increasingly, sees the likes of Serco and other private sector companies taking over the responsibility for running what used to be public institutions. The logic of public–private partnerships drives this strategy more deeply into the social fabric. Yet, the basic forms of citizen participation and active co-production at the heart of social democracy remain a clear and viable option for the provision of welfare and social security.

Note

1. See the recent public uproar at Serco's running of Mt Eden prison in Auckland with $1.5 million in anticipated penalty fines for various offences – http://www.radionz.co.nz/news/political/284397/minster-says-serco's-55-breaches-'fair'. For Serco see https://www.serco.com/ where it advertises its welfare business in education, healthcare, environmental services, justice and immigration, prisons, and the like.

Acknowledgement

This is an invited response to the special issue of Discourse based on AARE Invited Symposia 'Responsibility and responsibilisation in education' 2015. I would like to thank Christine Halse for constructive criticisms of this piece.

Disclosure statement

No potential conflict of interest was reported by the author.

References

Foucault, M. (2008). *The birth of biopolitics: Lectures at the Collège de France, 1978–1979*. (G. Burchell, Trans.). A.I. Davidson (Ed.). New York, NY: Palgrave Macmillan.
Hamann, T. (2009). Neoliberalism, governmentality, and ethics. *Foucault Studies*. Retrieved from http://rauli.cbs.dk/index.php/foucault-studies/article/view/2471
Keddie, A. (2016). Children of the market: Performativity, neoliberal responsibilisation and the construction of student identities. *Oxford Review of Education*, *42*(1), 108–122. doi:10.1080/03054985.2016.1142865
Lemke, T. (2001). 'The birth of bio-politics': Michel Foucault's lecture at the Collège de France on neoliberal governmentality. *Economy and Society*, *30*(2), 190–207.
O'Malley, P. (1992). Risk, power and crime prevention. *Economy and Society*, *21*(3), 252–276.
O'Malley, P. (2009). Responsibilization. In A. Wakefield & J. Flemming (Eds.), *Sage dictionary of policing* (pp. 276–277). London: Sage.
O'Malley, P., & Palmer, D. (1996). Post-Keynesian policing. *Economy and Society*, *25*(2), 137–155.
Peters, M. A. (2001). Education, enterprise culture and the entrepreneurial self: A Foucauldian perspective. *Journal of Educational Enquiry*, *2*(2), 58–71.
Peters, M. A. (2005). The new prudentialism in education: Actuarial rationality and the entrepreneurial self. *Educational Theory*, *55*(2), 123–137.
Shamir, R. (2008). The age of responsibilization: On market-embedded morality. *Economy and Society*, *37*(1), 1–19.

Index

abuse 48, 63
Academic Performance Reviews 128
academic responsibility 97–108, 110–12, 116–20, 124, 126, 128–36, 138, 143
accountability 123, 126, 130, 133–4, 139, 143–4; and contractualism 109–10, 114–15, 118–20; and feminist ethics 46; and governance 88, 92–3; and homo-/transphobia 31, 33, 35, 37–8, 40–1
accounting 1
activism 18, 21, 100, 135
Adappt initiative 22
aesthetics 143
affiliations 35–6
Afghanistan 4
Africa 4
agential realism 50
Ahmed, S. 47
alienation 92
Allan, J. 70–82, 138
Allen, L. 30–42
Almeida, D.J. 97–108, 138
Altbach, P. 110
alumni 22
Amin, A. 12
Amsler, M. 123–38
Andreotti, V. 19
Anti-Discrimination Laws 9
Aotearoa see New Zealand
Applebaum, B. 12, 32, 34, 40
Arab Spring 60, 100
Asia 20, 24–5
Asia Education Foundation 21, 23
assemblages 70–82
assessment 70, 73, 76–7, 83–96, 98, 101–2, 104–6, 128, 139, 141
Assessment and Reporting Authority (ACARA) 23
assimilation 9, 12–13
asylum seekers 5, 9–10
atomisation 24–5, 103, 106
Audit Commission 70
audit culture 126, 132–3, 142
austerity 58–9, 68, 76–7, 126

Australia 1, 4–6, 8–11, 60, 67, 139; and contractualism 109–11, 116–18; and cultural politics 98; and feminist ethics 43–4, 46, 48; and GCE 20–1; and global citizenship 17, 23–5; and governance 88; and homo-/transphobia 34–5
Australia and New Zealand (A/NZ) 30, 34
Australian Agency for International Development 21
Australian Bureau of Statistics (ABS) 23, 60
Australian Curriculum 3, 9, 20, 23, 48
Australian Values Statement 9
Australian Youth Foundation 22
authoritarianism 104, 130, 132
autonomy 3, 7, 12, 20, 77, 87; and contractualism 110, 112–13, 115–20; and cultural politics 98, 103; and feminist ethics 45–7, 49, 51; and governance 87; in New Zealand 124, 126–7, 133–5; post-GFC 57, 62, 66–7; and self-responsibilisation 138, 140–1, 143–4

Bacchi, C. 50
Bailey, C.W. 31
Baker, J. 51
Ball, S.J. 17
Bank of England 58
banks 58, 126
Banks, J.A. 20
Bansel, P. 36–7
Barad, K. 50
bargaining 116–18
Bauman, Z. 58, 111–13, 115, 117
Beasley, C. 50
Beck, U. 45, 111–13, 115, 117, 138
Benhabib, S. 47
Bergson, H. 12
Berlant, L. 44, 54
A better world for all 20
biculturalism 128
biopolitics 124–7
Black, R. 21
Blackmore, J. 109–22, 138

INDEX

Blair, T. 112, 126
blame 83–96, 102, 123–4, 138, 140
Bono 18
$20 Boss initiative 22
Bourdieu, P. 104, 127
Boyd, D. 12
Braverman, H. 105
Bretton Woods 64
Britain *see* United Kingdom
British Telecom 132
Bromdal, A. 30–42
Bully Stoppers 7
bullying 7–8, 30–1, 33–4, 38–41
Burchell, G. 66
bureaucracy 13, 64, 72, 112, 126, 133
burkas 9–10
business/business models 1, 109, 114, 124, 127, 130
Butler, J. 30–2, 34–5, 37, 40

Calvinists 65
Canada 33, 36, 39
Cantillon, S. 48
capitalism 19, 57–8, 62–8, 99, 124–5, 134
care work 45, 52
case studies 22, 24–5
celebrities 18, 31
Chicago school 125
China 4, 25, 97
Christians 9
Cisco Systems 23
cisgenderism 32
citizenship 9, 16–29, 47, 51, 101, 129
civil society 20, 76, 85, 127, 141
Clarke, J. 112
class 44–5, 52, 59–60, 63, 89, 102–3, 112
Clinton, B. 126
Code of Practice for Special Educational Needs and Disability 70–4, 76–81
coding/decoding 71, 73–4
collegiality 117–18, 126–7, 129, 135, 143–4
colonialism 19
commercialisation 127, 129–31, 133, 139
Common Core Standards (CCS) Initiative 88
communitarianism 127
competing responsibilities 16–29
conservatism 103–4, 110, 120
contractualism 103, 109–22, 138, 143
control societies 70, 72, 76–7, 79–81, 138
Cooper, D. 141
core-periphery links 63
Corporate Social Responsibility (CSR) 126–7
corporations 17–18, 22–5, 62, 71–2, 77, 81, 101, 110, 123–7, 131–3, 139
cosmopolitanism 18
Cover, R. 38
credentialism 92, 110
critical theory 19, 26–7, 45–6, 50, 52–3, 102, 124, 128, 134, 136

cultural politics 97–108, 138
Cumming-Potvin, W. 39

Davies, C. 32
de-responsibilisation 8
Dead Poets' Society syndrome 45
Dean, M. 130
debt 58–62, 68
deficit models 18–19, 23, 34
Deleuze, G. 71–3, 77–80, 138
Deloitte 109
democracy 3, 9–10, 18, 52–3, 59, 62; and contractualism 117; and cultural politics 98, 101–2, 105–6; in New Zealand 127, 135–6; and self-responsibilisation 143–5
denial 8–9, 11–13
Denneny, M. 106
Department of Immigration and Citizenship 23
Department of Industry, Innovation, Science, Research and Tertiary Education 23
Derrida, J. 74
determinism 6
deterritorialization 74
Development Dimensions International 133
deviance 7–8, 12
diagnoses 71–2, 75, 77
Diagnostic and Statistical Manual of Mental Disorders (DSM) 70, 72, 75
disability 59, 63, 70–82, 115, 138
discipline 45, 72, 79, 81, 84, 90, 98, 102, 126, 132–3, 135
discourse analysis 4, 21, 26, 124, 126–35; of assimilation 9–11; and cultural politics 102–3, 106; and feminist ethics 44, 50; and governance 92; of mutual responsibility 11; of racism 6–8; and responsibilisation 11–13; and responsibility 11–13; and self-responsibilisation 138–40; of white victimhood 8–9
dispositif 71
dispositional knowledge 102
diversity 2, 6, 12, 18, 20, 30, 34, 37
doctoral supervision 113, 118–19
dominant discourse 5, 21, 26

Eckersley, R. 46–7
ecology 47
economics 1
education 16–29, 43–56, 138–45; higher education 1, 52, 60, 89, 93, 109–22, 126–7, 131–2, 134, 139; tertiary education 23, 83, 97, 100, 116
Education, Health and Care (EHC) Plans 76–7, 80
Education for Intercultural Understanding 3
Education and Skills Committee 70
egalitarianism 6
Einstein, A. 23
elites 84, 90, 116
Employment Relations Authority 132

INDEX

empty architecture 72, 75–6, 79–80
engaged intellectuals 105
Engels, F. 62
England 58, 67, 83, 88–9
English language 4, 9, 25
enterprise 52, 57–8, 65–8, 92, 113, 116–18, 126, 129, 133, 138
entrepreneurs 18–19, 22, 25–6, 59, 66–7, 87; and contractualism 112; and cultural politics 104; and governance 91–2; and neo-liberalism 124–7, 129, 131, 133–6; and self-responsibilisation 139–43
environment 18, 20, 25
epistemology 53–4, 102, 128
equal responsibility 6
Equality Act 78
Ernst & Young 109
ethics 1, 13, 20, 25, 67, 102; of care 49–53; and contractualism 112–13; and feminism 43–57; and homo-/transphobia 32, 37, 39–40; and neo-liberalism 123, 130; post-GFC 67; and self-responsibilisation 141–3; work ethic 65
ethnicity/ethnic groups 2–6, 10–12, 32, 52, 60, 103
ethnography 34
Europe 1, 3, 58
European Union (EU) 58–60
Eurozone 126
evaluation 76, 93, 98, 101–2, 104, 110, 117, 125–6, 128, 133
everyday talk 2–15, 139
evidence-based practice 75
examinations 83–96, 101
Excellence in Research in Australia (ERA) 110, 117
exclusion 11, 18, 20–1, 60, 74, 84, 101, 113, 116–17

Fataar, A. 104
fatalism 100
fear 31–2, 40, 61, 78, 92
feminism 43–56, 138
fetishisation 64
financial services sector 58
flexible capitalism 57–8, 63–6
flows 70–82
focus groups 4–5, 10–13, 34–5
Foucault, M. 7, 19, 21, 26, 46, 58; and contractualism 113; and cultural politics 103–4; and governance 84, 87, 90, 92; and neo-liberalism 124–7, 130, 134; post-GFC 65–6; and self-responsibilisation 138–41, 143; and SEN/disability 71–2
Foundation for Young Australians (FYA) 17, 21–2, 26–7
Franklin, B. 65
Fraser, N. 51
freedom 1, 9, 46–7, 49, 58, 62; ambivalence of 65–7; and contractualism 112–13, 115–17,
119; and governance 86–7; and neo-liberalism 126, 135; post-GFC 64; and self-responsibilisation 138, 140–1, 143; and SEN/disability 75
Freud, S. 80
Furedi, F. 49
further research 139

Geertz, C. 99
gender 18, 25, 30–42, 44–5, 47, 49, 52, 60, 89, 102–3, 112, 141
Germany 59, 124–6
ghostings 70–82
Giddens, A. 45, 111–13
Gilligan, C. 46, 49
Gilroy, P. 2
Giroux, H.A. 105–6
global citizenship 16–29
global citizenship education (GCE) 16–29
Global Financial Crisis (GFC) 57–69, 109–10, 112, 126, 138
Global perspectives: a statement on global education for Australian schools 20
globalisation 17, 20, 25, 57–8, 62, 64, 66–8, 89–90, 97–106, 112, 114, 125
good practice 19
governance 16–17, 48, 53, 71–4, 77, 83–96, 110–11, 114–17, 126, 131, 133–6, 142–4
governmentality 13, 19, 67, 91–2, 94, 103–6, 113, 124–5, 131, 134–5, 138, 140–2
Governmentality Studies 140
grade inflation 89
Graduate Careers 23
Great Recession 58
Greece 59, 67
grit 98–9, 102–6
Grit Scale 102
Grunberg, I. 101
Guattari, F. 71–3, 77
Guide to the University of Auckland Leadership Framework (GLF) 128–9, 131–5
Gulson, K.N. 104
Gunter, H. 26
Gutek, G. 100

Hage, G. 46–7
Halse, C. 1–15, 139
Hamann, T. 141
Haraway, D. 58
Harris, J. 58–9
Harrison, L. 20
Hartung, C. 1, 16–29, 139
hate speech 39
Health and Well-being Boards 76
hegemony 12–13
Held, D. 99
Hello Sunday Morning initiative 24–5
heteronormativity 32, 36
High Resolves initiative 22

INDEX

higher education 1, 52, 60, 89, 93, 109–22, 126–7, 131–2, 134, 139
Homo œconomicus 125, 140–2
homophobia 30–42, 138
homosexuality 32–3
House of Commons Treasury Committee 58
human rights 18, 39
Human Rights Commission (Australia) 5

iconography 129, 131
identity 3, 8–9, 12–13, 21, 33–7, 39; and contractualism 111; and cultural politics 100, 103–4; and feminist ethics 50; and governance 92; and homo-/transphobia 41; and neo-liberalism 129; and post-GFC 62–4; and self-responsibilisation 139
ideology 19, 52, 84, 90, 99, 105–6, 125, 131, 134–5
ignorance 34, 40
Illich, I. 141
imperialism 25
inclusion 70–2, 75–6, 81, 85, 91, 128–9
India 4
Indignados 60
individualised responsibility 3, 7–9, 12–13, 18, 26; and contractualism 111–15, 117–20; and cultural politics 98–9, 102–4; and feminist ethics 45, 49, 53; and governance 87–8, 92–4; and homo-/transphobia 32, 40; and neo-liberalism 125, 133–4; post-GFC 58, 65–6; and self-responsibilisation 138–44
industrialisation 97–101
inequality 21, 26, 33, 51, 53, 116, 120, 127
inspiration 43
instrumentalisation 126, 129, 132–3
integrity 97–108, 129, 138
Intercultural Understanding 3
intergenerational theft 59, 68
internalisation 102
International Baccalaureate 20
International Monetary Fund (IMF) 126
international relations 18, 46
internships 61–2
invisible labour 117, 135
Islam 8, 10, 35
Islamophobia 35

Joint Strategic Needs Assessment 76

Kant, I. 138, 144
Kaul, I. 101
Kelly, P. 20, 57–69, 103, 138
Kentz and Laing O'Rourke 22
Keynes, J.M. 23, 101–2, 112, 139, 142, 144
King, M. 58
knowledge economy 84, 86, 89, 97, 100, 110, 112
Korea 4
Kromidas, M. 6

labour markets 57–8, 60, 62–3, 65–8, 87
laissez faire 125
Lauder, H. 89
leadership 22, 84, 110, 123–38
Leadership Framework (LF) 124, 128–35
league tables 88
learning difficulties 78
legislation 71–2, 76, 78, 88
Lemke, T. 87, 92, 103
lesbian, gay, bisexual and transgender (LGBT) 38
Levinas, E. 50
Lewis, A. 11
liability model 47
liberalism 3, 86, 88, 106, 112, 124–7, 138, 141–4
Liebenberg, L. 104
lifelong learning 91
Lindley, J. 90
litigation 79
lived experience 12
Local Offer 76–7, 79
localism 77
Lotterywest 22
Lynch, K. 48–51
Lyons, M. 48

McGrew, A. 99
Machin, S. 90
McInnes, D. 32
McKinsey & Company 100
McLaren, P. 105
McLeod, J. 43–56, 138–9
Malaysia 97
managerialism 114, 124–6, 130–4, 143
Mann, H. 97
Māori language 128–30
marginalisation 25, 60, 104, 106, 113
market 13, 20, 24–5, 66, 68, 72; and contractualism 109–10, 112, 114–20; and cultural politics 102, 104; and governance 86–8, 94; and neo-liberalism 125–7, 129, 131–5; and self-responsibilisation 138–45; and SEN/disability 75, 80–1
Martino, W. 39
Marx, K. 62, 87
masculinity 31
materialisations 70–82
media 9, 13, 18, 135
Melbourne Declaration on Educational Goals for Young Australians 20, 48
Melbourne University 23
metrics 45
micro-aggressions 3, 5
migration 2–5, 9–10, 12, 63, 100, 110
modernism 3, 7, 12–13
Mok, K.H. 100
morality 5–6, 12, 33, 37, 46, 49–50, 52, 67, 139, 141–4
mortgaged futures 57–69, 138
MTV 23

INDEX

multiculturalism 3, 5–6, 10, 12–13
mutual responsibility 11–13, 103
Myer Foundation 22

National Audit Office (NAO) 59
National Australia Bank 22
National Curriculum and Assessment 88
nationalism 32
Nature 6–8, 12
neo-liberalism 19–20, 24–6, 45–6, 52, 58, 62; and contractualism 112–14, 117; and cultural politics 98–9, 102–5; and governance 83–96; in New Zealand 123–37; post-GFC 65–8; and self-responsibilisation 138–44; and SEN/disability 72, 81
networks 16–17, 21, 26–7, 37, 62, 72, 109, 119, 124
New Deal 125
new work orders 64
New Zealand 1, 30, 34, 38, 88, 123–37, 139
New Zealand Education Act 135
New Zealand Qualifications Authority (NZQA) 129
Newcastle City Council 59
NGOs 21
No Child Left Behind (NCLB) 88
Noddings, N. 49
norms/normativity 3, 6–7, 9–10, 12–13, 18, 32; and cultural politics 103, 105; and feminist ethics 45, 47–8, 53; governance 90–1; and homo-/transphobia 36, 40; and neo-liberalism 128, 130, 133; post-GFC 64, 68; and self-responsibilisation 139, 141
Northern Territory Government 22

Obama, B. 100
Occupy movement 60–1
OECD 23
Office for Standards in Education 70
Oliver, J. 18
O'Malley, P. 140
ontology 3, 142
Organisation for Economic Co-operation and Development (OECD) 58, 60, 62–3, 110, 118, 134
Other 3–4, 8–9, 12, 31, 40, 50–2, 54, 90
outsourcing 140
Owen, J. 23
Oxfam 21

panopticon 72, 76
Parker, W.C. 20
Pascoe, C.J. 30
paternalism 31, 102–3, 114, 116, 118–20
pathology 7, 44
patrimonialism 115
pedagogy 20, 30, 39–40, 44, 48, 50–3; and contractualism 117; and cultural politics 98, 104; and governance 91; and neo-liberalism 135; and SEN/disability 72, 75–6

Peeters, R. 87–8
pensions 63–4, 87, 140–1
performativity 51, 53, 111, 140
Personal Budgets 80
personal responsibility *see* individualised responsibility
Peters, M. 1, 138–45
Peters, R.S. 47
Peters, T. 65–7
philosophy 12, 47, 49–50, 53, 65, 74; and contractualism 114, 117; and cultural politics 98, 100, 102, 106; and neo-liberalism 135
Piketty, T. 127
pollution 112
positivism 102
poststructuralism 21
poverty 25, 45, 87, 92, 103, 112, 125, 141–2
power relations 19, 24, 31–3, 37, 46, 53, 92, 105–6, 113, 117, 127–8, 134
precariat 63
precariousness/precarity 44, 49, 54, 57–8, 60, 62–8
Primary English Teaching Association Australia 21
private sector 73, 77, 101, 126, 132, 141, 144
private sphere 49–50
privatisation 77, 98, 109, 133, 138–9, 143–4
professionalism 129, 143–4
profit 22, 113, 139
progressivism 134
Protestants 65
Prout, A. 19
prudentialism 141–2
psychoanalysis 1, 50
psychology 7, 47, 59, 84, 91, 99, 102
psychopathologisation 75, 81
public good 44, 98–9, 101, 110, 112
public sector 73, 77, 87, 97–8, 126, 139, 144
public sphere 49–50, 106, 112, 126, 134
Puritans 65

qualifications 84, 89, 110, 129
The Queen's Trust 22
queer youth suicidality 38–40
Quinlivan, K. 30–42

Race to the Top 88–9, 91
race/race-thinking 2–3, 6–9, 11–13, 102–3, 112
Racial Discrimination Act (Australia) 5
racism/racist bullying 2–15, 31–4, 139
Raine, C. 24
Rasmussen, M.L. 30–42, 138–9
Rawolle, S. 109–22, 138–9
Reagan, R. 58, 126
Reclaim Australia 8
records of achievement 93
refugees 2, 4, 9
relationality 31–3, 37, 46–7, 49–54, 114–20, 139
religion 3, 5–6, 20, 32–5, 37, 40, 45

INDEX

repetition 31–3
responsibilisation 1, 3–4, 11, 20, 24, 53; and biopolitics 124–7; and contractualism 109–22; and cultural politics 98–9, 102–6; and GFC 57–69; and governance 83–96; and market 138–45; and neo-liberalism 123–37; post-GFC 66; for racism 5; and reframing responsibility 43–56; and scope in education 46–9; self-responsibilisation 138–45; and SEN/disability 72, 76–7, 79–81; techniques of 45–6
responsibility 1, 4, 11, 62, 66–8, 71; academic responsibility 97–108, 110–12, 116–20, 124, 126, 128–36, 138, 143; affirming 46–9; ambiguities of 123–4; and bullying 33–4; competing responsibilities 16–29; contradictory responsibilities 23–5; and ethics of care 49; and governance 84, 87–9, 91–4; and homo-/transphobia 30–42; and market 138–45; post-GFC 57–8; and queer youth suicidality 38–40; for racism 2–15; reframing 43–56; and scope in education 46–9; and SEN/disability 76–7, 79–80; sense of 45–6
rhizomes 72, 76
risk societies 111–13, 138
Rose, N. 27, 45, 67, 112–13
Rowlands, J. 109–22, 138
Ruddick, S. 19–20

Samsung 22
Sanjakdar, F. 30–42
scientism 7
Scott, G. 131–2
Second World War 87, 124
secondary students 2–15, 30, 139
self 3, 49, 138–45; as enterprise 57–8, 62, 65–8; self-responsibilisation 138–45; technologies of 46, 57, 103, 132, 139
self-harming 35, 38
Sennett, R. 63–4
Serco 139, 144
Sevenhuijsen, S. 52
sexuality 30–1, 33–5, 38, 40
Shamir, R. 127, 139
Shaw, G.B. 23
Shell 22
Shore, C. 123–38
short-termism 64
Sklair, L. 100
Smith, A. 124, 141
social connection model 47
social justice 18, 32, 34, 50, 52–3, 85, 102, 106, 113
social media 62, 98, 100
social relations 13, 32, 106, 128, 139
social sciences 140
social services 76
socialisation 84, 87
socialism 98, 127
sociocultural theory 103
sociology 1, 7, 19, 30–1, 45, 48–9, 51, 62, 64, 113

solidarity 50–3
sovereign debt crises 58–9, 68
Spain 60, 67
special educational needs and disability (SEND) 70–82
special educational needs (SEN) 70–82, 138; SEN industry 70–1, 80
Sri Lanka 4
Standing, G. 63
state 10, 12, 16–19, 21–3, 26, 45–7; and contractualism 110, 112, 116; and cultural politics 97–106; and governance 86–7, 92; and neo-liberalism 125–7, 133; post-GFC 58, 64; and self-responsibilisation 138–45; and SEN/disability 72, 74–7, 79
stereotypes 9, 13, 25
Stern, M.A. 101
Stiglitz, J. 127
student loans 60–1
subjectification 46, 78, 90–1, 94
subjugated knowledges 25–6
suicidality 38–40
Sulkunen, P. 113
Sure Start 59
surveillance 90–1, 124, 132, 140

Tasmania 60
Taylorism 89, 132
teacher educators 43–6, 48–53
technologies of the self 46, 57, 103, 132, 139
tertiary education 23, 83, 97, 100, 116
Thatcher, M. 58, 126
therapeutic culture 49
Thiem, A. 30, 37, 40
Third Way 112
Thompson, G. 105
Tierney, W.G. 97–108, 138
Timblr 61
Todd, S. 50–1, 53
Tomlinson, S. 70
Torrance, H. 83–96, 138
transcendence 3
transphobia 30–42, 138
Trnka, S. 112
Tronto, J.C. 49, 52
Trundle, C. 112
Trust Company 22
tuition fees 60
Tumblr 61, 67
Turkey 97
Twitter 100

UBS 22
UCLA 131
unemployment 4, 58–60, 87, 92, 103, 125, 141–2
unions 98, 116, 132–3, 135, 144
United Kingdom (UK) 1, 32, 49, 58–60, 83–4, 86–7; and contractualism 109, 112, 118; and governance 89, 93; and neo-liberalism 132;

INDEX

and self-responsibilisation 138; and SEN/disability 70–82
United Nations Education, Scientific and Cultural Organization (UNESCO) 3, 18
United Nations (UN) 134
United States (US) 1, 31, 49, 58, 64–5, 88, 93, 97–8, 100–1, 109, 118, 125
universities 60, 84, 86, 88–90, 100, 104; and contractualism 109–11, 113–14, 116–19; future of 134–6; and neo-liberalism 123–37; and self-responsibilisation 142–4
University of Auckland (UoA) 128, 133
University of Bristol 131
University of California-Berkeley 131
University College London 131
University of Hong Kong 131
University of Manchester 131
University of Sydney 131
University of Toronto 131
University of Western Sydney 131
Unlimited Potential 17, 22, 27
utopianism 106

values 3–4, 9–10, 12, 18, 20, 24; and cultural politics 102–3; eroding of 135; and feminist ethics 47, 50–1; and homo-/transphobia 40; and neo-liberalism 127, 129–30, 134; post-GFC 67; and self-responsibilisation 140–1, 144
victims 8–9, 12–13, 31, 83–96, 138, 140
Vietnam 4
violence 31–3
vocation 45
voluntary sector 17, 25, 73, 98
vulnerability 18, 38–41, 44, 49, 54
Vygotsky, L. 103

Walker, M.U. 50
Walton, G. 33–4, 36, 39
Walzer, M. 127
War on Terror 126
Washington, I. 31
We Are the 99% 61–2
Weber, M. 63–5, 67, 133
welfare 138–45
welfare state 72, 75, 101–2, 112, 138–40, 142, 144
West 3, 18, 86, 117, 124, 127, 144
Westernisation 99
white supremacism 8
wilful subjects 47
word counts 129
work ethic 65
work experience 17, 25
workload allocation 116–19, 143
World Bank 23
World Vision 21
World of Work initiative 25
Wright, J. 1

Xerox 22

Yeatman, A. 102–3, 111, 114–15, 118
Yip, A.K.T 32–3
Youdell, D. 70–82, 138
Young, I. 12, 47, 50–1
young people 30–42, 102–4, 138–9
Young People Without Borders (YPWB) initiative 22, 25
Young Social Pioneers initiative 22
YouTube 100

Zembylas, M. 52